New Language Learning and Teaching Environments

Series Editor
Hayo Reinders
Department of Education; Department of Languages
Anaheim University; King Mongkut's University
of Technology Thonburi
Anaheim; Bangkok, USA

New Language Learning and Teaching Environments is an exciting new book series edited by Hayo Reinders, dedicated to recent developments in learner-centred approaches and the impact of technology on learning and teaching inside and outside the language classroom. The series aims to:

- Publish cutting-edge research into current developments and innovation in language learning and teaching practice.
- Publish applied accounts of the ways in which these developments impact on current and future language education.
- Encourage dissemination and cross-fertilisation of policies and practice relating to learner-centred pedagogies for language learning and teaching in new learning environments.
- Disseminate research and best practice in out-of-class and informal language learning.

The series is a multidisciplinary forum for the very latest developments in language education, taking a pedagogic approach with a clear focus on the learner, and with clear implications for both researchers and language practitioners. It is the first such series to provide an outlet for researchers to publish their work, and the first stop for teachers interested in this area.

Diego Mideros
Nicole Roberts
Beverly-Anne Carter • Hayo Reinders
Editors

Innovation in Language Learning and Teaching

The Case of the Southern Caribbean

palgrave
macmillan

Editors
Diego Mideros
Centre for Language Learning
The University of the West Indies
St. Augustine, Trinidad and Tobago

Beverly-Anne Carter
St. Augustine, Trinidad and Tobago

Nicole Roberts
St. Augustine, Trinidad and Tobago

Hayo Reinders
King Mongkut's University of
Technology Thonbur
Bangkok, Thailand

ISSN 2946-2932   ISSN 2946-2940   (electronic)
New Language Learning and Teaching Environments
ISBN 978-3-031-34181-6   ISBN 978-3-031-34182-3   (eBook)
https://doi.org/10.1007/978-3-031-34182-3

© The Editor(s) (if applicable) and The Author(s), under exclusive licence to Springer Nature Switzerland AG 2023
This work is subject to copyright. All rights are solely and exclusively licensed by the Publisher, whether the whole or part of the material is concerned, specifically the rights of translation, reprinting, reuse of illustrations, recitation, broadcasting, reproduction on microfilms or in any other physical way, and transmission or information storage and retrieval, electronic adaptation, computer software, or by similar or dissimilar methodology now known or hereafter developed.
The use of general descriptive names, registered names, trademarks, service marks, etc. in this publication does not imply, even in the absence of a specific statement, that such names are exempt from the relevant protective laws and regulations and therefore free for general use.
The publisher, the authors, and the editors are safe to assume that the advice and information in this book are believed to be true and accurate at the date of publication. Neither the publisher nor the authors or the editors give a warranty, expressed or implied, with respect to the material contained herein or for any errors or omissions that may have been made. The publisher remains neutral with regard to jurisdictional claims in published maps and institutional affiliations.

Cover credit: 24BY36 / Alamy Stock Photo

This Palgrave Macmillan imprint is published by the registered company Springer Nature Switzerland AG.
The registered company address is: Gewerbestrasse 11, 6330 Cham, Switzerland

Contents

1 Foreign Language Education in the Southern Caribbean: An Overview   1
Diego Mideros, Nicole Roberts, Beverly-Anne Carter, and Hayo Reinders

2 Increasing Intercultural Competence in the Anglophone Caribbean: Experiences and Recommendations   23
Carmen Céspedes Suárez

3 Teaching English Pronunciation in a Blended Environment: Feedback on a Pedagogical Innovation   43
Frank Bardol

4 Teaching Beyond the Classroom: A Project-Based Innovation in a Language Education Course   57
Pamela Rose

5 Values-Based Innovation in the Caribbean Context: Grounding a Postcolonial Pedagogy for the Cave Hill Spanish Section of The University of the West Indies   83
Ian S. Craig

vi   Contents

6   Innovation in Language Education Partnerships: The
Confucius Institute at The UWI, St Augustine   107
Beverly-Anne Carter

7   Issues and Challenges of Continuing Education for
Teachers of French as a Foreign Language in the English-
Speaking Caribbean   129
Sabrina Lipoff

8   Learning Spanish Beyond the Classroom in a Corporate
Setting   151
Diego Mideros and Paola Palma

9   "Guess I have no choice but to do the e-book": Non-
specialist Learners' Perceptions in Spanish and Other
Languages during the Pandemic   175
Beverly-Anne Carter, Avian Daly, and Mathilde Dallier

10   Foreign/Second Language Learning and Teaching in the
Southern Caribbean: Future Directions   203
*Diego Mideros, Nicole Roberts, Beverly-Anne Carter,
and Hayo Reinders*

Index   221

Notes on Contributors

Frank Bardol is an associate professor at the University of Aix-Marseille. He taught English in secondary schools in Martinique before becoming a language teacher trainer. He holds a PhD in Applied Linguistics. He is currently teaching applied linguistics to future EFL teachers. His research focuses on the development of phonological competence using digital technology for the benefit of students specialising in other disciplines as well as on supporting teachers in finding methods and tools to teach English pronunciation.

Beverly-Anne Carter served as director of the Centre for Language Learning, The University of the West Indies, St. Augustine, from 2005 until her retirement in 2022. Professor Carter has researched and published on learner autonomy, technology applied to language learning, language policy and planning, and methodology in the teaching of English as a second language. Her research has appeared in local, regional, and international publications. Her work to expand the teaching of Mandarin Chinese resulted in the establishment of a Confucius Institute at the St. Augustine Campus. She has been honoured by the French and Japanese governments for her promotion of those languages.

Carmen Céspedes Suárez holds a PhD in Language and Literature Didactics from the University of Granada. She also holds a BA in viii **Notes on Contributors**

Translation and Interpreting as well as MAs in Teaching Spanish as a Foreign Language and Teaching English as a Foreign Language. She has worked as Spanish Lectora MAEC-AECID at the University of the West Indies in Barbados and was a Fulbright Teaching Assistant at the University of Scranton, Pennsylvania. She currently works at Universidad de Las Palmas de Gran Canaria in Las Palmas de Gran Canaria, Spain.

Ian S. Craig holds a doctorate in Hispanic Studies from the University of London. His most recent research centres on study abroad, university internationalisation, and innovative foreign language pedagogy in the Caribbean context. He is currently Senior Lecturer in Spanish at the University of the West Indies, Cave Hill Campus, Barbados, where he teaches Spanish language and Latin American Film.

Mathilde Dallier is an assistant lecturer in French and Coordinator for French, Portuguese, and German at the Centre for Language Learning, The University of the West Indies, St. Augustine. Presently a PhD candidate in linguistics (UWI), she holds an MPhil in Teaching French as a Foreign Language (FFL) from the Université des Antilles in Martinique. Her research interests include beliefs in FFL and their influence on teaching/learning, French grammar, art as a language teaching tool, technology in the FL classroom, and the role of the L1 in teaching/learning FFL.

Avian Daly is a project specialist at the Centre for Language Learning. She holds a masters' degree in English Language Teaching, specialising in ICT and Multimedia. Her current interests include course design and the pedagogical applications of technology in adult, foreign language learning. She is passionate about applying her skills and competencies to help learners maximise their learning. Although not currently engaged in teaching, Ms Daly has taught English in Martinique, France, and Italy, as well as French and Spanish in Trinidad at the primary, secondary, and tertiary levels.

Sabrina Lipoff is a teacher of French as a foreign language and trainer of trainers. She has been working in the field of French teacher training in the Caribbean since 2016. In 2020, she co-founded the association *On Continue*, which works to promote the teaching and learning of French in the region. She is in charge of the conception and implementation of international cooperation projects related to languages.

Diego Mideros is a lecturer in Spanish at The University of the West Indies, St. Augustine Campus, in Trinidad and Tobago. He holds a PhD in Linguistics awarded by the same university. His research interests include learner autonomy and qualitative approaches to language learning research. He is the author of the book *Am I an Autonomous Language Learner? Self-perceived Autonomy in Trinidad and Tobago: Sociocultural Perspectives*, published by Candlin & Mynard, 2021.

Paola Palma is an instructor of Spanish at The University of the West Indies, St. Augustine Campus. She has been teaching foreign languages for several years to young people and adults. Her experience in the classroom has shaped her research interests around topics such as student centred approaches to teaching, motivation, flipped classroom, and the use of technology in the classroom, topics that she has presented at various conferences and on which she has co-authored papers.

Hayo Reinders (www.innovationinteaching.org) is TESOL Professor and Director of Research at Anaheim University, USA, and Professor of Applied Linguistics at KMUTT in Thailand. He is founder of the global Institute for Teacher Leadership and editor of *Innovation in Language Learning & Teaching*. His interests are in out-of-class learning, technology, and language teacher leadership.

Nicole Roberts is a senior lecturer in Spanish at The University of the West Indies (UWI), St. Augustine campus. She is the Director of the Centre for Language Learning. Her research work in foreign/second language centres on social and sociocultural factors that impact reading comprehension and writing in Spanish as well as the importance of study abroad on FL acquisition. She is currently working on two book-length studies; one on *Cuba/Trinidad and Tobago: Language, Literature and Culture* and another on the poetry of the Puerto Rican author Mayra Santos Febres.

Pamela Rose is a lecturer in the Departments of Language and Cultural Studies, and Curriculum and Instruction at the University of Guyana,

x   Notes on Contributors

Berbice Campus. She teaches courses in language education and supervises undergraduate research in the Bachelor of Education (English) programme. Her academic journey began with a BA (English) from the University of Guyana, a postgraduate diploma, and an MA in Language Teaching and Learning from the University of Auckland. Her research interests include transformative pedagogy, innovative approaches to language teaching and learning, quality teacher preparation and professional development, and, more recently, using Principled Innovation to support educators' professional development.

List of Figures

Fig. 3.1	Diagram of the operation of the model (Bardol, 2020)	46
Fig. 4.1	An overview of the language arts course in which the project-based assessment was implemented	62
Fig. 4.2	Overview of the cycles of the initial project-based assessment	64
Fig. 4.3	Overview of the five phases of the initial project	66
Fig. 8.1	Which did you find more helpful?	168
Fig. 8.2	Which did you enjoy more?	168
Fig. 9.1	The learners' initial responses/thoughts	189
Fig. 9.2	Benefits of the online experience	189
Fig. 9.3	Challenges	191
Fig. 9.4	Lessons learnt/takeaways	193
Fig. 9.5	Fulfilment of initial expectations about ERT	194
Fig. 9.6	Going forward	195

List of Tables

Table 2.1	Instruments to develop ICC	29
Table 3.1	Dashboard summary of the three cycles (Bardol, 2020)	49

1

Foreign Language Education in the Southern Caribbean: An Overview

Diego Mideros, Nicole Roberts, Beverly-Anne Carter, and Hayo Reinders

For the editors of this volume based in the Southern Caribbean, it is a privilege to have the opportunity to join this *Innovation in Language Learning and Teaching* series, which to date has featured the cases of Thailand (Darasawang & Reinders, 2015), China (Reinders et al., 2017), Japan (Reinders et al., 2019b), and the Middle East and North Africa (Reinders et al., 2019a). In keeping with how innovation has been construed in previous volumes, our take on innovation is closely related with change; that is, change that comes from particular contextual needs seeking to enhance language learning and teaching. Although both

---

D. Mideros (✉) • N. Roberts • B.-A. Carter
Centre for Language Learning, The University of the West Indies,
St. Augustine, Trinidad and Tobago
e-mail: diego.mideros@sta.uwi.edu; nicole.roberts@sta.uwi.edu

H. Reinders
King Mongkut's University of Technology Thonburi—KMUTT,
Bangkok, Thailand

© The Author(s), under exclusive license to Springer Nature Switzerland AG 2023
D. Mideros et al. (eds.), *Innovation in Language Learning and Teaching*, New Language
Learning and Teaching Environments, https://doi.org/10.1007/978-3-031-34182-3_1

innovation and change are closely related, Hyland and Wong (2013) stress that innovation is a carefully planned process in which process is the keyword, whereas change can simply happen to us, most times under circumstances beyond our control. As such, innovation should always have clear outcomes in mind and a detailed plan to achieve such outcomes. Innovation is also often associated with the introduction of something new or a new idea. However, Hyland and Wong (2013) see novelty as residing in individuals' perceptions "how something is seen by teachers, headmasters, administrators or others involved in its implementation" (p. 2), and we should also add how novelty is perceived by learners themselves. In other cases, change is a mandate "from above by policymakers in government offices and at other times by classroom practitioners trying to make their students more active or their lessons more effective" (Hyland & Wong, 2013, p. 2). Nevertheless, the expectation of any innovative initiative is undoubtedly a positive and effective learning and teaching outcome.

The different regional cases that the *Innovation in Language Learning and Teaching* series has featured stress the fact that innovation is indeed a universal phenomenon that language teachers and practitioners experience in other parts of the world. The case of the Southern Caribbean, just like the previous volumes in the series, presents a unique perspective from an underrepresented region in the Global South. All previous volumes have addressed issues related to English language teaching in territories where English is not the official language and where gaining proficiency in English is perceived as an asset for academic and professional purposes. The case of the Southern Caribbean features four different countries in the region, namely Barbados, Guyana, St Lucia, and Trinidad and Tobago, as well as Martinique, an island located just north of St Lucia which is an overseas region of France. With the exception of Martinique, where French is the official language, the four countries in this volume have English as their official language, which means that in those countries the foreign/second (L2) languages that learners study in formal or informal settings are different from English. This volume documents innovations in learning and teaching Spanish, French, and Chinese in the case of the English-speaking countries, and English as a foreign language (EFL) in the case of Martinique.

The Caribbean Region

The Caribbean region boasts a plurality of languages where English, French, Spanish, and different creoles are widely spoken. The languages of the different colonisers that occupied different territories were instituted as the language of schooling, that is, education. Dutch, Haitian Creole, and Papiamento coexist with various other Creoles across the Caribbean. This region is a potpourri of multilingualism but not necessarily bilingualism; it is one where languages coexist and where, unfortunately, some eventually cease to be spoken and die (Alleyne & Hall-Alleyne, 1982).

Academics across the Caribbean have written about the necessity for foreign language (FL) education (see, for example, Jennings, 2001, Carter, 2004, 2009, Peters & Nzengou-Tayo, 2006) in the Caribbean. Invariably, at the macro level, their comments centre on the need for governments to make policy changes for the inclusion of FLs in curricula or at the more foundational level, the need for increased and better classroom resources regarding L2 teaching. At ground zero, many learners engage in studying L2 languages for a myriad of reasons and more so today, as the region navigates the twenty-first century replete with issues of economic woes, natural disasters, and food insecurity, which have in turn produced increased numbers of migrants and refugees within the region. All in all, the Caribbean region continues to have large numbers of learners who are constantly engaging with the study of foreign/second languages for a variety of reasons and in a wide range of settings, both formal and informal.

The call for papers that preceded this volume sought submissions by researchers and practitioners who had tackled specific challenges in L2 education, in their classrooms. We asked that the papers not only describe the area of innovation but also the impetus for the innovation. One of our main objectives was not only to highlight some examples of successful pedagogical interventions across the Caribbean region but also to indicate areas that were not necessarily successful and to discuss the lessons learnt from the broad experiences. The responses to the call came overwhelmingly from the countries of the southern cone of the Caribbean, perhaps based on our own geographic location in Trinidad and Tobago, the most southern of the island nation states of the Caribbean archipelago.

When we began this project, our original intention was to capture the kind of research and innovation taking place throughout the entire Caribbean region, which, as we have stated, is a region of great linguistic variety and rich multicultural and multilinguistic dimensions. In addition, we felt it important to feature the kind of innovative practices taking place in L2 classrooms and wider contexts where teacher-researchers could present and discuss their innovations in their first language (L1). As colleagues at The University of the West Indies (UWI), St Augustine, we had discussed, researched, and published on the context of the Caribbean in various issues related to L2 learning and teaching. Later, in discussions with Hayo Reinders on the notion of innovation, we acknowledged that we were particularly interested in looking beyond what we are currently doing in our L2 teaching practice, so as to examine the novel ideas that we (and fellow researchers) were using that were particularly helpful in improving the work environment for L2 learning and teaching. Accordingly, Darasawang et al. (2015) point out that at the heart of innovation lies the pairing of old ideas so as to yield new results.

In the end, the chapter contributions that we received for the volume came from *Barbados, Martinique, St. Lucia*, and *Trinidad and Tobago* as well as *Guyana*. Notably, these five territories are all located in the southern cone of the Caribbean region. Specifically, these contributions feature and give representation to the small-island territories in the Southern Caribbean, some of them also known as the Lesser Antilles in the Caribbean region. We strongly believe that there is a clear and present need to illustrate innovative pedagogical efforts made in this area of the Caribbean region that is very much underrepresented in the L2 research literature and overshadowed within the region by the larger islands and territories to the north. We see the absence of the countries of the Greater Antilles (Cuba, Dominican Republic, Haiti, Jamaica, and Puerto Rico) as an advantage to make a case and show what innovation looks like in small-island territories that may not have access to as many resources such as the larger and even the developed countries. The chapters in this volume illustrate that innovation in this part of the world is closely tied to human capital and the tremendous efforts made by teachers, practitioners, and researchers to improve L2 learning and teaching is carried out with limited material resources.

By centring our focus specifically on the Southern Caribbean, we seek to shed light on the relationship between sociocultural agency and innovation. Given that innovation must be looked at and assessed in context, this focus enables us to explore what innovative practices teacher-researchers are able to do in their context with the resources they have available, and how they find new ways of going about their L2 practices to promote more effective learning and teaching. In addition, we examine issues concerning FL educational contexts.

The Contemporary Situation in the Southern Caribbean

Over the decades, there can be no doubt that L2 learning and teaching in the Caribbean seem to have varied with the whim and fancy of particular local governments. Martinique sits as the exception to this context as the island remains as an overseas territory of France, officially called the *Collectivité Territoriale de Martinique*. Thus, the island is European in cultural heritage. However, in the other countries in this volume (including Guyana), the local Ministries of Education are the governing bodies which oversee L2 education. They control not simply which subjects are studied but also at what levels and to what degree of competence. In this light, Trinidad and Tobago's Secretariat for the Implementation of Spanish, established in 2005, was created to drive the Spanish as the First Foreign Language initiative. However, despite its somewhat impractical decision to oversee the effective use of Spanish throughout the nation by 2020, the goal is far from realised (Hoyte-West, 2021).

Nonetheless, attitudinal change in language learning across the region has slowly been taking place. For example, given the recent migrant influx of Venezuelan nationals to Trinidad and Tobago and other Caribbean territories, there can be no doubt that communicative competence in the Spanish language is now a much-sought-after skill. Thus, the contemporary context of the region as well as the global competitiveness demand

6   D. Mideros et al.

that we pay close attention to the innovative changes that are taking place in higher education in the Southern Caribbean and across the entire Caribbean with respect to L2 learning and teaching. Now more than ever, we need to train competitive graduates who are not simply competent in an L2 but, rather, are also citizens who can compete globally in the job market, who are highly trained, and who are proficient in all regional languages as well as the trending South-Asian languages, which in turn can enhance trade and the economic climate of the region. Moreover, the cultural understanding which is brought to bear on the L2 learner provides new ways of seeing and interpreting the world.

L2 Research and Innovation in the English-Speaking Caribbean

Historically, linguists in the English-speaking Caribbean region have devoted their research efforts to the study of local vernacular languages or Creole languages in relation to the role of standard English as the official language, particularly in formal education settings (Christie, 2010; Allsopp & Jennings, 2014). A clear example is the volume *Language Education in the Caribbean: Selected Articles by Dennis Craig*, which is a compilation of works of the late Creole linguist Dennis Craig where various dimensions of language teaching and learning in the English-based Creole-speaking territories of the Caribbean are covered. The focus of Craig's volume is the continuum from Creole-influenced varieties to standard English and how to better and adequately teach standard English by means of what Craig called "Bidialectal Education," which is a way of raising awareness among learners of the existing similarities of both systems. However, the study, teaching, and learning of other L2s are not issues addressed in this book.

Another example of the strong regional research focus on Creoles is Christie's (2010) thorough review of the Caribbean language situation as represented in the *Caribbean Journal of Education*. She reviewed all the language-related articles published for a period of 35 years in the journal in an effort to discuss the kinds of research reported and their implications particularly for the teaching of English. In her review, she found that the studies published in the journal "reflect recognition of Creoles as real languages and also increasing appreciation of them as symbols of culture and national identity" (Christie, 2010, p. 1). It is also worth noting that many of these studies report the situation of Jamaica, the largest English-speaking Caribbean island.

The study and research of the L2s taught in the region have not been central in comparison to the research interest and output of the different regional Creoles. French and Spanish have been taught in secondary schools even before independence from Britain in many English-speaking countries in the Caribbean (Bakker-Mitchell, 2002). There is an examination body—Caribbean Examinations Council—in charge of overseeing the formal examinations of these languages. However, scholarly research reporting on studies and innovations in the field of L2 learning and teaching is rather limited in regional and international journals. Furthermore, in many cases university professors of French and Spanish tend to be literary scholars, which results in more research output on the literatures of these languages and not necessarily on L2 learning and teaching.

Published accounts of issues relating to L2 learning and teaching in the Southern Caribbean region are scarce. Significantly, this not only diminishes the input of Caribbean L2 learners, teachers, and researchers from ongoing global conversations on L2 learning and teaching research, but it also prevents researchers and practitioners from other parts of the world from learning about the unique experiences and ideas that have emerged in these small-island states. Despite the scarcity of L2 research in the region, a few researchers and practitioners have explored a number of L2 learning and teaching issues such as study abroad (Carter, 2006a; Craig, 2010, 2016, 2018; Roberts, 2019), autonomy in language—French and Spanish—learning (Carter, 2006b; Villoria Nolla, 2020; Mideros, 2021), technology in the L2 classroom (Nzengou-Tayo, 2006; Stewart, 2006), peer feedback (Gea Monera, 2006), tandem and telecollaboration (Neva et al., 2010), listening comprehension (Mideros & Carter, 2014; Mideros, 2015, 2018), interlanguage corpus of Jamaican learners of French (Peters, 2006), L2 teachers and teacher education (Williams & Carter, 2006;

Yamin-Ali, 2006, 2010), learning styles and multiple intelligences in L2 learning (Luengo-Cevera, 2015), among others. All these studies were conducted mostly in university settings. Other studies have explored the implementation of Spanish in primary schools in Jamaica (Lingo, 2020) and Trinidad (Wilson, 2016) or the teaching of Spanish in secondary schools in Jamaica (Stewart-McKoy, 2020). The learning and teaching of languages such as Hindi (Moodie-Kublalsingh, 2006) and Mandarin Chinese (Carter et al., 2018) have also been documented.

All the aforementioned studies have been published in regional or international journals, or are books or book chapters. Unpublished L2 research projects produced by postgraduate students in the region are not captured in this brief review. Interestingly, a few of the above studies resulted from a special issue titled *Foreign language teaching and learning in the Caribbean* (Peters & Nzengou-Tayo, 2006) published by the *Caribbean Journal of Education*. Unfortunately, after that special issue, there have not been similar regional initiatives to capture and document the kind of L2 research taking place in the Caribbean region, thus underscoring the importance of this volume.

Another noteworthy exception to the lack of L2 research is Jennings (2001), which is a study that enables us to take a historical look at how FL learning and teaching have evolved in the region after two decades. At the turn of the century, Jennings provided a comprehensive account of FL teaching in a number of countries in the Commonwealth Caribbean (CC). Her study sought to explore the kind of training that both English and FL teachers had received in terms of the teaching materials, teaching methodologies, and technologies employed in the classroom, as well as how adequately low achievers and underachieving males were catered to in primary and lower secondary school levels (forms 1–3/grades 7–9). This exploration resulted from the imperative need to assess the ideals of educational policies and the realities that take place in classrooms and teacher training programmes. Back in 1997, as a result of a heads of governments conference, a few ideas that became policy described the ideal Caribbean person as one "with multiple literacies, foreign language skills, independence and critical thinking" and the kind of Caribbean education as one with "student-centred teaching; universal quality secondary

1 Foreign Language Education in the Southern Caribbean... 9

education; and the application of technology as an aid to teaching and learning" (Jennings, 2001, p. 131).

This is the backdrop against which Jennings found that Trinidad and Tobago rationalised the introduction of the modern language syllabus for lower secondary schools arguing that FL learning "contributes to the intellectual and moral development of the learner" (Jennings, 2001, p. 123). Countries like Barbados and Guyana also initiated projects to promote the teaching and learning of Spanish. Furthermore, the region viewed the need to expand "regional diplomacy, trade and foreign policy interests," which in turn made it necessary to increase "diplomatic contacts with non-English-speaking countries. Being able to communicate with these countries has assumed an added significance" (Jennings, 2001, p. 123). Despite this view, the treatment of FL learning and teaching was inadequate back then. "The fact that so little information on FL teaching in schools was made available by the ministries of education for this study may well be indicative of the marginalisation of foreign languages in the curriculum of schools in CC countries" (Jennings, 2001, p. 123). Yet, another major difficulty found in this study was that often parents discouraged their children from studying a foreign language in secondary school because they could not see the value that French or Spanish might bring to their future professional or working careers. "The fact that parents and their children perceive themselves as speakers of English, which is perhaps *the* universal language of communication, provides little if any motivation for them to contend with the rigour of learning a second language" (Jennings, 2001, p. 124) (emphasis in original). Jennings concluded:

> National education policy documents may advocate the teacher as facilitator and guide but the reality is that the teaching and learning tradition in the Caribbean has entrenched didactic classroom practices which support teacher dominance while a shortage of material resources tends to bolster passivity on the part of the learner. What in the longer term may bring about a shift in this pedagogical mode are the application and use of new technology. But this would require technological as well as human resource inputs into teachers' colleges and schools in all Caribbean countries on a

scale which highly indebted poor countries in the region will be unable to afford. (2001, p. 131)

Undoubtedly, attempts to address some of the concerns and recommendations posed by Jennings have slowly been taking place. We see the ways in which the increasing use of technology is now part of the everyday learning and teaching realities of both learners and teachers in L2 classrooms, particularly during the COVID-19 emergency response, but even prior to that. Studies discussing issues of study abroad and learner autonomy also seem to address concerns about "teacher dominance" and "passivity on the part of the learner," as teachers and practitioners are making more concerted efforts to put students at the centre of learning and teaching. Yet, it is interesting not only to see how the innovations presented in this volume may address some of the issues that Jennings stressed more than 20 years ago and also to see how 20 years after we still face similar issues.

Language Policy: The Case of Trinidad and Tobago

Initially commissioned by the Ministry of Education of Trinidad and Tobago to produce a policy report of relevance to the primary sector, Robertson (2010) produced "Language and Language Education Policy" at the end of widespread consultation with a variety of stakeholders. The final report addressed policy and recommended an implementation plan for all education sectors under the remit of the Ministry of Education, from Early Childhood Care and Education, to secondary education. There was no specific focus on tertiary education, which at the time was located in a different ministry.

Robertson's thesis is premised on language education as a significant component of a sound education and a way to achieve sustainable development goals. The report focuses primarily on Trinidad and Tobago Standard English (TTSE), Trinidadian English lexicon Creole (TCE), and Tobagonian English lexicon Creole (TOB). While lesser prominence is given to heritage and community languages, Robertson is clear that national, regional, and global imperatives require greater commitment to and investment in second and foreign language education. For example, the report strongly advocates for the introduction of Spanish as a core subject in the primary curriculum and competence in Spanish by the end of compulsory (16+) schooling.

Although the policy makes the case for language education as a contributor to sustainable development goals, there is a clear attempt to avoid a utilitarian view of language. Thus, the policy underscores the social value of all local languages, including Trinidad and Tobago Deaf Sign Language (TTDSL), in forming national identity and for social cohesion and foreign/second languages for enhancing reflection and critical thinking skills. While the policy excluded recommendations and an implementation plan for the tertiary sector, the articulation between the secondary and tertiary sectors in the local context ensures that curriculum changes in foreign language education at the secondary level would result in changes to teaching and learning in higher education.

Agency: A Sociocultural View of Innovation

In this volume we choose to view innovation as a sociocultural phenomenon. Each of the attempts at innovating is framed under particular conditions and circumstances that both enable and constrain researchers and practitioners to successfully implement an innovative idea with the aim of improving language learning and teaching. In this light, agency plays a critical role, the agency of those attempting to effect change. Recently, agency has attracted quite a lot of attention in L2 learning and teaching research (Lantolf & Pavlenko, 2001; van Lier, 2008; Huang & Benson, 2013; Deters et al., 2015; Kayi-Aydar et al., 2019; Larsen-Freeman, 2019). From the field of anthropological linguistics, Ahearn (2001) provisionally defines agency as "the socioculturally mediated capacity to act," which means that individuals' actions cannot be viewed or even assessed in a vacuum without considering the elements available in the context that can foster or hinder action. Lantolf and Pavlenko (2001) stress that "agency is never a property of the individual but a relationship that is constantly constructed and renegotiated with those around the individual and with society at large" (p. 148).

More recently, Larsen-Freeman (2019) provided an extended view on agency from the perspective of a complex dynamic systems theory where social and contextual elements are key in understanding this construct. Although her discussion addresses issues of language learning and learner agency, her views on agency can also be applied to language teacher agency. Just as Lantolf and Pavlenko (2001), Larsen-Freeman argues that agency is relational and not inhered in a person. Agency is always related to the particular context and to the affordances available in that context. She also views agency as an emergent phenomenon; once we realise we are capable of making things happen or causing change in the world around us by means of our actions, agency emerges. Another one of her views of agency is its spatial and temporal nature; agency is influenced by past events, one's engagement with the present, and an orientation to the future. Given that agency emerges when we realise we can cause change, this also means that agency is achievable. From an ecological perspective, Larsen-Freeman argues that agency "is not a power that one has…, but rather is something one achieves *by means of* an environment, not simply *in* an environment" (Biesta & Tedder, 2007, p. 137) (emphasis in original). In other words, the environment and the affordances available in it must be conducive for one to achieve and exercise agency. Larsen-Freeman's last take on agency concerns its multidimensional nature. Agency is related to the relevance and significance we attach to events and things. As such, agency takes account of a person's perceptions of things and what beliefs, emotions, motivations, and so on a person holds when faced with a particular situation in a particular context. The multidimensional view means that to understand agency requires an assessment of multiple components which can be interrelated with one another within a system.

Our attempt to look at innovation through the lens of agency in this volume is a way of reminding our audience that language teachers and practitioners in this part of the world seek to innovate in contexts that are filled with more constraints than affordances. This volume makes a conceptual and practical contribution to the field of L2 learning and teaching in the Southern Caribbean region. Initially, it was inspired by our broad concerns regarding what innovation was being produced in the region and how we could best share both the foundational issues and the challenges presented as well as reflect on the pedagogy described in terms of what worked and what may not have been successful. We hope that this volume puts the Southern Caribbean on the L2 research map by allowing us to actively join international conversations on L2 learning, teaching, and innovation, where we should stress that innovation in the Global South is strongly linked to human capital. Our volume seeks to remind very strongly that L2 learning and teaching is a human endeavour where teachers, practitioners, and researchers work with limited resources to make L2 learning a worthwhile and successful experience. At the same time, the contributors to the volume describe innovation in L2 teaching and learning as they explore Caribbean realities and by extension increase their understanding of their own. Very often when thinking about innovation, we imagine rather sophisticated advances that mimic practices in many developed countries that have the privilege to have access to resources. However, it would be unfair to assess the efforts presented in this volume solely in terms of innovations that are produced in developed countries where teachers and practitioners have access to a wider range of material and financial resources.

Our volume shows that innovation may not look the same from the perspective of Small Island Developing States and that the efforts to promote change are tied to sociocultural factors that illustrate the level of agency that teacher-researchers exercise in their contextualised realities. The innovative ideas presented in this volume must be assessed through the perspective of the teachers-practitioners' agency, which in turn might resonate with language teachers in other developing countries in the Global South or underrepresented countries in the L2 language and teaching research literature. In this light, this volume may serve as a source of information to language practitioners across the Caribbean region and globally.

In This Volume

Overall, this volume features eight different innovations from different territories of the Southern Caribbean. Some chapters focus on teaching in the classroom and beyond, while other chapters focus on teachers and teacher education, and yet others describe innovations at larger institutional settings. What follows is a brief outline of each of the chapters.

The volume opens with Chap. 2, "Increasing Intercultural Competence in the Anglophone Caribbean: Experiences and Recommendations." In this chapter, Carmen Céspedes Suárez explores the promotion of intercultural communicative competence amongst advanced university learners of Spanish in Barbados. The author describes the different stages—from needs analysis, to design, to implementation and evaluation—of a project that sought to raise students' awareness of intercultural communicative competence in Spanish as a foreign language. The project was explicit in its effort to bring together different cultural elements of both the Spanish-speaking world and the English-speaking Caribbean. This pedagogical implementation also served to reassess and shift negative cultural stereotypes that at times learners held for the target culture and in turn realised that such stereotypes were also existing in their own cultures.

Chapter 3 is entitled "Teaching Pronunciation in a Blended Learning Environment." In this chapter, Frank Bardol uses action research to reflect on an English language course for specialists from other disciplines (LANSAD in French), offered at the University of the Antilles (Martinique). The chapter describes the various stages of the pedagogical innovation that was implemented to teach pronunciation in a blended class environment while respecting flexibility in learning for the student. The analysis reflects on the impact of the blended environment on the students' learning process. The chapter concludes that digital tools are necessary to service learning and that student autonomy can be achieved through self-reflection, and teacher support and guidance.

In Chap. 4 "Teaching beyond the Classroom: Project-based Assessment in a Language Education Course," Pamela Rose describes how she went about implementing project-based assessment as part of the course

1 Foreign Language Education in the Southern Caribbean...

Teaching of language arts at the primary level, which is a teacher education course at the University of Guyana. Rose discusses the process of innovation of this implementation and the different stages necessary to make this project a reality with three different cohorts of students. Collaboration was a key element for the success of the project in which student-teachers were tasked to promote reading for pleasure amongst primary school children. Undoubtedly, this chapter presents an extraordinary example of what project-based learning and assessment looks like and how student-teachers can learn to solve practical problems that they will face as practitioners. The chapter also illustrates service-based learning.

Chapter 5 is entitled "Values-Based Innovation in the Caribbean Context: Grounding a Postcolonial Pedagogy for the Cave Hill Spanish Section of The University of the West Indies." In this chapter, Ian Craig takes the implementation of the foreign language policy at the UWI and uses it as a starting point for his self-reflection on the foreign language program at the Cave Hill Campus in Barbados as well as his own sense of vocation as a language teacher-researcher. The chapter describes initial efforts to harness the foregrounding of values in the Spanish programme to drive innovation, informed by critical, decolonial, and transformative approaches to language learning. It further charts a pathway towards a clearly defined, value-based identity for the Cave Hill Spanish Section and will be of particular use to language educators and leaders seeking to orient innovation towards strategic alignment within a postcolonial context.

In Chap. 6, entitled "Innovation in Language Education Partnerships: The Case of the Confucius Institute at The UWI, St Augustine", Beverly-Anne Carter provides an engaging discussion of how a Confucius Institute was established at her home university in Trinidad and Tobago. What is truly innovative about this chapter is the notion of *glocality*, as she describes how a conscious effort was made to merge the global nature of an international organisation like the Confucius Institute and the local characteristics and culture of her home university. Carter walks the reader through the entire process, taking into account all the stakeholders at play in what truly is an innovation at an international and institutional levels.

Chapter 7 is entitled "Issues and Challenges of Continuing Education for FLE Teachers in the English-Speaking Caribbean." In this chapter, Sabrina Lipoff covers a much-needed area of innovation in the region: teacher training for teachers of French. Lipoff paints an invaluable picture of the need to strengthen the teaching of French through the improvement of teaching skills among teachers. The chapter describes a project entitled Integrating French as a Language of Exchange (IFLE) funded by the French Ministry of Europe and Foreign Affairs in Saint Lucia. The IFLE project sought to integrate ten countries of the English-speaking Caribbean for which the goal was to bring together both the English and the French Caribbean by means of exchanges and mobility through the promotion of the French language. The innovation that resulted from this project was an asynchronous online training that benefited 120 French teachers from nine countries. The chapter discusses the process of innovation, the successes, and the areas for improvement for future innovations of this nature.

Chapter 8 is entitled "Learning Spanish Beyond the Classroom in a Corporate Setting." In this chapter, Diego Mideros and Paola Palma explore the benefits and challenges to the incorporation of learning beyond the classroom (LBC) in a blended course designed for a company in the aviation industry in Trinidad and Tobago. More than simply creating an inclusive learning environment, they sought to best engage the learners and thereby enhance the learner experience. In their analysis of the innovative process, they explore how LBC is promoted, then they analyse a teacher's narrative regarding the process, and ultimately they conclude that the most important lesson for LBC is the pivotal role of the teacher and the need to sensitise teachers to that role in providing more engaging and relevant out-of-class learning.

In Chap. 9, which is entitled "Student Responses to Remote Teaching during the Pandemic," Beverly-Anne Carter, Avian Daly, and Mathilde Dallier examine the impact of the Covid-19 pandemic on language classes at the Centre for Language Learning (CLL) at the UWI, St Augustine. This chapter discusses learner perceptions in various classes at the Centre following the move to emergency remote teaching (ERT) arising out of the Covid-19 pandemic. They draw heavily on data from student responses to a review survey, to analyse foreign language learning and teaching during the pandemic through the lens of innovation in teaching and learning, the central theme of this volume.

Chapter 10 is entitled "Foreign/Second Language Learning and Teaching in the Southern Caribbean: Future Directions." In this chapter, the editors of this volume discuss the lessons learned from each of the chapters from the sociocultural point of view of agency and look ahead to make pedagogical and research recommendations for the future.

Conclusion

Innovation in Learning and Teaching: The Case of the Southern Caribbean is a timely research and innovation effort to put the region on the map of L2 learning and teaching research internationally. As we have discussed in this introductory chapter, we identified a gap in terms of L2 research output that needs to be filled. Probably this volume can be the beginning of a new era where more L2 research and innovation in the entire Caribbean region takes place. As editors of this volume, it is our hope to begin a conversation with local L2 teachers and practitioners so that L2 research from the Caribbean can also be viewed as a serious and rigorous applied linguistics enterprise.

The chapters in this volume are just a few examples of what takes place in classrooms and beyond where learners engage in learning foreign/second languages and cultures that geographically are not that far from their contexts and realities. In fact, it is through L2 learning and teaching that we can activate in our students their "imagined communities" (Kanno & Norton, 2003) and encourage them to see themselves speaking other languages in other places—and in the case of the Caribbean, students do not have to travel that far to be able to speak English, French, or Spanish. The chapters in this volume discuss and illustrate timely issues that Jennings (2001) discussed in her thorough review of FL learning and teaching in some countries of the CC. Robertson's (2010) policy document is also referential as it sought to push more investment in FL learning and teaching in Trinidad and Tobago, in particular.

In closing, we hope that this volume inspires local and regional L2 teachers and practitioners to engage in more L2 research that documents innovations regardless of how big or small they may seem. The Caribbean region will benefit if more L2 teachers become researchers and seek to innovate learning and teaching from their classrooms. The examples provided in this volume represent a limited number of L2 learning and teaching issues in need of further exploration, and they are of relevance to the region. We hope that international audiences in both developed and developing regions appreciate the voices presented here, voices of Southern Caribbean learners and teachers who make efforts to improve L2 learning with the resources they have available in this small part of the world.

References

Ahearn, L. (2001). Language and agency. *Annual Review of Anthropology, 30*, 109–137.

Alleyne, M. C., & Hall-Alleyne, B. (1982). Language maintenance and language death in the Caribbean. *Caribbean Quarterly, 28*(4), 52–59. https://doi.org/10.1080/00086495.1982.11829334

Allsopp, J., & Jennings, Z. (Eds.). (2014). *Language education in the Caribbean: Selected articles by Dennis Craig.* University of the West Indies Press.

Bakker-Mitchell, I. A. (2002). Foreign language education in post-colonial English speaking Caribbean. *Journal of Instructional Psychology, 29*(3), 192–202.

Biesta, G., & Tedder, M. (2007). Agency and learning in the lifecourse: Towards an ecological perspective. *Studies in the Education of Adults, 39*, 132–149.

Carter, B. (2004). Some trends in foreign language education. *Caribbean Journal of Education, 25*(1), 37–63.

Carter, B. (2006a). Language learning beyond the classroom: The contribution of study abroad. *Caribbean Journal of Education, 27*(2), 1–19.

Carter, B. (2006b). *Teacher/student responsibility in foreign language learning.* Peter Lang.

Carter, B. (2009). Reconceptualising the agenda for language education: Languages for all. *Caribbean Curriculum, 16*, 41–55.

Carter, B., He, M., & Kawasaki, T. (2018). Using YouTube and WeChat to promote communicative and intercultural competence in Japanese and

Mandarin. In C. H. Xiang (Ed.), *Cases on audio-visual media in language education* (pp. 219–239). IGI Global.

Christie, P. (2010). Caribbean language as represented in the Caribbean Journal of Education. *Caribbean Journal of Education, 32*(1), 1–12.

Craig, I. (2010). Anonymous sojourners: Mapping the territory of Caribbean experiences of immersion for language learning. *Frontiers: The Interdisciplinary Journal of Study Abroad, 19*(1), 125–149. https://doi.org/10.36366/frontiers.v19i1.277

Craig, I. (2016). Overseas sojourning as a socioeconomic and cultural development strategy: A context study of The University of the West Indies. *Study Abroad Research in Second Language Acquisition and International Education, 1*(2), 277–304. https://doi.org/10.1075/sar.1.2.06cra

Craig, I. (2018). Student-centred second language study abroad for non-traditional sojourners: An anglophone Caribbean example. In J. Plews & K. Misfeldt (Eds.), *Second language study abroad: Programming, pedagogy and participant engagement* (pp. 83–121). Palgrave Macmillan. https://doi.org/10.1007/978-3-319-77134-2

Darasawang, P., & Reinders, H. (Eds.). (2015). *Innovation in practice: Lessons from Thailand. Palgrave Macmillan.* https://doi.org/10.1057/9781137449757

Darasawang, P., Reinders, H., Waters, A. (2015). Innovation in language teaching: The Thai context. In P. Darasawang & H. Reinders (Eds.) *Innovation in Language Learning and Teaching: The Case of Thailand*. Palgrave Macmillan. https://doi.org/10.1057/9781137449757_1.

Deters, P., Gao, X., Miller, E., & Vitanova, G. (Eds.). (2015). *Theorizing and analyzing agency in second language learning*. Multilingual Matters.

Gea Monera, M. (2006). Peer feedback in the language classroom. *Caribbean Journal of Education, 27*(2), 67–80.

Hoyte-West, A. (2021). A return to the past? The Spanish as the first foreign language language policy in Trinidad & Tobago. *Open Linguistics, 7*, 235–243. https://doi.org/10.1515/opli-2021-0018

Huang, J., & Benson, P. (2013). Autonomy, agency and identity in foreign and second language education. *Chinese Journal of Applied Linguistics, 36*(1), 7–28. https://doi.org/10.1515/cjal-2013-0002

Hyland, K., & Wong, L. L. (Eds.). (2013). *Innovation and change in English language education*. Routledge. https://doi.org/10.4324/9780203362716

Jennings, Z. (2001). Teacher education in selected countries in the Commonwealth Caribbean: The ideal of policy versus the reality of practice. *Comparative Education, 37*(1), 107–134.

Kanno, Y., & Norton, B. (2003). Imagined communities and educational possibilities. *Journal of Language, Identity and Education, 2*(4), 241–249.

Kayi-Aydar, H., Gao, X., Miller, E., Varghese, M., & Vitanova, G. (Eds.). (2019). *Theorizing and analyzing language teacher agency*. Multilingual Matters.

Lantolf, J., & Pavlenko, A. (2001). (S)econd (l)anguange (a)ctivity theory: Understanding second language learners as people. In M. Breen (Ed.), *Learner contributions to language learning: New directions in research* (pp. 141–158). Routledge.

Larsen-Freeman, D. (2019). On language learner agency: A complex dynamic systems theory perspective. *The Modern Language Journal, 103*, 61–79. https://doi.org/10.1111/modl.12536

Lingo, D. (2020). Evaluation of national curriculum strategies for Spanish at the primary level in Jamaica. *Caribbean Journal of Education, 41*(2), 215–249.

Luengo-Cevera, E. (2015). Learning styles and multiple intelligences in the teaching-learning of Spanish as a foreign language. *Enseñanza & Teaching: Revista Interuniversitaria de Didáctica, 33*(2), 79–103. https://doi.org/10.14201/et201533279103

Mideros, D. (2015). The social dimension of FL listening comprehension: From theory to practice in higher education. *The Caribbean Teaching Scholar, 5*(2), 111–124.

Mideros, D. (2018). Social dimensions of listening. In J. Liontas (Ed.), *TESOL Encyclopedia of English Language Teaching*. Wiley. https://doi.org/10.1002/9781118784235.eelt0593

Mideros, D. (2021). *Am I an autonomous language learner? Self-perceived autonomy in Trinidad and Tobago: Sociocultural perspectives*. Candlin & Mynard. https://doi.org/10.47908/20

Mideros, D., & Carter, B. (2014). Meeting the Autonomy challenge in an advanced Spanish listening class. In G. Murray (Ed.), *Social dimensions of autonomy in language learning* (pp. 135–151). Palgrave Macmillan.

Moodie-Kublalsingh, S. (2006). The teaching of Hindi in Trinidad. *Caribbean Journal of Education, 27*(2), 125–152.

Neva, C., Landa-Buil, M., Carter, B., & Ibrahim-Ali, A. (2010). Telecollaboration in Spanish as a foreign language in Trinidad. *Ikala, Revista de Lenguaje y Cultura, 15*(24), 75–102.

Nzengou-Tayo, M. J. (2006). Computer-assisted language learning: Using the technology. *Caribbean Journal of Education, 27*(2), 21–42.

Peters, H. (2006). Developing of a longitudinal oral interlanguage corpus of Jamaican learners of French. *Caribbean Journal of Education, 27*(2), 81–102.

Peters, H., & Nzengou-Tayo, M. J. (2006). Introduction. *Caribbean Journal of Education, 27*(2), 1–19.

Reinders, H., Coombe, C., Littlejohn, A., & Tafazoli, D. (Eds.). (2019a). *Innovation in language education: The case of the Middle East and North Africa.* Palgrave Macmillan. https://doi.org/10.1007/978-3-030-13413-6

Reinders, H., Nunan, D., & Zou, B. (Eds.). (2017). *Innovation in language education: The case of China.* Palgrave Macmillan. https://doi.org/10.1057/978-1-137-60092-9

Reinders, H., Ryan, S., & Nakamura, S. (Eds.). (2019b). *Innovation in language teaching and learning: The case of Japan.* Palgrave Macmillan. https://doi.org/10.1007/978-3-030-12567-7

Roberts, N. (2019). Assessing the value and effectiveness of study abroad and exchange programs in foreign language degree programs: A case study. *International Journal of Educational Excellence, 5*(1), 15–28.

Robertson, I. (2010). *Language and Language Education Policy.* Unpublished report.

Stewart, M. (2006). 'The games people play': Utilising PowerPoint games in foreign-language delivery. *Caribbean Journal of Education, 27*(2), 43–66.

Stewart-McKoy, M. (2020). An evaluation of the teaching of Spanish in selected secondary schools in Jamaica. *Caribbean Journal and Education, 41*(2), 191–214.

van Lier. (2008). Agency in the classroom. In J. Lantolf & M. Poehner (Eds.), *Sociocultural theory and the teaching of second languages* (pp. 163–186). Equinox.

Villoria Nolla, M. T. (2020). Working towards autonomy in second language acquisition: Shifting roles and learning by doing at The University of the West Indies, Mona. *Caribbean Journal of Education, 41*(2), 66–83.

Williams, V., & Carter, B. (2006). Arriving at a (self-)diagnosis of the foreign language teaching situation in Trinidad and Tobago. *Caribbean Journal of Education, 27*(2), 103–123.

Wilson, D. (2016). *The teaching of Spanish as a modern foreign language in Trinidad: A case study of the Spanish initiative implementation in the primary school.* [Unpublished doctoral dissertation]. University of Leicester.

Yamin-Ali, J. (2006). Meeting professional language standards in the FL classroom in Trinidad and Tobago. *Caribbean Curriculum, 13*, 23–44.

Yamin-Ali, J. (2010). 'Context'—The magic of foreign language teaching. *Caribbean Curriculum, 17*, 17–32.

2

Increasing Intercultural Competence in the Anglophone Caribbean: Experiences and Recommendations

Carmen Céspedes Suárez

Introduction

Intercultural communicative competence (ICC) has grown in importance due to international mobility and migration processes in recent years. Many communities have experienced a process of transformation as a result of globalization. They have become more culturally plural and diverse. Hence, the encounter of different cultural groups in "such sensitive places from a human point of view" (Landone, 2014, p. 114) requires us to raise awareness so we can all learn to live with the "exotic" and the "foreign."

Various professionals in the business, health, or education sectors have been involved to a greater or a lesser extent in situations in which they did not know about certain habits or behaviors of the target culture (C2), thus leading to a cultural clash or misunderstanding. That is why most

---

C. Céspedes Suárez (✉)
Faculty of Education, Universidad de Las Palmas de Gran Canaria,
Las Palmas de Gran Canaria, Spain
e-mail: carmen.cespedes@ulpgc.es

© The Author(s), under exclusive license to Springer Nature Switzerland AG 2023
D. Mideros et al. (eds.), *Innovation in Language Learning and Teaching*, New Language
Learning and Teaching Environments, https://doi.org/10.1007/978-3-031-34182-3_2

institutions are encouraging learning and teaching intercultural communicative competence (ICC) (Vilà Baños, 2005).

ICC has been defined in a number of ways. Nevertheless, this study follows the definition provided by Meyer (1991). According to this author, ICC refers to someone's capacity to act flexibly and appropriately in a situation in which members of other cultures are involved, all of them manifesting different cultural behaviors, attitudes, or expectations (Meyer, 1991, cited in Oliveras, 2000, p. 38). This capacity entails knowing these dissimilarities so we can make up for the lack of correspondence between their cultural patterns and ours. Byram (1995) divided this competence into five types of knowledge so we know what to expect and develop: intercultural attitudes; knowledge; skills of interpreting and relating; skills of discovery and interaction and critical cultural awareness.

In order to acquire these skills, teachers and students should start relativizing and reflecting upon their own identities (Neuner, 1997). This process might require that they distance themselves from their cultural values and even question them. However, this might be the best way to stimulate self-concept, empathy (Neuner, 1997), open-mindedness, tolerance, and a nonjudgmental attitude (Chen & Starosta, 2000). All these components would positively contribute to the concept of "global citizenship," which ultimately denotes the capacity of living peacefully with Others (Morgan, 1998; Iglesias Casal, 1998; Miquel, 2003).

When considering ICC in the English-speaking Caribbean, it is evident that most countries in the region would benefit from getting to know their Latin American neighbors from a more pragmatic point of view, especially when it comes to strengthening commercial and tourist relations. Furthermore, implementing courses in intercultural competence at different educational levels would help reduce racist attitudes towards migrants coming from Latin America and other Caribbean islands, especially towards Venezuelan and Guyanese migrants settling down in Trinidad and Tobago and Barbados respectively.

Similarly, given the wide range of nationalities that coexist at The University of the West Indies' (The UWI's) five campuses—Mona in Jamaica, Cave Hill in Barbados, St Augustine in Trinidad and Tobago, Five Islands Campus in Antigua and Barbuda, and Open Campus remotely—instilling these values becomes even more crucial, with

2 Increasing Intercultural Competence in the Anglophone...

classrooms being the best space to serve that purpose (Trujillo Sáez, 2005; Barros García & Kharnásova, 2012). Moreover, as there is an indissoluble link between language and culture (Masello, 2002; Martín Peris, 2008), teaching the language component alongside the customs and traditions of the target culture usually raises motivation (Dörnyei & Ushioda, 2013), as well as learners' affective filter (Krashen, 1987; Arnold, 2000). Thus, combining both elements is likely to increase students' language levels in the long term.

However, it is worth noting the methodological change that has taken place over the last few decades in the area of foreign language teaching. In general, language teachers no longer conceive culture as a secondary or anecdotal component in textbooks or foreign language courses. The most innovative educational trends have come to acknowledge that conveying the "4 F's" (*facts, folklore, food*, and *festivals*) (Kramsch, 1993), as well as solely teaching formal and highbrow culture (Areizaga, 2001), is rather counterproductive and detrimental.

Despite broadening and enhancing learners' general culture, knowledge in highbrow culture does not help them act successfully in encounters with native speakers. Such encounters require that learners pay attention to other procedural aspects such as the speaker's intention or the context in which the interaction occurs. On the contrary, knowing what snacks to bring to lunch with friends, how to react and respond to certain compliments, or how punctual we must be to a formal event is much more useful than knowing the names of lakes or the famous writers of the C2. This explains why language teachers are currently focusing on teaching lowbrow culture and paralinguistic aspects such as kinesics (body gesture and movements), nonverbal communication (visual contact and facial expressions), chronemics (time perception), and proxemics (personal space perception). Ideally, language teachers should teach both highbrow and lowbrow cultures equally (Kramsch, 1988), and that is what the next section addresses.

Justification

The University of the West Indies expressed its wish to become a multilingual institution as part of its strategic plan conceived for 2022. In order to accomplish this, it is important we pay attention not only to language skills but also to sociocultural and paralinguistic aspects that will determine the success or the failure of the communication process. Thus, it is essential to start teaching these elements through language courses as well as through a holistic intercultural methodology that prepares students to perform in intercultural settings. Bearing this desire in mind and the theoretical framework discussed above, I found it relevant to design a specific course in intercultural communicative competence for the Anglophone Caribbean, especially because there was little contact between students from Cave Hill Campus and the Spanish-speaking community in Barbados.

Although the number of speakers of Spanish has increased its presence as a result of migration from Venezuela and the visit of diplomats and staff working in international organizations, the reality is that both communities barely interact with one another. In fact, Li (2018) found that the Spanish language is more popular in Barbados (62.3%) than French (22.1%) and other languages. Nonetheless, when she asked students how best they learn Spanish, more than 85% mentioned their instructors as the only means to practice it, and a negligible percentage mentioned family members or friends. Consequently, if students do not have access to speakers of Spanish by natural means and they plan to travel to a Spanish-speaking country (55.4%) or work in one in the future (47.3%) (Céspedes Suárez, 2020, 2021), it is our responsibility as teachers to expose them to sociocultural elements of the language on a more regular basis.

Once I noticed these factors, I decided to conduct a thorough analysis of students' immediate needs as well as their language and cultural interests at the beginning of the academic year (Semester 1, 2018). I carried out several surveys addressed to local students and Spanish instructors locally and internationally asking specific questions related to intercultural competence. I also inquired about what language skills they found the hardest. They answered oral comprehension and oral expression

2 Increasing Intercultural Competence in the Anglophone... 27

unanimously. In most cases, students claim that these skills are tougher to develop because they do not have access to or do not know native speakers with whom they can organize language exchanges. They expressed that Barbados is a nonimmersion context, and even if they could practice these skills through the infinite world of the internet and digital apps, less self-taught learners confessed they preferred to attain these skills face-to-face. Therefore, since most students expect to practice both language and intercultural skills in the classroom, the teacher should devise an eclectic methodology that mixes both preferably.

After inquiring about language perception, students were asked about their preferences between the different Spanish varieties, that is, Latin American and Peninsular (Spain). A vast 93.1% expressed a marked preference for Latin American Spanish varieties. Similarly, students were asked about their preferences between lowbrow and highbrow cultures. A wide 83.3% perceived the learning of the lowbrow culture (habits, traditions, behaviors, etc.) more fruitful than the study of the highbrow culture (politics, geography, or history) (Céspedes Suárez, 2020, 2021). Consequently, these preferences confirmed the need for emphasizing both varieties in the classroom.

Another issue of concern was the textbook employed for the course SPAN 1001, *Aula Internacional 3* (B1.1 CEFR level) (Corpas et al., 2014), which on certain pages showed a Eurocentric vision (Gimeno Sacristán, 1992; Besalú Costa, 2002). This phenomenon has been widely criticized by other instructors too:

> When we encounter groups of Jamaican university students, the clash breaks out as most of them are black and live in developing countries. The vast majority of positive images [in some textbooks] correspond to the developed Western world. Thus, it highlights the negative aspects of those less favored countries. (González Boluda, 2015, p. 4) (my own translation)

Overall, the textbook was relatively new (2014), and it visibly attempted to integrate Latin American accents and some intercultural aspects such as greetings or punctuality in Spanish-speaking countries (lowbrow culture). However, this content only appeared in Unit 3 and on a few pages. Thus, it was not sufficient to develop intercultural competence in a

28   **C. Céspedes Suárez**

consistent manner. Furthermore, as expressed by González Boluda (2015), few images or pictures displayed the black population or the idiosyncrasy of the Anglophone Caribbean. Most students in Barbados were African descendants. Many of them also came from other islands in which black is the predominant race (St Kitts and Nevis, Grenada, Bahamas, etc.). Thus, acquiring intercultural competence in a miscellaneous context would be more meaningful if their cultures, races, and accents were taken into account. Moreover, as most of them are eighteen years old and onwards, their level of maturity usually allows them to embark on reflection and introspection processes that are highly rewarding and instructive.

In light of these factors, I concluded that developing an ad hoc formative course could compensate for the absence of these elements in the textbook. I also analyzed a set of fifteen Spanish textbooks as a model of reference to look at the way intercultural competence was incorporated in order to conceive more suitable activities. The ultimate goal was to integrate lowbrow culture and Hispanic American variety in a more organic manner to respond to learners' explicit demands.

Implementation

As mentioned above, all these variables prompted the design of a formative course consisting of twenty-three didactic units intended to develop the ICC throughout an entire academic year (around eleven or twelve weeks each semester). It comprised intercultural activities that were implemented during formal classes (lectures) and conversation classes (tutorials/discussions). Although I sought to focus on lowbrow culture on a more frequent basis, I did not want to neglect highbrow culture at its expense. Thus, I decided to design two instruments with an equal distribution of both highbrow and lowbrow cultures. On the one hand, the instrument *Anécdotas* (anecdotes) comprised short stories in which their protagonists either described an aspect of the lowbrow culture of their own culture (C1) or explained a misunderstanding or cultural clash

2 Increasing Intercultural Competence in the Anglophone... 29

they experienced in any of the countries of the cultures involved (Spain, Caribbean, or Latin America). I used this instrument during an hour of class, as it was a brief and dynamic story that triggered a stimulating debate afterwards. On the other hand, the instrument *Entrevistas* (interviews) focused on the highbrow culture (arts, sports, literature, etc.) of the twenty-one countries where Spanish is spoken as an official language. Therefore, an individual with a typical accent was interviewed. This exercise was conceived as homework since it consisted of a listening comprehension and a writing expression activity that required more time and reflection on the students' side (Table 2.1):

The most meaningful aspect is that both instruments conveyed the intrinsic characteristics that intercultural theories promote, such as the increase of knowledge about us and others, relativization of one's own identity, and assessment of someone else's, as well as the discovery of knowledge that would contribute to the increase of tolerance and empathy towards the unique or the unprecedented. From a pedagogical perspective, *Anécdotas* errors were seen and addressed as learning opportunities (Iglesias Casal, 1998). In fact, many life experiences constitute authentic testimonials based on books such as *Culturas cara a cara* (Grupo CRIT, 2007) or *How strange! The use of anecdotes in the development of intercultural competence* (Camilleri-Grima, 2002). Many authors support the benefits deriving from downplaying errors. It is a fun way to learn from what happened to others with humor and curiosity. In this way, hypotheses can be checked and both teachers and students can dismantle the so-called stereotypes.

Table 2.1 Instruments to develop ICC

Instrument	Modality of culture	Language skills	Place
Anécdotas (23)	Lowbrow culture	Reading comprehension + oral expression	In the classroom
Entrevistas (23)	Highbrow culture	Listening comprehension + writing expression	At home

Note: This table shows the instruments used to develop ICC in the classroom, the modality of culture present in each instrument, language skills gained through each one, and the place where they were implemented

Planning

As for the methodology and planning, SPAN 1001 and SPAN 1002 courses of intermediate level are usually taught in seven hours at The UWI. These courses are addressed to students enrolled in Spanish Majors or minors or as elective subjects for those enrolled in other undergraduate degrees (Law, Medicine, etc.). The aim of these courses is to build a solid language foundation before enrolling in more specific courses such as Introduction to Hispanic Literature and Business Spanish. Six of the contact hours are face to face, four of them being lectures and two of them tutorials. Thus, I had one noncontact hour left at my disposal. Traditionally, this hour was used to reinforce language aspects at home or in the language lab under the modality of blended learning.

As a major methodological change, I decided to use this period of time and change the "non-contact hour" to "full contact hour" in order to fully exploit the cultural component. I split up this newly named "cultural class" into four segments: (1) exposure to highbrow culture through a PowerPoint on a Spanish-speaking country, (2) explanation of the instrument/sheet *Entrevistas* that students had to complete as homework, (3) exposure to lowbrow culture by means of *Anécdotas*, and (4) intercultural debate after reading *Anécdotas*.

To be more specific, I dedicated the first twenty minutes of every Monday to work on the highbrow culture of a Spanish-speaking country by means of a cultural presentation on history, geography, politics, and so on of that particular country. Right after, students had to write down the most surprising five aspects they had learnt from the PowerPoint on a small piece of paper and hand it to me. I only allowed five minutes for this activity, as I wanted to stimulate active listening comprehension and synthesis. Subsequently, I urged students to read the short section *Anécdotas* in approximately ten minutes. Lastly, I encouraged students to comment on the cultural features mentioned in *Anécdotas* and actively participate in a group oral debate for over fifteen minutes. By the end of the class, I explained the topic of *Entrevistas* (listening and reflection sheet) they would have to complete and hand in on Thursday of the same week. It is worth mentioning that the country shown in the PowerPoint

2 Increasing Intercultural Competence in the Anglophone... 31

always corresponded to the country later shown in *Entrevistas* so students were more motivated towards the completion of the activity. After a while, students got used to these time dynamics and the cultural class worked effectively as students were enthusiastic and eager to know about the next country.

We must emphasize that even if the weight of the cultural component was concentrated on this cultural class, we wanted this construct to permeate the rest of the lessons too. As the Spanish syllabus at The UWI is built on the communicative approach, tutorials/ conversation classes were planned so that discursive features and typical gestures of the Spanish culture were practiced (lowbrow culture). Thus, students engaged in different speech acts such as directive speech acts in which they encouraged their classmates to accomplish actions aimed at preserving the environment; commitment acts in which they had to perform the role of a politician and promise civic reforms; plus inviting, offering, complimenting, or praising among many others.

For instance, in those cases in which students had to invite or make an offer following some examples read in *Anécdotas*, the other interlocutor had to reject on more than one occasion, to imitate the way Spanish speakers act. As this reaction is deemed "appropriate" in Spanish lowbrow culture, they had to come up with a believable excuse and apologize to relieve their interlocutor's uneasiness. In other cases, students and I expressly worked with images from advertisement campaigns and utilized genuine resources of the C2.

Assessment

Regarding the assessment of these tasks, most experts agree that this component is the main obstacle that prevents this competence from fully evolving. ICC is inherently subjective, and it is generally challenging to assign exact numerical values to the *cognitive, attitudinal,* and *affective* dimensions that comprise it (Imahori & Lanigan, 1989).

Given that no accurate tool has been designed to assess ICC yet, authors like Lázár et al. (2007) and Bordón (2007) recommend assessing ICC in a formative, qualitative, and subjective manner instead of a summative or final one. The main reason is that the first modality (formative) enables us to collect pieces of evidence of intercultural consistency by using a set of direct and indirect evidence tools (portfolios, self-assessments, learning diaries, etc.) over a longer period of time (Deardorff, 2011).

Other authors like Landone (2014) suggest applying a "triangulation of pieces of evidence of different nature: qualitative and quantitative, experiential and attitudinal/psychological profile and self-reflective combined with hetero-assessments" [own translation] (Landone, 2014, p. 121), since they could provide us with more information about learners' intercultural progress in the long run. Therefore, daily work with these two instruments was added to the assessment component that the official syllabus of SPAN 1001 and SPAN 1002 establishes. The grade corresponding to *Anécdotas* was added to the grade from the oral expression section and the grade for *Entrevistas* to the listening comprehension grade.

Results

In order to collect data, I employed tools commonly associated with the ethnography of communication. Firstly, I took notes of all the relevant comments students made in class after reading *Anécdotas*. I wrote them in a diary and combined them with on-the-spot observations. Secondly, I selected the most revealing reflections students had written in the sheet *Entrevistas*. I later categorized these testimonials following Byram and Zarate's (1994) classification of intercultural objectives and Vinagre Laranjeira's (2014) telecollaborative work. From a qualitative perspective, I summarize below a set of anonymous testimonials that evinced progressive assimilation of ICC. As most students possessed B1 level in Spanish, I edited and translated their written excerpts to make them more understandable to the readership:

Objective 1. Attitudes of Curiosity and Openness

This first objective includes both curiosity towards foreign culture and the enthusiasm students ordinarily express when they want others to experience their idiosyncrasy. They normally share their cultural products:

> —*Barbadians are friendly and receptive. We sometimes say, "Why you hay" ("Why are you here?") but far from being impolite, it is a way to start a conversation with tourists and foreigners—.*

> —*I would recommend the movie "Panama Canal Stories" about the Panama Canal construction and its connection to Barbados as many Bajans migrated to build it—.*

Students wanted to prove that Caribbean society is warm and friendly. They also wanted us to participate in their history. We later used this topic to explain the "brain drain" and the prevailing migration trends in Spain, Central, and South America.

Objective 2. Knowledge about Social Groups and Their Products

This knowledge involves recognizing that some products stem from popular beliefs or ancient traditions, so learners can research the historical or socioeconomic origins behind some of them. In order to accomplish this task, students read several Chilean legends related to the Unit 12 "Mysteries and enigmas" in *Aula Internacional 3*, such as the Pincoya or Millalobo's myths, which students compared to their oral tradition:

> —*We know the legend of the "Steel Donkey" in Barbados. It emerged around the 20th century, and it is a curse. This donkey is supposed to have its eyeballs on fire. It can breathe fire and drags steel chains along its way. My grandma told me that if you did not pay the "coolie" (an Indian trader), he would curse you and send the Steel Donkey to your house until you paid off the debt—.*

Remarkably, this student referred to the migrants from India by explicitly calling them "coolies," despite it being a derogatory term in some countries like the UK. We asked her whether she considered this was a random legend or whether there might be some sort of rejection and discrimination towards the Indian population of the Muslim faith on behalf of the Barbadian community. This led to a parallel discussion about voodoo in Haiti, Santeria in Cuba, or the evil eye in some Hispanic countries.

Regarding students' ability to distinguish common cultural products and compare them, we found a wide repertoire of contrastive analyses between the source and target cultures (C1 and C2). Following the coverage of Unit 3 about celebrations and festivities in the Hispanic world, we looked at typical meals linked to each ceremony:

> —*When somebody thinks of "fishcake" here, s/he automatically thinks of a family event, a birthday party, a social event, etc., as it is an easy dish to make. It is not "asado" or "mate"* [Argentinian foods] *but the social idea behind it is the same—.*

Following this activity, I asked students to investigate their origins and many of them informed us that the search dated back to the slavery era. They confirmed that many Caribbean dishes were imported from Africa. Therefore, it was not a superficial or playful exposure, but a formal approach that required researching, knowledge deepening, and autonomous learning.

Objective 3. Skills to Discover and Interact

Byram (1997) states that these skills increase when apprentices travel and visit other regions substantially different to their own:

> —*I traveled to Cuba a few years ago. When I got into a shop, the shop assistants did not pay the least attention to me, and they kept assisting other customers. However, as soon as they heard me talking and noticed I was a tourist, they quickly approached me to help me out diligently—.*

2 Increasing Intercultural Competence in the Anglophone... 35

This student revealed that this incident had happened merely due to his skin color. Undoubtedly, this testimonial was useful to hold an intense debate about racism and colorism in the Caribbean and other Spanish-speaking countries. This is convenient as we can resort to personal experiences to explain controversial phenomena. As teachers, we must convey these singularities to students so they are warned about potential causes of uneasiness or misunderstandings in the countries of the L2/C2.

Objective 4. Interpretation and Relation Skills

Vinagre Laranjeira (2014) claims that these skills can be observed when students relate what they know is appropriate in the C2 and apply it to counteract conflicts. For instance, when we were dealing with the topic of "Botellón" in Spain (massive social gatherings to drink outdoors), we asked learners if they agreed with the reasons youngsters cited to defend this type of entertainment. One student replied:

—If I look at it from the perspective of my culture, my answer would be no, but I do not want to sound ethnocentric. I agree with some of the reasons, as it is the only way to gather with friends and socialize. It is a norm in Spanish culture—.

Clearly, this reflection was a sign of her intercultural progress. Human beings tend to adopt an ethnocentric posture prone to criticism and negative prejudices when they face something unusual or radically different, which was reversed in this case.

Objective 5. Critical Consciousness Awareness

Byram (1997) maintains that individuals wholly develop this awareness when they are able to distance themselves from their source culture and be neutral, even if that entails judging distinctive conventions of their C1. This was exhibited when we were dealing with the topic of work, labor, and professions in Unit 1. The sheet *Entrevista con Honduras* included a listening activity about unemployment levels in that country. A student noted:

36   C. Céspedes Suárez

—Youth are significantly affected and hit by unemployment in Barbados. There are not enough measures or initiatives to stimulate employment or internships among us. There are not sufficient scholarships either—.

This awareness about what works better or less well in our homelands is vital and represents the path towards progress. Praising with excessive patriotism and without analyzing critically the areas that need improvement ultimately hinder distancing and attaining intercultural competence.

Objective 6. Awareness about One's Own Identity

We wanted to make students aware of unique aspects of their C1 they might have never noticed before assimilating the C2. The sheet *Entrevista con Nicaragua* included a listening exercise about the loss of identity, artisan products, and traditional attire as a result of globalization and the influence of foreign trends, especially from North America. A student claimed:

—I think I spent part of my past life wishing to look "more American" than Tobagonian. However, I try to feel proud of my roots now that I am older. I no longer think that my African background is a synonym of poverty but rather a symbol of cultural wealth, emancipation, and freedom—.

This listening exercise allowed us to highlight the fact that other Hispanic countries are coming across a similar transformation. For instance, the presence of English words grows rapidly inside the Spanish language in Mexico and in Spain due to the cinema industry, social media, or mass media influence.

Objective 7. Empathy, Tolerance towards Ambiguity and a Nonjudgmental Attitude

Both Neuner (1997) and Chen and Starosta (2000) located these concepts at the "intercultural pyramid" summit. In the sheet *Entrevista con*

2 Increasing Intercultural Competence in the Anglophone... 37

Bolivia, a newsreader with an indigenous background was interviewed. When exposing students to certain ethnic minorities, I perceived students had internalized some intercultural dimensions in the following excerpts:

> —*There are lots of myths, negative connotations, and stigma around the Rasta group. If the audience progressively sees Rasta on TV, elderly people for example might stop being so narrow-minded and they might understand their lifestyle and religion better—.*

Students maintained that some members of the Rasta community used to isolate themselves from the rest of the society. Some chose to live in an antisocial or almost hermit-like way, at least in Barbados, which somehow led to their ostracism. This sparked a debate about those minorities who suffer higher rates of discrimination. Apparently, this xenophobia is more pressing if their lifestyle or religious beliefs differ more from the ones of the recipient community.

Objective 8. Stereotypes and National Rivalries

The capacity to reject negative stereotypes and the national rivalries associated with them also constitutes a noteworthy sign of ICC increase and the achievement of the complete or transcultural level (Meyer, 1991). In *Entrevista con las Islas Canarias*, the protagonist stressed the persisting rivalries between the inhabitants of Gran Canaria and Tenerife. One student expressed:

> —*Caribbean countries have rivalries in the same way siblings have. We fight against each other from time to time. However, whenever a foreign country attacks the Caribbean nation, we join forces to fight against the entire world—.*

This comment manifested that even if negative stereotypes constitute the basis of most national disagreements and represent a coping mechanism when we face something unknown (Iglesias Casal, 1998), it is important to analyze the historical reasons or context in which those stereotypes arose. Once we do that, we can determine whether they should be replaced by a less-biased image nowadays.

Conclusions

Once I implemented both instruments and examined students' testimonials, I verified a perceptible and steady increase of ICC. Overall, this didactic proposal did not interfere with the development of the remaining language skills, nor did it require a substantial methodological change that might have jeopardized the goals of the official syllabus. On the contrary, having only one hour to work on the cultural component together with the rest of the lessons at our disposal was sufficient to consolidate this competence more efficiently. Likewise, the possibility to include this proposal in the assessment system through the oral expression and the listening participation components was also an advantage as students started to comprehend that culture is a key component, thus taking the cultural tasks more seriously. There is no doubt that students tend to work harder if that effort is later reflected in their grades, which I managed to do in a more comprehensive and sensible way.

To confirm the effectiveness of the project I conducted several tests and used a final intercultural sensitivity questionnaire to check intercultural competence acquisition at the end of the academic year. After nine months, students confirmed they had enjoyed the activities, they had learnt meaningfully, and they had developed most of the intercultural items we had set out to achieve by the end of the second semester. Ultimately, this proved the feasibility of this proposal and, more importantly, it proved the systematic work was worthwhile.

From a sociocultural point of view, it goes without saying that strengthening this sociocultural content would reap enormous rewards as it aligns with the new language policies both *Caribbean Examination Council* (CXC) and The University of the West Indies plan to implement in the near future. In fact, the latter announced its desire to become a multilingual academy in 2019 within the "Ten in Two" Austerity Plan. This initiative has paved the way for a more ambitious language policy aimed at emphasizing the value of studying a foreign language, regardless of the student's degree. To this end, we also must take government aspirations into account, as Barbadians authorities, for instance, want minors to develop bilingual competence so that they can interact and strive in a more interconnected world.

Bearing all this in mind, methodological suggestions such as the one presented in this chapter favor more practical didactics of language and culture following the latest and the most innovative methods in second language didactics. In this way, we forge a more faithful and closer vision of Hispanic culture and a more sociolinguistic and instrumental approach to the Spanish language from which the entire Caribbean community can benefit.

References

Areizaga, E. (2001). Cultura para la formación de la competencia comunicativa intercultural: El enfoque formativo. *Revista de Psicodidáctica*, (13), 157–170.

Arnold, J. (2000). *La dimensión afectiva en el aprendizaje de idiomas*. Cambridge University Press.

Barros García, B., & Kharnásova, G. M. (2012). La interculturalidad como macrocompetencia en la enseñanza de lenguas extranjeras: Revisión bibliográfica y conceptual. *Porta Linguarum, 18*, 97–114.

Besalú Costa, X. (2002). *Diversidad cultural y educación*. Síntesis.

Bordón, T. (2007). La evaluación de adultos por medio de los cuadros propuestos en el PEL. *Carabela*, (60), 73–98.

Byram, M. (1995). Acquiring intercultural competence: A review of learning theories. In L. Sercu (Ed.), *Intercultural competence* (pp. 53–70). Aalborg University Press.

Byram, M. (1997). *Teaching and assessing intercultural communicative competence*. Multilingual Matters.

Byram, M., & Zarate, G. (1994). *Definitions, objectives and assessment of sociocultural competence*. Council of Europe.

Camilleri-Grima, A. (2002). *How strange! The use of anecdotes in the development of intercultural competence*. Council of Europe.

Céspedes Suárez, C. (2020). Perceptions and attitudes of Spanish learners towards the intercultural communicative competence in the Anglophone Caribbean: A didactic proposal to develop it. *Tonos Digital*, (38), 1–35.

Céspedes Suárez, C. (2021). *Desarrollo y evaluación de la competencia intercultural en la clase de ELE: diseño de un curso formativo de mejora.* Doctoral dissertation, Granada University. https://digibug.ugr.es/handle/10481/66690

Chen, G. M., & Starosta, W. (2000). The development and validation of the Intercultural Sensitivity Scale. *Human Communication, 3*(1), 2–14.

Corpas, J., Garmendia, A., & Soriano, C. (2014). *Aula 3 Internacional. Curso de español.* Difusión.

Deardorff, D. K. (2011). Assessing intercultural competence: New directions for institutional research. *Wiley Periodicals, Inc,* (149), 65–79.

Dörnyei, Z., & Ushioda, E. (2013). *Teaching and researching motivation.* Routledge.

Gimeno Sacristán, J. (1992). Currículum y diversidad cultural. *Educación Sociedad, 11,* 127–153.

González Boluda, M. (2015). Hacia una perspectiva intercultural en los manuales de español lengua extranjera (ELE). *Zona Próxima,* (22) (online journal).

Grupo CRIT. (2007). *Culturas cara a cara. Relatos y actividades para la comunicación intercultural.* Edinumen.

Iglesias Casal, I. (1998). Diversidad cultural en el aula de E/LE: La interculturalidad como desafío y como provocación. In K. Alonso, F. Moreno Fernández, & M. Gil Bürmann (Eds.), *El español como lengua extranjera: Del pasado al futuro. Actas del VIII Congreso Internacional de ASELE* (pp. 463–472). Servicio de publicaciones de la Universidad de Alcalá de Henares.

Imahori, T. T., & Lanigan, M. L. (1989). Relational model of intercultural communication competence. *International Journal of Intercultural Relations, 13*(3), 269–286.

Kramsch, C. (1988). The cultural discourse of foreign language textbooks. In A. Singerman (Ed.), *Towards a new integration of language and culture* (pp. 63–88). Northeast Conference Reports.

Kramsch, C. (1993). Language study as border: Experiencing difference. *European Journal of Education, 28*(3), 349–358.

Krashen, S. D. (1987). *Principles and practice in second language acquisition.* Prentice-Hall International.

Landone, E. (2014). Más allá de la evaluación de la competencia lingüística en la acreditación. In J. De Santiago Guervós & Y. Gonzalez Plasencia (Eds.), *El español global. Actas del III Congreso Internacional del Español en Castilla y León, Salamanca* (pp. 112–123). Junta de Castilla y León.

Lázár, I., Huber-Kriegler, M., Lussier, D., Matei, G. S., & Peck, C. (Eds.). (2007). *Developing and assessing intercultural communicative competence: A guide for language teachers and teacher educators.* Council of Europa.

Li, Y. (2018). Foreign language education policy in the Commonwealth Caribbean and proposals on Chinese language teaching. In R. Herrero-Martín & P. González García, *Hands on conference on foreign language teaching* [PowerPoint, slides 1–42]. The University of the West Indies and Confucius Institute.

Martín Peris, E. (2008). La autoevaluación: Nuevas consideraciones sobre un viejo tema. In S. P. Cesteros & S. Roca Marín, *La evaluación en el aprendizaje y la enseñanza del español como lengua extranjera / segunda lengua. Actas del XVIII Congreso Internacional de la ASELE* (pp. 27–44). Servicio de publicaciones de la Universidad de Alicante.

Masello, L. (2002). *Español como lengua extranjera: Aspectos descriptivos y metodológicos*. Universidad de la República.

Meyer, M. (1991). Developing transcultural competence: Case studies of advanced foreign language learners. In D. Buttjes & M. Byram (Eds.), *Mediating languages and cultures* (pp. 136–158). Multilingual Matters Ltd.

Miquel, L. (2003). Consideraciones sobre la enseñanza de español lengua extranjera a inmigrantes. *Carabela*, (53), 5–24.

Morgan, C. (1998). Cross-cultural encounters. In M. Byram & M. Fleming (Eds.), *Language learning in intercultural perspective: Approaches through drama and ethnography* (pp. 224–241). Cambridge University Press.

Neuner, G. (1997). Le rôle de la compétence socioculturelle dans l'enseignement et l'apprentissage des langues vivantes. In M. Byram, G. Zarate, & G. Neuner (Eds.), *La compétence socioculturelle dans l'apprentissage et l'enseignement des langues* (pp. 45–107). Council of Europe.

Oliveras, À. (2000). *Hacia la competencia intercultural en el aprendizaje de una lengua extranjera. Estudio de los choques culturales y los malentendidos*. Edinumen.

Trujillo Sáez, F. (2005). En torno a la interculturalidad: Reflexiones sobre cultura y comunicación para la didáctica de la lengua. *Porta Linguarum*, (4), 23–39.

Vilà Baños, R. (2005). *La competencia comunicativa intercultural. Un estudio en el primer ciclo de la ESO*. Doctoral Dissertation, Barcelona University. www.tesisenxarxa.net/TDX/TDX_UB/TESIS/AVAILABLE/TDX1216105135329

Vinagre Laranjeira, M. (2014). El desarrollo de la competencia intercultural en los intercambios telecolaborativos. *Revista de Educación a Distancia*, (41), 1–22.

3

Teaching English Pronunciation in a Blended Environment: Feedback on a Pedagogical Innovation

Frank Bardol

Origin of the Innovation

The LANSAD sector does not enjoy as good a reputation as the specialty disciplines, with the diversity that can be observed at the level of the following:

- The content of the lessons, which show a certain disparity in most LANSAD sectors in French Universities.
- The terms of its organization: the training takes place either face-to-face or entirely remotely or according to a blended learning modality

---

Translated to English by Nicole Roberts

F. Bardol (✉)
Research Laboratory: ADEF UR4671, Aix-Marseille University,
Aix-en-Provence, France
e-mail: Frank.Bardol@univ-amu.fr

© The Author(s), under exclusive license to Springer Nature Switzerland AG 2023
D. Mideros et al. (eds.), *Innovation in Language Learning and Teaching*, New Language
Learning and Teaching Environments, https://doi.org/10.1007/978-3-031-34182-3_3

As a result, teaching in the LANSAD unit welcomes various teacher initiatives that aim to promote the development of communication skills in general. It is also an environment that is conducive to innovative practices, because the constraints at the macro level (European and national language policies) are minimal. This made it easier for us to innovate to meet our needs (limited time, a high number of students, heterogeneity of levels) at middle and micro levels. Hence the implementation of a blended learning environment to encourage students to improve their English pronunciation. Our project can be described as innovative, because rare are research projects that articulate the teaching of pronunciation through multisensoriality and reflexivity and its implementation in a blended learning environment. We endeavored to teach pronunciation so that students could "feel," "see", and hear the sounds from the works of various researchers such as Celce-Murcia et al. (2010), Underhill (2005) and Roach (2009) to mention a few researchers. This research project was born out of the observation that the level of oral English of students on the brink of graduating with BA degrees was below the level of some students at the end of the baccalaureate, where those students in the degree program are supposed to have reached the level of independent speaker B2 (North & Piccardo, 2016). According to the evaluations at the end of the first term, the majority of first-year students reached level B1 (independent user, threshold level) or even A2 (elementary user) in speaking. We therefore wanted to innovate to draw the attention of institutional leaders and researchers to the relevance of LANSAD teaching for developing language skills, especially with regard to English pronunciation.

Description of the Specific Context

Our action research project was carried out from January 2018 to December 2019 in the LANSAD unit, where students are divided according to various disciplines. Several teachers with various statuses (university professors, associate professors, readers, contract and part-time, to mention a few) are in charge of teaching. We selected the following groups of learners for whom we were responsible:

3 Teaching English Pronunciation in a Blended Environment... 45

- 2017–2018, semester 2: 26 BA Spanish students (second year)
- 2018–2019, semester 1: 17 BA Information and Communication Sciences (SIC) students (first year)
- 2019–2020, semester 1: 29 BA Educational Sciences (SED) students (third year)

Our research project was intended to be relevant enough to provide a solution to meet the conditions for setting up the teaching of English pronunciation. If the blockages at the macro level were minimal, several obstacles at the middle level (the organization of the LANSAD unit within the Faculty of Arts and Humanities) and micro level (teaching in the classroom) could be observed to carry out our project. It was a question of overcoming the obstacles linked to the following:

- The limited amount of time allocated to teaching EFL: 24 hours per semester do not allow communication objectives to be achieved, and particularly with English pronunciation.
- The heterogeneity of level: experienced learners (levels B2-C1) develop alongside learners of elementary level (A2) in similar groups, with large numbers.

We are responsible for the organization of the LANSAD unit. The main actors of this research project are the teachers, the students and the members of the information technology services, who helped us to set up the Moodle platform for educational and organizational purposes. In fact, some lessons took place remotely. The digital training was mainly concerned with the following:

- Creating online working groups
- Giving students the opportunity to upload their work in the form of written and oral files
- Providing students with the opportunity to evaluate their peers
- Observing the digital records to assess the attendance rate of learners on the Moodle platform
- Facilitating training and learning by allowing students to access digital resources related to content

In short, the information technology unit helped us strengthen the coherence between face-to-face and distance learning, publicize knowledge online and support learners in their autonomy. From the onset of the course, we shared the project with students so they could cooperate in this action research, and we strived to support their efforts to improve their pronunciation, step-by-step. This required both attendance at face-to-face and online class sessions.

The Implementation Phase

Three research cycles were carried out between 2018 and 2019. The aim was to encourage learners to improve their English pronunciation. To do this, we relied on three main poles of a model (Fig. 3.1) that emerged at the end of the research cycles, which were as follows:

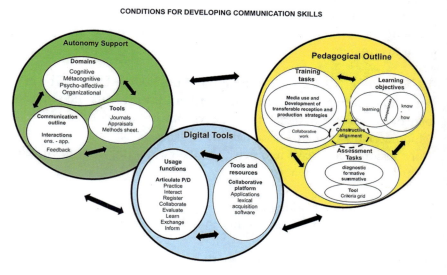

Fig. 3.1 Diagram of the operation of the model (Bardol, 2020)

- Pedagogical Outline: phonological learning objectives are linked to learning and evaluation tasks according to Biggs' constructive alignment (2003).
- Support for Autonomy: the communication scenario and the support tools (journals, assessment grids, etc.) are used to meet various needs (cognitive, metacognitive, psycho-affective, etc.) linked to learners' autonomy.
- Digital Instruments: these include digital tools and their usage functions. These were designed to facilitate the appropriation of phonological knowledge and to support learners' efforts to improve their pronunciation online.

As we can see in Fig. 3.1, each pole contains elements that interact with each other and also between the elements of the other poles. We observe the complexity at stake throughout the project, together with its dynamic and evolving trait.

Emergence of Problems and Means Implemented to Overcome Them

Several pedagogical and organizational obstacles arose during the three research cycles. We have tried to provide answers that are intended to be as appropriate as possible. First of all, the coherent articulation of face-to-face and remote modes proved to be a thorny issue. We mainly relied on the work of researchers such as Rivens Mompean (2013), Nissen (2019) on language teaching in blended learning environments, and feedback from Peraya et al. (2012). The research enabled us to propose a course organization that respected the coherence between the face-to-face and remote modes with regard to English phonology and phonetics. Thus, a four-step approach to teaching pronunciation was created (PDAE), which is described below:

1. **Perceiving**: phonological facts (sounds and connected speech) from the perspective of auditory, visual and kinesic sensoriality to facilitate memorization. This phase is guided by nonverbal techniques. It is therefore favored in the classroom.
2. (Auditory) **Discrimination**: using minimal pairs exercises. This is carried out at a distance depending on the learner's availability.
3. **Appropriation**: includes a conceptualization phase of phonological facts in the classroom, followed by a consolidation phase at a distance to give learners time to produce them properly.
4. (Free) **Expression**: students are encouraged to speak from various situations using the phonological facts they have learned. This final step occurs at a distance to save time in the classroom for more communicative activities.

Despite efforts to encourage learners to improve their phonological competence skills, some of them did not achieve the learning outcomes because they lacked motivation or were discouraged from the start, according to the interviews carried out. We became aware of the importance of psycho-affective support (Albero, 2003) throughout the course, by acknowledging that "pronunciation is much more rooted in the learner's personality than any other aspect of language" (Krashen, 1988, p. 35). As a result, we set up journals through which we interacted with learners to allow them to regain confidence.

Furthermore, the evaluation of progress, which was our original goal, is another question that arose. However, we had to revise our objectives somewhat because it is unrealistic to expect significant progress after only eight weeks of the course. Additionally, the absence of a control group would have made this undertaking inconsequential in terms of scientific reliability. Therefore, we decided to observe the following:

- Student impressions with regard to the implementation of the blended learning environment
- The effects of the elements introduced on the development of English pronunciation

3 Teaching English Pronunciation in a Blended Environment... 49

We finally tried to answer three questions that summed up our research objectives. Has the project succeeded in:

1. facilitating phonological appropriation?
2. individualizing the learning approach?
3. optimizing phonological training time?

The (in)validation of these objectives was made possible by the implementation of several data collection methods (questionnaires, performance tests, interviews, journals and digital records on *Moodle*) that we reviewed to obtain the most reliable results, as we can observe in Table 3.1.

Moreover, we were concerned with the objectivity of this research project. Indeed, we were designers, practitioners and evaluators all at the same time. We considered how to be objective despite wearing all of these hats. Overall, we determined that we were interested in the attributes of action research according to the work of Catroux (2002), Narcy-Combes

Table 3.1 Dashboard summary of the three cycles (Bardol, 2020)

Criteria/ Cycles	Cycle 1	Cycle 2 (*new items in bold and in italics*)	Cycle 3 (*new items in bold and in italics*)
Presentation of context	Université des Antilles Semester 2, 2017/18	Université des Antilles **Semester 1, 2018/19**	Université des Antilles **Semester 1, 2019/20**
Targeted audience	26 students Licence 2, heterogeneous level	***17 students Licence 1**, heterogeneous level*	***29 students Licence 3**, heterogeneous level*
Instruction	Spanish	*SIC*	*SED*
Evaluation of the project			
Course assessment tools	End of course questionnaire: 22 Pretest and posttest: 13 Journal: 13	End of course questionnaire ***modified focus tool: 16*** Pretest and posttest ***revised: 16*** Journal: 7 ***Statistical data Moodle: 20 Revision– clarification: 5***	***Start and end of course questionnaire modified focus support: 21/25*** Pretest and posttest ***(different support): 21*** Journal: 25 Statistical data Moodle: 29

(2005) and Grosbois (2012), who advocate the "scientific nature" of research. This is done by the following:

- The variation of experimental contexts: according to Narcy-Combes (2005, p. 117), research must provide as much detail as possible about the context of the experiment. These conditions could contribute to the reliability of the data.
- The involvement of as many people as possible (colleagues, engineers, administrators, etc.): this can make the experiment reliable, according to Catroux (2002, p. 15); that is why we tried to implement the PDAE method in a blended learning environment to overcome the obstacles inherent in teaching and learning English pronunciation. If this action research meets the needs of teachers in the field, it will be all the more authentic and accepted by the community of practitioners.
- The triangulation of data: cross-referencing the data would allow for better validation of the results obtained. As less than 30 students make up our research grouping, this sample proved to be much too small for the evaluations per se to constitute quantitative evidence.
- Distance in the interpretation of results: this is recommended, taking into account the specific context of the action research (Narcy-Combes, 2005, p. 120).

These recommendations, far from being exhaustive, are areas of observation that we have tried to examine in order to reduce bias and underscore the scientific rigor of this project. A final question that seemed important to take into account is the comparison between the three research cycles that we carried out. Each cycle was similar as well as different from the other. This is one of the main attributes of action research according to Susman (1983). We have carried out this action research project step-by-step that took into account the strengths and weaknesses of each previous cycle.

Analysis and Implications

Has the action research project made it possible to bring together favorable conditions for the development of English pronunciation? A cross analysis of all the results across the three cycles made it possible to answer this research question. Following the methodology used in Table 3.1, we can observe to what extent our three research objectives have been achieved.

Objective 1: Has the Action Research Succeeded in Facilitating Phonological Appropriation?

We were able to validate this first objective over the three cycles. Indeed, according to the 63 questionnaire responses, we observed that 86% of learners in cycle 1, 100% for cycle 2 and 92% for cycle 3 declared that the action research project contributed to the improvement of English pronunciation. These results coincide with those of the 45 journals where 95% of learners attested to this fact. According to them, three elements facilitated phonological appropriation. These were:

- The multisensory approach (PDAE) found in the two modes
- Formative assessment tasks
- Digital tools

Also, we observed that the action research project positively permitted support for cognitive autonomy, since 68% of learners indicated in their journals that they became aware of the usefulness of phonology to communicate efficiently.

Objective 2: Has the Project Managed to Individualize the Learning Path?

This research objective emerged at the end of the second cycle. As per the questionnaires, 80% of cycle 3 learners declared that their course was individualized based on the following:

- The communication plan accessed by journaling
- The criteria evaluation grids
- Digital tools

On the other hand, to observe whether there was an individualization of the learning path for cycles 1 and 2, we relied on a subsidiary research objective: that is, reflective learning. Indeed, the fact that a learner manages to reflect on his learning to explain his strengths, or weaknesses, and to propose remedial techniques is an indicator of the adequacy of support, and of the project in general in meeting their needs. We carried out a content analysis by themes from 45 journals. It revealed that 46% of learners for cycle 1, 28% for cycle 2 and 68% for cycle 3 managed to take the necessary step back to identify their mistakes and their strengths. Cycle 3 was mainly focused on students' autonomy support, hence the encouraging results. This is also a sign of the relevance of the elements used to individualize the course and support learners on the path to metacognitive autonomy. Thus, the second objective could only be validated for the third research cycle.

Objective 3: Has the Experimental Course Succeeded in Optimizing Phonological Training Time?

The 63 learners who answered the questionnaires declared that they were able to train remotely: 63% for cycle 1, 87% for cycle 2, 80% for cycle 3. The journals revealed similar data since more than 68% of learners said that they were able to study remotely according to their availability. The statistical data from the Moodle platform for cycles 2 and 3 support this observation and also indicate that the eight learners who did not achieve the phonological learning outcomes in these two cycles are below the average median level of the group. This is a sign of the relevance of the platform for the development of English pronunciation. Thus, we can validate this third objective across the three cycles. However, one of the limitations of our action research project is the introduction of the journal as an educational element. We used the journals to help students reflect on their progress in the learning path at various moments. They had to analyze their mistakes, point out their weaknesses and strengths and write about their efforts and the tools they used to improve their pronunciation. Our feedback was supposed to encourage their reflection and support their metacognitive autonomy. According to our analysis of the journals, only 19/62 learners found its integration into the course useful for improving their pronunciation. Successful learners may not need this type of guidance as much as learners with difficulties in improving their English pronunciation. The journal should therefore be offered to the latter, and a formative interview with the teacher would complete this reflective work.

The first results are encouraging and tend to consolidate our research hypotheses and validate a few elements of the model (Fig. 3.1). However, this model will only be relevant if and when the practitioners who use it follow training on the following:

- The teaching of English pronunciation and its nonverbal techniques
- The creation of collaborative platforms such as Moodle to evaluate, interact, inform and facilitate distance learning

Recommendations

We now wish to highlight a few key elements by reviewing the three poles of the model (Fig. 3.1):

- **The Pedagogical Outline:** It would be more appropriate to review the phonological objectives through the cycles, according to the starting level of the learners. We recommend always integrating them into the communication objectives for the purpose of contextualization. The multisensory approach implemented should be adapted to the objectives set and articulated according to the hybrid modality, taking care to include the tasks most appropriate to the remote mode. Constructive alignment would not only promote coherence between the objectives and the training and evaluation activities, but it would also make it possible to point out inconsistencies during the preparation phase of the pedagogical outline.

- **Support:** Assessment grids should be shared and should serve as a tool for discussion with learners so that they can best position themselves in the learning pathway. We tried to do this with the use of the journal. The finding was ambivalent. Although the majority of learners demonstrated some degree of metacognitive autonomy, the format of the journaling was rejected. It would perhaps be more appropriate to interview students who are having cognitive, organizational, metacognitive, or psycho-affective difficulties, as per the clarification interviews that we carried out, but instead at the midpoint of the course. Support and guidance contribute to individualization. It should be maintained, but only for those students who need it the most. Based on this, we can make them more autonomous.
- **Digital tools** should be used to service learning and facilitate the performance of the tasks required from a pedagogical perspective.

We have offered avenues of exploitation on the layout of various elements of the course, according to our findings over the three research periods. The promising trends that have emerged should encourage the designer, the researcher and the practitioner who wish to transpose this model to another context. This would serve to (in)validate our hypotheses and generalize these initial trends.

References

Albero, B. (2003). L'autoformation dans les dispositifs de formation ouverte et à distance: Instrumenter le développement de l'autonomie dans les apprentissages. *Les TIC au cœur de l'enseignement supérieur.* Actes de la journée d'étude du 12 novembre 2002, Laboratoire Paragraphe, Université Paris

VIII—Vincennes-St Denis, 139–159. http://edutice.archives-ouvertes.fr/edutice-00000270

Bardol, F. (2020). *Les conditiondos de développement de la compétence phonologique dans un dispositif hybride: le cas de l'enseignement-apprentissage de l'anglais en LANSAD, à l'Université des Antilles.* Doctoral dissertation, Université de Lille.

Biggs, J. (2003). Aligning teaching for constructing learning. *Higher Education Academy, 1*(4). https://www.advance-he.ac.uk/knowledge-hub/aligning-teaching-constructing-learning

Catroux, M. (2002). Introduction à la recherche-action: Modalités d'une démarche théorique centrée sur la pratique. *Recherche et pratiques pédagogiques en langues de spécialité, 21*(3), 8–20. https://doi.org/10.4000/apliut.4276

Celce-Murcia, M., Brinton, D., Goodwin, J., & Griner, B. (2010). *Teaching pronunciation.* Cambridge University Press.

Grosbois, M. (2012). *Didactique des langues et technologies: De l'EAO aux réseaux sociaux.* PUPS.

Krashen, S. D. (1988). *Second language acquisition and second language learning.* Prentice Hall.

Narcy-Combes, J.-P. (2005). *Didactique des langues et TIC: Vers une recherche-action responsable.* Ophrys.

Nissen, E. (2019). *Formation hybride en langues: Articuler présentiel et distanciel.* Didier.

North, B., & Piccardo, E. (2016). *Developing illustrative descriptors of aspects of mediation for the CEFR.* Education Policy Division, Council of Europe. https://rm.coe.int/168073ff31

Peraya, D., Peltier, C., Villiot-Leclercq, E., Nagels, M., Morin, C., Burton, R., & Mancuso G. (2012). Typologie des dispositifs de formation hybrides: configurations et métaphores. *Quelle université pour demain?* 144–155. https://hal.archives-ouvertes.fr/hal-00703589

Rivens Mompean, A. (2013). *Le Centre de ressources en langues: vers la modélisation du dispositif d'apprentissage.* Presses Universitaires du Septentrion.

Roach, P. (2009). *English phonetics and phonology: A practical course* (4th ed.). Cambridge University Press.

Susman, G. I. (1983). *Action research: A sociotechnical systems perspective.* Sage Publications.

Underhill, A. (2005). *Sound foundations: Learning and teaching pronunciation.* Macmillan.

4

Teaching Beyond the Classroom: A Project-Based Innovation in a Language Education Course

Pamela Rose

Introduction

The use of problem-based learning (PBL) instruction is becoming more widespread in higher education because of its potential to yield higher gains in problem-solving and decision-making (Iwamoto et al., 2016; Clark, 2017). Skills in collaborative problem-solving and decision-making are in high demand for the rapidly evolving global environment (Sandeen, 2012). Thus, higher education institutions are using assessments that feature problem-based projects such as first-year seminars, undergraduate research, service learning, community-based learning, internships and capstone projects.

These project-based assessments are alternatives to traditional forms of assessment and are underpinned by the constructive approach to teaching and learning. Constructivists argue that learning is enhanced

---

P. Rose (✉)
Departments of Language and Cultural Studies & Curriculum and Instruction, University of Guyana, Georgetown, Guyana
e-mail: pamela.rose@uog.edu.gy

© The Author(s), under exclusive license to Springer Nature Switzerland AG 2023
D. Mideros et al. (eds.), *Innovation in Language Learning and Teaching*, New Language Learning and Teaching Environments, https://doi.org/10.1007/978-3-031-34182-3_4

when students have active roles in their learning (Liu & Chen, 2010). From this constructivist lens, students engaged in project-based assessments are expected to gain greater autonomy, develop more responsibility, build transferable soft skills and increase their motivation and success (Clark, 2017).

In light of the criteria for PBL projects proposed by Thomas (2000), not all project-based assessments can be considered PBL. According to Thomas, in PBL, teachers act as facilitators and guides as students work collaboratively on real-world problems and issues. Through its applied and reflective activities, PBL takes students outside of the classroom and into the real world. Framed from Thomas's perspective, assessments using projects that are based on academic challenges, scenarios and simulated problems do not count as PBL assessments. Accordingly, PBL project-based assessments must be based on authentic, real-life challenges. However, while there is a rich literature on PBL project-based assessments in the science, technology, engineering and mathematics (STEM) disciplines (Dolan, 2016; Barak, 2020), there is a paucity of literature on their use and potential capabilities in the humanities disciplines (Darling-Hammond, 2017; Grigg & Lewis, 2018).

Therefore, this chapter focuses on an innovation in the humanities in the higher education context. It describes the process of implementing a project-based assessment in a language education course. As a response to calls for more responsive and innovative higher education pedagogy (Grigg & Lewis, 2018; UNESCO, 2015), this chapter adds to the literature on innovation as transformative pedagogy in teacher education.

Background

In my context in the Faculty of Education and Humanities, even though projects are used as forms of assessments, many do not fulfill the criteria to be deemed problem-based assessments because they generally focus on simulated academic challenges with theoretical solutions that are rarely implemented. The nature of these assessments is of concern for two reasons. One is that teacher practitioners consistently express concerns about classroom challenges, which they seem incapable of managing. This

4 Teaching Beyond the Classroom: A Project-Based Innovation... 59

situation underscores the need for teacher education to focus on the real-life realities of classrooms (Afdal & Spernes, 2018; Darling-Hammond, 2017). Second, the unpredictable global landscape in which teaching occurs and new and complex challenges emerge suggests that key priorities in teacher education should include pedagogical innovation to support more collaborative and transformative ways of promoting learning (UNESCO, 2015).

As I read about changes in higher education that were happening elsewhere, I became motivated to seek alternative means of assessment that could have practical value to teacher practitioners in my language education course. I was drawn to project-based assessment because the literature suggests that apart from developing learner autonomy, soft skills and responsibility (Warren, 2016), these forms of assessment have been positively associated with deep approaches to learning and increased rates in retention and engagement across student groups (Clark, 2017; Grigg & Lewis, 2018). Examples of such projects include service-based learning (Kuh, 2008), course-based undergraduate research experience (CURE) (Dolan, 2016) and collective teacher efficacy (Bandura, 1997).

Service-Based Learning

Kuh (2008) defined service-based learning as community-based learning in which students work and solve problems collaboratively with community partners and give back to the community. Clark (2017) noted that this type of learning develops intellectual and practical competencies while increasing the rate of students' engagement and success.

Course-based Undergraduate Research

CURE is an emerging field in higher education, and it involves entire classes of students conducting research in their regular credit-bearing courses (Dolan, 2016). Unlike other types of traditional research, with CURE, students collaborate to design the project, analyse data and interpret findings as they engage with stakeholder communities (Corwin

60 P. Rose

et al., 2014). CURE has been successfully used in the STEM disciplines in higher education with collaboration and the integration of knowledge cited as its most appealing features (Shortlidge et al., 2016). CUREs are known to motivate students to actively engage with research and their learning because they are windows through which students can recognise the larger purpose and impact of their work, beyond classroom grades (Fukami, 2013; Freeman et al., 2014). While CURE has been successfully used in STEM disciplines, its use in other disciplines is yet to be generally documented (Corwin et al., 2018). Moreover, the blending of service learning and CURE has not yet received much attention.

Collective Teacher Efficacy

Collective teacher efficacy relates to group goals and how members of the group work together to achieve those goals (Bandura, 1997; Goddard et al., 2004). It draws on four sources of self-efficacy beliefs to shed light on how people working together develop beliefs and confidence that allow them to collectively succeed. Mastery experiences, vicarious experiences, social persuasion and affective states are all sources of self-efficacy and processes associated with collective efficacy (Bandura, 1997). Mastery experiences result from the success of individual teachers and occur at the individual and organisation level (Goddard et al., 2004). According to Bandura (1997), vicarious experiences relate to observing and modelling what works well, and social persuasion is associated with feedback from various sources such as colleagues and school leadership (Eells, 2011). Affective states, the emotional tone of the school, refer to how conducive organisations are to engaging with and accepting change (Tschannen-Moran & Barr, 2004). According to Ross et al. (2004), school processes in collective teacher efficacy relate to congruence of school plans with school needs, empowered school leadership, shared school goals and school-wide collaboration.

Although there is a rich body of literature on collective teacher efficacy (Eells, 2011; Goddard et al., 2004; Tschannen-Moran et al., 1998), there is renewed interest in it from the lens of teachers' professional development programmes because it has been recognised as a key driver of improvements in students' academic performance and school-wide systems (Thornton et al., 2020; Donohoo, 2018). Research has linked collective teacher efficacy to problem-solving in schools, pointing out that schools and teachers who accept collective responsibility for students' successes and failure become more critical of their teaching and learning environment (Donohoo et al., 2018; Hattie & Zierer, 2017). According to Donohoo et al. (2018), this approach helps to keep student learning in focus. It creates a school culture in which there is less appropriation of blame and more reflection that generates productive patterns of behaviours and courses of action conducive to implementing better, high-yielding innovative strategies. Framed from service-based learning and CURE, the project-based assessment appears to be an appropriate innovation to generate the productive patterns of behaviours (Donohoo et al., 2018) necessary to develop collective teacher efficacy for problem-solving in language education classrooms.

Context

The Berbice Campus is the smaller of two campuses of the University of Guyana, the single national university in Guyana. Berbice Campus is located in a rural area and has less than 1000 students enrolled in programmes in five divisions, namely the Divisions of Agriculture and Forestry, Natural Sciences, Social Sciences, Health Sciences and the School of Business and Entrepreneurship. These divisions are attached to their respective faculties or colleges at the larger campus, Turkeyen, which is located in the city.

The Division of Education and Humanities is mainly concerned with teacher preparation, offering degree programmes to early childhood, primary and secondary school teacher practitioners through the Departments of Curriculum and Instruction, Language and Cultural Studies, Foundation and Education Management and Social Studies.

In 2014, the Department of Curriculum and Instruction reviewed its course outlines for the language education courses with a view of including more contemporary approaches to language education. In one course, the Teaching of Language Arts at the Primary Level, changes were made

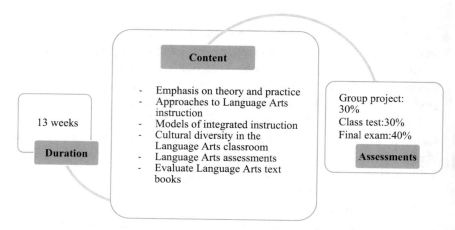

Fig. 4.1 An overview of the language arts course in which the project-based assessment was implemented

to the course content. Three in-class assessments were reduced to two for the course work component of the assessments because the semester was reduced from 15 to 13 weeks across the university. While a group assessment for 30% of the total course work score was stated on the course outline, the nature of the group assessment was not prescribed. Figure 4.1 provides an overview of the course in which the project-based assessment was implemented.

The Course

The Teaching of Language Arts at the Primary Level (EEN 4102) is one of many three-credit courses in the Faculty of Education and Humanities. It is a semester-long course (September to December) offered to teacher practitioners pursuing a bachelor's degree in primary education. It aims to help them acquire the skills and strategies necessary to understand the language arts needs of their learners and the environment in which they teach this subject. The course emphasises that language is best learned as an integrated process through purposeful activities in a language-rich environment.

4 Teaching Beyond the Classroom: A Project-Based Innovation...

In this course, teacher practitioners are expected to describe their language arts teaching and learning environment and identify needs of their learners framed from theoretical discussions on principles of contemporary language arts teaching. They also examine models of integrated instruction and different types of language arts assessment in addition to critiquing language arts text books.

Delivery of the Course

Teacher practitioners met with me once every week for three hours for a total of 13 sessions during which they engaged in theoretical discussions and considered practical applications of language arts principles to their language arts classroom. They were to complete two assessments for course work, one class test (30%) and one group-project (30%), and then one final exam (40%) at the end of the course. Consistent with the flipped method of teaching (Bergmann & Sams, 2012), I posted class readings and tasks on the Moodle platform prior to the classroom sessions so that more time was available to discuss how to apply the theory and principles to the language arts classrooms. As we attempted to connect theory to practice, we identified problematic issues and engaged in discussions of how to solve these problems.

It was during these discussions I recognised that teacher practitioners had more common problems than ideas for addressing them and that the assessments in the course appeared more theoretical than authentic and practical. One recurring problem was the declining literacy rates in their schools and the multidimensional nature of this specific problem. This observation was a key motivation to implement an innovative project-based assessment. I wanted to transform and contextualise learning in this course by making its assessment more meaningful and relevant to the real-life realities of teacher practitioners and the needs of students in their classrooms.

Implementing the PBL Assessment in the Teaching of Language Arts Course

A total of 118 teacher practitioners participated in the project-based assessments that were implemented and sustained across three academic years at the University of Guyana Berbice Campus, beginning during the academic year 2017–2018. In the latter years, the project-based assessment expanded to accommodate more stakeholders and additional features. At the beginning of each cycle of the project, we co-constructed the rubric to grade the assessment. We identified criteria for grading and assigned marks to each criterion depending on the volume of work to be completed for each task. Figure 4.2 presents an overview of the cycles of the initial project-based assessment conducted during the academic year 2017–2018.

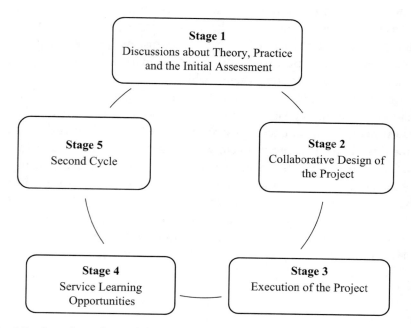

Fig. 4.2 Overview of the cycles of the initial project-based assessment

Cycle 1: Academic Year 2017–2018

Stage 1: Discussion about Theory, Practice and the Initial Assessment

During the first four weeks of the course, we engaged in discussions about the theory and practice of language arts teaching with specific attention to models of integrated instruction. For the first assessment, 42 teacher practitioners were put into groups of 8 and given one model of integrated instruction to present using any format they desired. One group used a panel discussion to make a presentation on literature-based models of language arts instruction. They delivered a very engaging, creative and insightful presentation that linked declining literacy rates in primary schools to factors that included students' lack of interest in reading for pleasure and the absence of books that target reading for pleasure in classrooms and the homes of students. As I listened to their presentation, especially how well and convincingly they articulated their ideas and how they engaged the class, I thought that their presentation needed to have greater reach beyond the walls of the classroom and that we could use it as a springboard to initiate a collective focus on literacy issues. I shared my thoughts with the class, and the teacher practitioners were receptive and very enthusiastic about creating a project-based assessment to address a real need.

Stage 2: Collaborative Design of the Project

We identified a focus for the project which was to promote reading for pleasure in primary schools through collaborative engagements with key stakeholders. Working collaboratively in one session, we identified five phases for the project. It was titled *Teachers in concert for literacy development*. Figure 4.3 shows the five phases of the project which were identified and later operationalised.

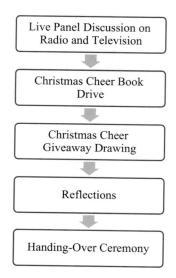

Fig. 4.3 Overview of the five phases of the initial project

Stage 3: Execution of the Project

Panel Discussion: We used the panel discussion presented by the group to raise awareness of the literacy issues, provide information for addressing literacy issues and advertise the other phases of our project. The panel discussion was done live, once on national television and once on the radio by the group of teacher practitioners who had created it. We then split the class into working committees such as finance with responsibility for budgeting and purchases, design with responsibility for creating donation boxes and decorating spaces, catering with responsibility for arranging snacks and meals and a planning committee with specific responsibility for coordinating the main events including a cultural programme embedded in a book drawing, a donor appreciation cocktail and a handing-over ceremony.

Christmas Cheer Book Drive: Following the panel discussion, we embarked on a book drive, collecting donations of story books or cash to purchase from willing donors in their business places. Teacher practitioners also split into groups and visited each outdoor market once with

4 Teaching Beyond the Classroom: A Project-Based Innovation... 67

their donation boxes to solicit donations from willing donors. Every group was involved in the book drive, soliciting donations and story books.

Christmas Giveaway Drawing: After the book drive, we held a Christmas Giveaway Drawing, which integrated a cultural programme, a drawing of winners (primary schools) for reading spaces and a donor appreciation cocktail. The donor appreciation event was cosponsored by the Department of Education and the university. Donations collected were not used for this event. We invited our key stakeholders including heads of schools to participate in the event by identifying winners and interacting with each other during the donor appreciation cocktail.

Reflections: Teacher practitioners were asked to reflect on their learning during the project-based assessments, identify highlights of their learning and what could be done better in another cycle of the project. Across two years, they reported gains in content, learning to integrate project-based, literature-based and task-based strategies in their classrooms, learning how to identify problems and find solutions, how to collect and analyse data, interview and transcribe data and discuss findings, how to collaborate with their classmates and community partners, how to solicit donations from vendors, shoppers, passers-by and the business community, how to do a live interview on television, how to develop resilience, determination and perseverance, how to accept both praise and criticisms, and how not to allow criticisms to dim their light and hope and proceed with optimism in the face of all the odds. In essence, they developed collective teacher efficacy for problem-solving, especially resilience and willingness to persist in difficult circumstances (Goddard et al., 2004).

Handing-Over ceremony: We created reading spaces which were handed over to the winners during the ceremony. Every group was involved in sorting books into levels and categories and setting up the spaces prior to the handing-over ceremony. Stakeholders were invited to distribute the reading spaces which identified them as sponsors (branding).

In the first year of the programme, teacher practitioners were able to distribute reading spaces to 25 primary schools across Region 6. Each reading space comprised several sets of story books, a book case and a carpet on which students can sit or lie when reading in the classrooms.

Stage 4: Building Service-Learning Opportunities in the Course through the Design of the Project

Service-learning opportunities were integrated into the course through its design. We identified and engaged stakeholders internally and externally. Internally, I pitched our project to the Coordinator of the Division of Education and Humanities and the Campus Board from which we engaged the heads of the Library and Bursary units, sought funding as partial contribution to the donor appreciation event and sought approval to engage external stakeholders during the project. Our external stakeholders were the members of the private and public sectors from whom we solicited either story books or funds to purchase, the regional department of education that provided snacks and the media from whom we accessed free air time. Collectively, through our engagement, we sought to give back to the communities in providing reading spaces to classrooms in primary schools to address the issue of literacy.

Cycle 2: Academic Year 2018–2019

During academic year 2018–2019, Stages 1 to 4 were repeated with a second cohort of 35 students. There were three key differences between this cycle and the previous cycle.

1. As a repeat of the previous project-based assessment, this cycle was titled *Teachers in concert for literacy development II*.
2. It expanded into another geographic region, engaging businesses, schools and the Department of Education in Region 5.
3. A course-based undergraduate research experience (CURE) was integrated to evaluate the initial project and use the findings to strengthen the current project.

Implementing CURE

CURE was implemented during Stage 1: Discussion of Theory, Practice and the Initial Assessment. Its implementation involved the following phases.

Phase 1: Document Analysis

Teacher practitioners viewed videos, financial statements, photographs, list of winners, donors, media reports and so on related to the previous project (2017–2018) to familiarise themselves with the nature and scope of the work conducted by the pioneers of the previous project and to begin formulating a research plan. One hour in each three-hour session was used to discuss project activities.

Phase 2: Research Plan

At the whole class level, we identified a research focus, purpose and research questions. The aim of this phase was for teacher practitioners to identify strengths and weaknesses in the previous project so that their project could be better planned and executed. We focused on the general impact of the spaces in the classrooms, perceptions of the spaces by the winners and how the spaces were used by them. Our three research questions were as follows:

1. What impact did the reading spaces have on learners in the classrooms?
2. What were teachers' perceptions of the reading spaces?
3. How did teachers use the reading spaces?

Data was collected from the previous winners through semi-structured interviews. Teacher practitioners were to record, transcribe and analyse the data for content.

Phase 3: Fieldwork

The class was divided into groups according to geographic locations. The teacher practitioners assigned research roles and tasks within each group. Data collection was completed during one week. The data was analysed and reported during the subsequent week.

Phase 4: Reporting

Groups presented their findings, and the class identified and selected findings they deemed useful to making decisions for their project-based assessment. Groups collaborated and collated their findings to produce one report which was shared with stakeholders during the handing-over ceremony of the second cycle of the project-based assessment. In the second cycle of the programme, teacher practitioners distributed 24 reading spaces to primary schools in Regions 5 and 6.

Cycle 3: Academic Year 2019–2020

This cycle was identical to the second cycle and was titled *Teachers in concert for literacy development III*. Forty-one teacher practitioners collected data from the winners in the second cycle. Data collection and analysis engaged similar methods used by their predecessors in the previous project-based assessment. This cohort of teacher practitioners distributed 46 reading spaces to primary schools in Regions 5 and 6.

Challenges of Implementing the PBL Assessment in the Course

Assessing Group Performance

In the initial and second cycles of the project-based assessment, assessing teacher practitioners while implementing the service-learning projects was a challenge. This problem is noted in the literature (Dolan, 2016). Teacher practitioners, who worked as teams/groups, monitored individual performance throughout the process, reporting instances when they believed team members were not making adequate contributions. This situation presented a challenge to assess group performance when the performance of individual members was below par. In addition, task groups were dynamic, reducing or increasing in numbers and having members working across multiple groups when required. For example, a member of a group formed according to geographic location served that group and was also a member of the finance committee or the social committee with responsibility for planning and executing the social events that were a part of the project.

However, when group products were extremely satisfying, teacher practitioners did not focus on individual performance. Nevertheless, we arrived at a consensus to award individual scores to team members who performed multiple roles and tasks. We adjusted the assessment rubrics so that they combined individual and group/team grading, which led to satisfactory outcomes. In the third cycle of the project-based assessment, although teacher practitioners complained about individual members' contribution, they preferred to have the assessment rubric focus on group performance rather than a combination of individual and group. Thus, cohorts varied in how they wanted to be assessed, and this finding underscores the importance of co-creating the rubric before the start of the project-based assessment instead of applying a standard rubric uniformly across successive projects.

Workload

The amount of energy and time required to integrate service-based learning and CURE into the course was sometimes overwhelming. This challenge aligns with findings in the literature that workload is a drawback of integrating such projects in courses (Shortlidge et al., 2016). Ensuring that the teacher practitioners were also not overwhelmed and that the project activities did not interfere with their regular schedule was also another challenge. To overcome these particular challenges, we created a rigid work plan, ensuring that all tasks adhered to the deadlines, and in all the cycles we moved the handing-over ceremony to the semester break.

As grades were due at the end of the semester, I approached the administration to have the mark sheet submitted at the conclusion of the project-based assessment. We also enlisted the help of the faculty secretary for record keeping. One notable feature that assisted with time management was that without my intervention teacher practitioners developed a rapid response approach where they would quickly troubleshoot issues which emerged, find solutions and seek my approval to implement solutions or provide information after the fact. This action allowed the project to flow without many encumbrances.

Transparency for Financial Activities

Another area of concern was ensuring that all financial activities were transparent and followed stipulated university protocols. In implementing the service-learning aspect of the project, some areas such as budgeting, maintaining financial records and providing clerical support were outside the scope of classroom instruction. We enlisted the help of support staff with those specific responsibilities at the university. This being a small campus, the support staff were willing to invest extra time and effort to manage those areas of the project as we progressed, and this helped to mitigate these challenges.

Opportunities

Creation of Synergies

Implementing service learning and CURE in the project-based assessment in the language arts course allowed us to create synergies within the institution and outside of the institution since the successful implementation of the project might not have been possible without widespread cooperation in these spheres. As noted in the challenges section, multiple members of different sections of the campus were willing to commit time and effort, staff from the Bursary who managed the finances, staff from the faculty office who assisted with clerical duties, staff from the library and computer centre who provided technical support for major events and staff from housekeeping who provided critical support before and after the events. In addition to the business communities, the departments of education in two regions played important roles in contributing to the project and making the primary schools available to participate in the book drive drawing and handing-over ceremony. As referred to in Dolan (2016), synergies between campus constituents are required for the successful execution of such projects in higher education institutions even though they are difficult to achieve. The synergistic efforts to address the literacy issue indicate that as a small campus its emotional tone (Bandura, 1997) is consistent with that required for developing collective teacher efficacy.

Developing Collective Teacher Efficacy for Problem-Solving

The integration of service-based learning and CURE yielded opportunities for teacher practitioners to develop research knowledge and collective teacher efficacy for problem-solving in the language education course. Collaborating in teams, engaging in relevant work, evaluating what went wrong and how improvements can be made contribute to outcomes in problem-solving. The successful outcome of the cycles of the project was highly dependent on teacher practitioners using research information and organising and working systematically as a team. In addition, they empirically evaluated projects of their predecessors, developed and applied persuasive strategies to solicit donations from sceptical donors, obtained support from stakeholders for their cause, reduced and managed risks when approaching potential donors, worked in groups to manage options, saw situations from different perspectives, identified and monitored potential issues and found collective solutions to problems as they emerged. In terms of language education, the skills developed reflect the project-based assessment as an innovation enabling teacher practitioners to develop mastery of experiences and to use vicarious experiences and social persuasion (Bandura, 1997) to accomplish a common goal. These are very important lifelong processes and problem-solving skills that are transferable to settings outside the classroom (Wiley & Stover, 2017).

Sourcing Funding

Funding is a major challenge identified in the literature when implementing such projects (Dolan, 2016). However, while the university was unable to provide all the necessary funding required for the project-based assessment, teacher practitioners engaged stakeholders. In addition, the departments of education played key roles. The departments in two geographical regions provided financial support in the form of snacks and meals for the donor appreciation event and the handing-over ceremony. Cash donations from the business community to purchase reading spaces and free air time on national television all formed a part of the funding which supported the successful implementation of the project-based assessment.

Impact on Students' Literacy Development and Engagement

The initial focus of the project-based assessment was to help teachers of language arts to improve the literacy rates in their classrooms by creating easily accessible resource rich reading spaces in classrooms. Teacher practitioners' feedback was collected and used at the end of each project to ensure that the resources provided met the needs of the students and the projects were making impacts to support continuation. Teacher practitioners conducting each project interviewed teachers who were awarded reading spaces to find out about the students' experiences with the reading spaces in their classrooms. Their summarised responses indicated what impacts the reading spaces were making on students' literacy development. First, we found that teachers were using the reading spaces in two main ways to improve their students' literacy levels:

4 Teaching Beyond the Classroom: A Project-Based Innovation...

1. Activity space embedded in classroom teaching

In some schools, the spaces were used as an activity space during routine reading sessions in the classrooms. Some teachers integrated the reading spaces in their story time activities. Students were encouraged to select books, tell stories and participate in whole class discussions about the stories.

2. Independent reading

In some schools, the students were encouraged to visit the reading spaces during their lunch or spare time and choose to read independently or with peers.

Second, we found that teachers perceived that the reading spaces improved students' literacy levels in three key areas.

1. Word recognition and vocabulary skills

The teachers reported that the reading spaces enhanced the students' word recognition and vocabulary skills as many of them who had difficulties in these areas and had actively engaged with the reading spaces showed improvements.

2. Comprehension skills

They also reported that many of the students improved their reading comprehension skills, performing better in tasks in which they were required to demonstrate understanding of what they read.

3. Self-confidence

Further, they reported that the reading spaces boosted students' self-confidence by motivating weak learners and encouraging peer teaching.

A few teachers reported that some students were so highly engaged and motivated to read that they wanted to spend most of their class time in the reading spaces, and thus they were a little distracted by the reading spaces during instructional periods.

Factors Enabling the Success of the Project

The feedback from teachers in primary schools that benefitted from the projects would suggest that reading spaces were helping to improve literacy in classrooms in which they were placed, and thus the project-based innovation was producing satisfactory outcomes. Noteworthy is that several factors were responsible for the successful implementation of this innovation in the teaching of language arts course. First, the flipped classroom approach enabled the multidimensional project design to be completed within the time frame. Second, the course outline was flexible in that it did not specify what should be done for the group assessment. Third, the approach to the assessment was flexible in that no specific format was prescribed for the group tasks conducted during the initial project when the idea for the project-based assessment emerged. Fourth, buy-in from the other units in the campus such as the Library and Bursary were instrumental in making the project activities less overwhelming for teacher practitioners. Finally, a flexible rubric that was co-created and that could have been adjusted at any cycle during the assessment enabled a fair and transparent process for grading. Despite the successful implementation of the innovation, there were some limitations.

Limitations

This innovation was implemented on a relatively small campus, and as a consequence some potential institutional barriers might not have been captured. There might be in other larger higher education institutions, institutional factors which might impact the successful execution of this kind of innovation. How successful this innovation is can only be determined if it is replicated in other higher education institutions in different contexts and with larger and more diverse populations and structures. In addition, when teacher practitioners complained about colleagues who were not making adequate contributions, no follow-up was done to find out whether they were not comfortable with the tasks especially since it involved them having to conduct activities with which they might not be comfortable. Future use of this type of innovation should follow up on any form of resistance to activities and tasks, either subtle or overt. Doing so might provide insights necessary for creating more effective collaborative spaces.

From a language teaching and learning perspective, reports on the success of the project were from the classroom's teachers' perspective on how students performed in classroom activities and tests. An evaluation of the impact of the innovation from more objective investigations of students' performance in literacy-based assessments would yield more insights into the impact of the project on a wider scale. This is another dimension for a future cycle of the innovation. Despite these limitations, there are useful implications for practice when the innovation is evaluated.

Evaluation

The previous sections have shown how the innovation was integrated organically into a language education course in the humanities discipline by blending service-based learning and course-based undergraduate research experience, although integrating such practices successfully into a curriculum is considered a major challenge (Dolan, 2016). The blending of service-based learning and course-based research experience in this assessment fostered theory–practice-related outcomes in teacher practitioners' professional development such as enabling them to develop skills in field research methodology and apply these skills to problem-solving to address challenges at a national level. This innovation also helped to foster collective teacher efficacy with teacher practitioners gaining opportunity to collaboratively identify common problems, reflect on others experiences, take action and reflect on their actions, all of which are germane to solving problems and improving student success in classrooms (Parker, 2018).

However, even though the innovation appeared largely successful, educators interested in implementing this type of innovation might want to consider several factors. First is the time frame. This innovation was time-intensive, and there would be instances when events such as national holidays could interfere with class schedules. Second is the weighting of

78   P. Rose

the assessment in the innovation. I always felt guilty about the weighting (30%) given to the assessment, considering the magnitude of the tasks involved. An intensive assessment with so many dimensions deserves a greater weighting. One might even want to consider making this assessment the only course work assessment given its aspects and duration. Fourth are the financial controls. Given that teacher practitioners solicited donations independently, there is need for financial accountability in the form of astute record keeping. Receipts prepared by the university were provided to donors, and all funds acquired were deposited into the account of the university to be retrieved through formal requests with adequate supporting documents. This process was sometimes lengthy and caused undue delays for some tasks, but it was necessary for transparency and ensuring that the university protocols governing finances were strictly adhered to.

Implications for Practice

By combining service-based learning with course-based undergraduate research experiences, instructors can promote problem-based learning in which teacher practitioners engage meaningfully with research and key community stakeholders to address national issues. This type of active, inquiry-based learning can empower teacher practitioners to help their students to develop academic and lifelong skills such as reading for pleasure. Through this type of innovation, higher education training can become more transformative.

With respect to improving literacy rates, this project-based innovation can help teacher practitioners to change the way they think about and approach literacy issues. Through this bottom-up process, in which they actively collaborated with multiple stakeholders, they could motivate students to engage with literature and foster reading for pleasure. This innovation can also encourage teacher practitioners to develop collective teacher efficacy to address literacy learning and improve students' learning gains in literacy. The innovation reflects one way in which traditional assessments could be redesigned to meet twenty-first-century professional development needs. It equips teacher practitioners with processes and methods that they can use to develop collaborative initiatives for addressing common everyday classroom challenges.

References

Afdal, H. W., & Spernes, K. (2018). Designing and redesigning research-based teacher education. *Teaching and Teacher Education, 74*, 215–228.

Bandura, A. (1997). *Self-efficacy: The exercise of control*. W. H. Freeman.

Barak, M. (2020). Problem, project- and design-based learning: Their relationship to teaching science, technology and engineering. *School Journal of Problem-Based Learning, 7*(2), 94–97. https://ejpbl.org/journal/view.php?number=53

Bergmann, J., & Sams, A. (2012). *Flip your classroom: Reach every student in every class every day*. International Society for Technology in Education.

Clark, B. (2017). Project based learning: Assessing and measuring student participation. *Research and Evaluation in Literacy and Technology, 39*, 1–29.

Corwin, L. A., Laursen, S. L., Branchaw, J. L., Eagan, K., Graham, M., Hanauer, D. I., Lawrie, G., et al. (2014). Assessment of course-based undergraduate research experiences: A meeting report. *CBE—Life Sciences Education, 13*(1), 29–40. https://www.lifescied.org/doi/full/10.1187/cbe.14-01-0004

Corwin, L. A., Runyon, C. R., Ghanem, E., Sandy, M., Clark, G., Gregory, C., Palmer, S., Reichler, S., Rodenbusch, E., & Dolan, E. (2018). Effects of discovery, iteration, and collaboration in laboratory courses on undergraduates' research career intentions fully mediated by student ownership. *CBE—Life Sciences Education, 17*(2), 1–18. https://www.lifescied.org/doi/10.1187/cbe.17-07-0141

Darling-Hammond, L. (2017). Teacher education around the world: What can we learn from international practice? *European Journal of Teacher Education, 40*(3), 291–309. https://doi.org/10.1080/02619768.2017.1315399

Dolan, E. L. (2016). *Course-based undergraduate research experiences: Current knowledge and future directions*. National Research Council.

Donohoo, J. (2018). Collective teacher efficacy research: Productive patterns of behaviour and other positive consequences. *Journal of Educational Change, 19*(3), 323–345.

Donohoo, J., Hattie, J., & Eells, R. (2018). The power of collective efficacy. *Educational Leadership, 75*(6), 40–44.

Eells, R. (2011). *Meta-analysis of the relationship between collective efficacy and student achievement.* Unpublished doctoral dissertation, Loyola University of Chicago.

Freeman, S., Eddy, S. L., McDonough, M., Smith, M. K., Okoroafor, N., Jordt, H., & Wenderoth, M. P. (2014). Active learning increases student performance in science, engineering, and mathematics. *Proceedings of the National Academy of Sciences of the United States of America, 111*(23), 8410–8415. https://doi.org/10.1073/pnas.131903011

Fukami, T. (2013). Integrating inquiry-based teaching with faculty research. *Science, 339*(6127), 1536–1537. https://science.sciencemag.org/content/339/6127/1536.full

Goddard, R. D., Hoy, W. K., & Woolfolk Hoy, A. (2004). Collective efficacy beliefs: Theoretical developments, empirical evidence, and future directions. *Educational Researcher, 33*(3), 3–13. https://journals.sagepub.com/doi/1 0.3102/0013189X033003003

Grigg, R., & Lewis, L. (2018). Moving the andragogy of teacher educators forward: The potential and challenges of Problem-Based Learning in teacher education. *Journal of Problem-Based Learning, 5*(1), 5–20. https://doi.org/10.24313/jpbl.2018.5.1.4

Hattie, J., & Zierer, K. (2017). *10 mindframes for visible learning: Teaching for success* (1st ed.). Routledge. https://doi.org/10.4324/9781315206387

Iwamoto, D. H., Hargis, I., & Vuong, K. (2016). The effect of project-based learning on student performance: An action research study. *International Journal for the Scholarship of Technology Enhanced Learning, 1*(1), 24–42.

Kuh, G. (2008). *High-impact educational practices: What they are, who has access to them, and why the matter.* Report from the Association of American Colleges and Universities.

Liu, C., & Chen, I. J. (2010). Evolution of constructivism. *Contemporary Issues in Education (CIER), 3*(4), 63–66.

Parker, J. (2018). Undergraduate research, learning gain and equity: The impact of final year research projects. *Higher Education Pedagogies, 3*(1), 145–157.

Ross, J., Hogaboam-Gray, A., & Gray, P. (2004). Prior student achievement, collaborative school processes, and collective teacher efficacy. *Leadership Policy School, 3*(3), 163–188.

Sandeen, C. (2012). High-impact educational practices: What we can learn from the traditional undergraduate setting. *Continuing Higher Education Review, 76*, 81–89.

Shortlidge, E. E., Bangera, G., & Brownell, S. E. (2016). Faculty perspectives on developing and teaching course-based undergraduate research experiences. *BioScience, 66*(1), 54–62. https://doi.org/10.1093/biosci/biv167

Thomas, J. W. (2000). *A review of research on project-based learning.* The Autodesk Foundation.

Thornton, B., Zunino, B., & Beattie, J. (2020). Moving the dial: Improving teacher efficacy to promote instructional change. *Education, 140*(4), 171–180.

Tschannen-Moran, M., & Barr, M. (2004). Fostering student learning: The relationship of collective teacher efficacy and student achievement. *Leadership and Policy in Schools, 3*(3), 189–209.

Tschannen-Moran, M., Woolfolk Hoy, A., & Hoy, W. K. (1998). Teacher efficacy: Its meaning and measure. *Review of Educational Research, 68*(2), 202–248.

UNESCO. (2015). *World education forum 2015: Final report.* http://unesdoc.unesco.org/images/0024/002437/243724e.pdf

Warren, A. (2016). *Project-based learning across the disciplines plan, manage, and assess through + 1 pedagogy.* Corwin Publishing.

Wiley, E. A., & Stover, N. A. (2017). Immediate dissemination of student discoveries to a model organism database enhances classroom-based research experiences. *CBE—Life Sciences Education, 13*(1), 131–138. https://doi.org/10.1187/cbe.13-07-0140

5

Values-Based Innovation in the Caribbean Context: Grounding a Postcolonial Pedagogy for the Cave Hill Spanish Section of The University of the West Indies

Ian S. Craig

This chapter explores an attempt to redefine the values of the Spanish Section of the Cave Hill (CHSS) (Barbados) Campus of The University of the West Indies (The UWI), the public university of the CARICOM region, as a primary driver of ongoing processes of innovation. The attempted innovation here thus concerns the ethos of an academic unit, which as its senior member I have sought to infuse with a self-consciously *critical* impetus in order to inform other more specific processes of change; here, "'critical' signals a concern with power, and with theories of society, language and the person in which democracy and equity are fundamental" (Abednia & Crookes, 2019, p. 242). The attempted innovation might therefore also be described as a *cultural* one, in the sense that it constitutes an intervention designed to address assumptions

---

I. S. Craig (✉)
Department of Language, Linguistics and Literature,
The University of the West Indies, Bridgetown, Barbados
e-mail: ian.craig@cavehill.uwi.edu

© The Author(s), under exclusive license to Springer Nature Switzerland AG 2023   **83**
D. Mideros et al. (eds.), *Innovation in Language Learning and Teaching*, New Language Learning and Teaching Environments, https://doi.org/10.1007/978-3-031-34182-3_5

and to make explicit factors that have hitherto been implicit. Given that cultural changes usually take time, it should be stated from the outset that the process of change outlined herein is in a relatively early stage, so that the analysis also seeks to map terrain for future progress deriving from the initial self-reflective stock-taking exercise. Put at its simplest, this innovation constitutes a set of decisions taken by me as the senior member of the CHSS:

1. To make explicit the values that underpin my own pedagogy, to myself and to students, by declaring these at the beginning of the final-year language course I teach (Craig, 2017, 2018).
2. To elicit from students and staff a statement of their own values.
3. Drawing on steps 1 and 2, to draft a statement of Mission and Values for the CHSS and explore whether there is sufficient consensus on values among teachers and students of the CHSS and the Cave Hill Discipline of Modern Languages (CHDML) to craft a collective statement of Mission and Values for publication on the institutional website.
4. In light of steps 1 to 3, to imagine and plan for a Cave Hill Spanish program that is fully decolonial, critical and transformative, and thus fit for purpose in its context.

The process described herein thus draws on the notion of innovation as "an informed change in an underlying philosophy of language teaching/learning brought about by direct experience, research findings, or other means, resulting in an adaptation of pedagogic practices such that instruction is better able to promote language learning as it has come to be understood" (DeLano et al., 1994, p. 489). In addition to foregrounding "underlying philosophy," the project also draws on notions of innovation that emphasize specific contexts and eco-systemic integration, such as "Wedell (2009), [who] has argued that we need to put people and contexts at the core of the innovation process, and similarly Carless (2011), [who] puts forward the case for 'contextually grounded approaches' to pedagogic innovation" (Carless, 2012). In the postcolonial context of The UWI, these approaches from within applied linguistics resonate with broader critiques from the field of international education

5 Values-Based Innovation in the Caribbean Context...

concerning the "uncritical international transfer of policy and practice" that often afflicts educational contexts located in the hegemonically designated "periphery" of world affairs, including the Caribbean region (Crossley, 2010, p. 422). A key objective of this project was thus to ensure that the new articulation of a philosophy and the definition of strategic decisions emanating from it were consonant with the interests of stakeholders across the dimensions of the ecosystem in which the CHSS operates: students, teachers, the institution, the nation and the CARICOM region at large.

In what ways, we might ask, is the articulation of a new philosophy and the definition of strategic decisions a student-centered endeavor? It is clear that the existence of an agreed set of principles and objectives for the academic unit in which a student is enrolled forms the basis of her understanding of how her personal motivations for pursuing a course of study cohere with the goals of the collective. This seems fundamental to any sense of belonging, a known predictor of positive outcomes in educational contexts (Strayhorn, 2019). This factor is likely to be particularly important in our context, given the pattern of foreign language education in the Anglophone Caribbean, where students are most likely to have come through primary and secondary levels overwhelmingly dominated by co-national teachers, of both foreign languages and other subjects, before entering a regional university with a considerably higher proportion of foreign teachers. On entering The UWI, most students are thus entering an educational space dominated by cultural others for the first time, potentially generating anxiety and concern around possible cultural dissonance or even the imposition of metropolitan ideologies alluded to above. The existence of an explicitly stated unit-level philosophy that cleaves to the stated objectives of the institution as a whole, and is thus recognizably relevant to the ecosystem in which it operates, can thus serve to allay such anxieties and enhance a sense of belonging.

Equally, the emphasis on values in the project—and initially the term "values" was deliberately preferred over "vision" in the statement of identity—connects with the emphasis on deep learning and understanding in student-centered approaches: as the basis of ethics, a statement of values builds the foundation of a pedagogy for the section that reflects humanist interpretations of student-centered learning, incorporating notions of personal growth, consciousness-raising and empowerment (Tangney, 2014).

Why Turn to Values?

A confluence of factors in various domains motivated the nascent process of innovation described herein: personal and professional, institutional and geohistorical. As the sole senior lecturer in the CHSS, I am its longest-standing member after twenty-one years of service, and the only member who has held administrative office. When the CHSS is called upon to reflect on its strategic direction as part of Quality Assurance Review processes, therefore, I am expected to lead such exercises. Given the status of Barbados as a former British colony that became independent three years before I was born, it is perhaps inevitable that a central evolutionary driver of my professional trajectory has been both self-conscious interrogation and sometimes unwilled exposure of my own cultural biases as a privately educated, white Englishman, now in middle age. After two decades, it is now my personal conviction that the adoption of an *explicitly* decolonial and critical pedagogy and strategic vision is a desirable innovation in this context. As discussed below, this will serve both to align the CHSS's endeavors with broader institutional imperatives and to orient and induct new staff and students into a clearly defined ethos with transparent aims.

My research endeavors accord with the biographical and broader professional trajectory outlined above. A particular current of research in a number of fields over recent decades has invited educators to ask questions about the values, ethics and ideologies that drive their activities and to take an explicit stance on relations of power. These questions came to the fore in my own case through research in the field of study abroad, where matters of equity and social justice have recently become overwhelming concerns (Contreras, Jr. et al., 2020). As noted above, the term *critical* often characterizes the subfield names that arise from this foregrounding of the axiological dimension of the given field, in reference to the Critical Pedagogy movement associated most commonly with

Paulo Freire (1970). The field of applied linguistics has embarked on a similar self-examination, with collaborators of Freire such as Donaldo Macedo (2019) and others inviting language educators to question the oft-overlooked reproduction of assumptions that commonly underlie language teaching, entailing uncritical approaches to issues such as hierarchies of language prestige, the inclusion of *difficult* material or the ideological—these days mostly neoliberal—underpinnings of textbook materials (Block, 2009; Bori, 2018; Canagarajah, 2005; Kamasak et al., 2020).

Along with *critical*, the terms *decolonial* and *decolonizing* frequently appear in texts that propound a radical critique of Western epistemology and call for explicit attention to the structural and systemic power relations underlying established practices such as education (and by extension language education). In the context of a postcolonial region of small-island states such as the Anglophone Caribbean, the relevance of such critiques is self-evident and informs the Mission of The UWI to "advance learning, create knowledge and foster innovation for the positive transformation of the Caribbean and the wider world." While the institutional context is outlined further below, in discussing motivations for the innovation described herein, it is relevant to adduce further The UWI's current Strategic Plan, subtitled "Revitalizing Caribbean Development," which explicitly identifies the need to "rekindle the activist academy that addresses the regional agenda in the context of each national community that constitutes the Caribbean world" (The University Office of Planning, 2017). The double "re" in "revitalize" and "rekindle" strongly suggests a subtext of stalled regional development as a result of a decline in activism, which is a values-driven endeavor par excellence. Part of the impetus for the attempted innovation described herein, then, was a sense that the institution wished and expected its employees to reflect on how they might communicate and embody values that questioned a status quo characterized by a certain ideological stagnation and acquiescence—whether unwitting or willed—to the dominant neoliberal vision of power relations and social organization.

These institutional imperatives reflect those of the CARICOM region in general, which in its formally adopted description of the "Ideal Caribbean Person" includes characteristics that echo The UWI Strategic

Plan's injunction to think both innovatively and with due recognition of historical conditionings: "[The Ideal Caribbean Person] demonstrates multiple literacies, independent and critical thinking, questions the beliefs and practices of past and present and brings this to bear on the innovative application of science and technology and to problem solving" (CARICAD, 2014). Though framed over twenty years ago, this formulation has acquired a distinct urgency over the past nine months since the novel Coronavirus pandemic began to affect the region directly. As elsewhere, the pandemic has entailed tragic loss of life, widespread threat to personal livelihood, very significant macro-economic strain and generalized disruption of societal wellbeing. Alongside these logistical and socio-psychological pressures, however, the disruption caused by the pandemic has also generated a climate that is arguably more fertile for innovation and, particularly, for newly urgent considerations around values in education. The gigantic impact of COVID-19 and the relative success of certain polities over others in mitigating its effects have resulted in a generalized questioning of the neoliberal meta-narrative of our age, particularly regarding the role of a strong and empathetically oriented state in resisting macro-shocks of this kind (Morrissey, 2020; Navarro, 2020). From a more subjective perspective, the radical reorientation of relationships, both interpersonal and between human societies and the natural world, together with the experience of a marked slowing of time under lockdown, for some at least, have caused ever more widespread questioning of the absurdities of a late-capitalist lifestyle previously taken for granted by many (Humphrys, 2020; Samuel, 2020).

Other globally resonant phenomena have recently brought matters of value and the assumptions behind them squarely into view. The return to prominence of the Black Lives Matter movement, and particularly the widespread social discord in the United States following the death of George Floyd (1973–2020) at the hands of the police, emerged as the only phenomenon capable of toppling the pandemic from its prime spot in the news agenda. As a result, disparities and commonalities in the experience of racism between the United States and the Anglophone Caribbean were thrown into relief in public forums in Barbados (and doubtless elsewhere in the region) (Binyon, 2020). The sense that a sociohistorical tipping point has been reached, favoring the confrontation of unaddressed assumptions and habits of interaction, is thus very much in the air. All of these developments have created a strong sense that all of us need to choose a side and adopt a committed position, eschewing both the shield of postmodern skepticism and the evasions of neoliberal notions that frame education primarily in terms of purely technical training.

The Context

Adapting an analogy with Third Cinema, theorist la paperson (2017) posits a typology of universities spanning: "the first world university [...] characterized by an ultimate commitment to brand expansion and accumulation of patent, publication, and prestige;" the second world university or "liberal arts" college, whose "libertarian mode of critical thinking displaces the possibility of sustained, radical critique;" and finally "the third world university [, which] defines itself fundamentally as a decolonial project—as an interdisciplinary, transnational, yet vocational university that equips its students with skills toward the applied practice of decolonization." He further observes that "each mode appropriates or contains within itself elements of the other two. There is a third university in every first and second university, and vice versa" (p. 46).

This notion of various, contradictory universities within one is useful in characterizing the institutional context of the CHSS. Founded in 1948, The UWI was born as a colonial project that was subsequently instrumental in shaping the discourse of Anglophone Caribbean independence processes in the 1960s and the subsequent, ongoing endeavor of building truly sovereign societies in the region. As a postcolonial institution par excellence, it inevitably retains traces of its colonial origins, which may be more or less visible or self-acknowledged, while simultaneously acting as a focal point for theorizations and actions that seek both to transcend latent coloniality—its own and that of the societies it serves—and to map alternatives to the reformulated subjugations apparently rendered inevitable by neoliberalism. The activist role of its current vice chancellor as chairman of the CARICOM Reparations Commission ("*Not Enough to Say Sorry*" *for Slavery Links*,

2020) or the Other Universals Project (Marketing and Communications Department, 2019) are recent examples of its leading role in anti-colonial contestation as a "third university;" on the other hand, the press release charting the path of the "The New UWI: A Global System for the Future" from 2020 onwards fluently speaks the language of the dominant contemporary neoliberal ethos of higher education, apparently signaling an unashamed aspiration to consolidate "first-world university" status (Beckles, 2020).

From the vantage point of a language educator, these competing energies within the institution are potentially confusing, to the extent that they embody incompatible notions of the relation between the Self and the Other, a central concern of those who educate students for engagement with cultural Others. Put bluntly, we might be moved to ask the following questions: Am I teaching a foreign language primarily to ensure for my students the best possible chance of "succeeding on the world stage" by acquiring maximum competitive advantage as individuals in the employment marketplace? Or am I teaching a foreign language because it may favor certain forms of collective solidarity that might ultimately form a bulwark against the zero-sum, competitive vision of international engagement asserted by the prevailing neoliberal ideology?

The answer to these questions is clearly "both," in a certain sense: while all universities must somehow meet the equally essential goals of equipping students both to thrive materially in an imperfect and unequal world and to transcend that status quo through engaged action, this latter imperative is much more existentially urgent in the postcolonial context. Though all subject areas must seek to reconcile and integrate these aims into a coherent experience, there is some evidence in recent developments that the location of foreign language learning within The UWI has moved decidedly toward the terrain of decolonial contestation and transcendence of the postcolonial predicament. This is evident in the drafting of a new Language Policy, still in approval phase at the time of writing, which directly addresses the linguistic bind created by postcolonial status, asserting that "learning the language of the colonizer has been seen to be an important asset in the process of deciphering, challenging and undermining colonial power." The Policy also valorizes Caribbean Creoles on a par with languages of empire and cites as its first desired outcome "to

5 Values-Based Innovation in the Caribbean Context...

contribute to the UWI Project of fostering critical global citizenship skills, thus enhancing students' capacity to engage ethically, empathetically and critically, with cultural 'others' both whilst on campus and after graduation."

An October 30, 2020 press release entitled *UWI and ACS through MOU commit to sustainable development, decolonisation and regionalism* (2020) points in a similar direction. It reports that the agreement in question "made The UWI a Social Partner of the ACS" (the Association of Caribbean States, a body encompassing all Caribbean language communities and thus seeking to overcome colonial schemes of interaction determined by cultural and linguistic inheritances), and quotes UWI Vice Chancellor Professor Sir Hilary Beckles's opening remark, "This day we take another critical step in the deconstruction of the colonial Caribbean." In this text, the project of institutionalized multilingualism, of which the abovementioned Language Policy forms a significant part, is explicitly linked to sustainable development through decolonization and regional integration:

> Noting "this MOU between The UWI and ACS will give greater sustainability to our integration activities," Sir Hilary underpinned the centrality of this alignment between The UWI and ACS beyond an English-based framework, and within the context of the greater Caribbean region. He explained that this began with The UWI's bold move, last year, to forge partnerships with Cuba's University of Havana and Universidad de los Andes (UNIANDES) in Colombia. It was further cemented with the University of St. Maarten's incorporation into The UWI system earlier this month. He made special reference to the University's strategic priority to be multilingual by 2023 as part of the "preparation of an entire generation of students and young people to take command and control of their Caribbean space." (*UWI and ACS through MOU commit to sustainable development, decolonisation and regionalism*, 2020)

The broader context of The UWI would thus seem clearly to favor the adoption of a values-oriented approach in language teaching and learning that foregrounds decolonial and critical approaches. However, the degree of alignment of this approach with the personal value systems and pedagogical convictions of the teachers of languages at the institution is, naturally, another matter altogether. As noted above, the CHSS comprises one Barbadian and four non-Caribbean nationals, three Spanish, and one English. It is located within a Discipline of Modern Languages that also includes a French Section offering a Major and a Minor in that language (one Congolese lecturer, one French, one Martinican, one Jamaican, and one Barbadian), a single Brazilian Portuguese lecturer (from Brazil) and a single Chinese lecturer (from China).

As in many language departments, this diversity supplies not only an exceptional cultural richness but also a complexity of interaction that can defy predictability and hinder a sense of common cause: no one member could ever become sufficiently familiar with *all* the cultures of *all* the members to identify cultural misunderstandings or points of tension with any degree of confidence, complicating the already-fraught business of arriving at consensus among academics. The strong sense of hierarchy in the institution at large may also be at issue here: though I am the longest-serving member of the Discipline of Modern Languages and senior in Spanish in all senses, I am outranked academically by two professors in French and no longer hold any position of executive responsibility. My proposal to explore an explicitly values-driven philosophy for the entire Discipline of Modern Languages, rather than merely the CHSS, thus emerges somewhat "from the trenches," with its own merits alone to propel it forward.

Implementation

In practice, I took the following steps to reorient the CHSS's Mission and Values in a critical direction:

1. Conducting a survey of CHSS staff members.
2. Eliciting student values by incorporating them as a required component in a video introduction exercise in a final-year Spanish-language course required for the Major and Minor in Spanish.
3. Drafting a statement of Mission and Values consonant with those expressed by staff and students, but also coherent with both the broader critical vision outlined above and with the institution's existing value statements.

4. Eliciting feedback on the new statement of Mission and Values from both staff and students, then amending accordingly.

The initial proposed text was as follows:

Mission and Values of the Spanish Section 2021

Mission

The mission of the CHSS is to make a key contribution through its programs and activities toward fulfilment of the stated aims of The UWI Language Policy, namely to:

- foster critical global citizenship skills, thus enhancing students' capacity to engage ethically, empathetically and critically, with cultural "others" both while on campus and after graduation.
- create UWI students who are marketable, not just within CARICOM but also across the global community.

Values

The Section thus declares the following values that guide its pursuit of this Mission:

1. The Spanish Section values the capacity of language- and culture learning to foster a broad range of transferable skills that favor both gainful employment and collective endeavor toward civic, social, political and developmental goals.
2. The Spanish Section values academic rigor, vocational and social relevance and the cultivation of opportunities to engage in activities that are creative, immersive and service-oriented.
3. The Spanish Section values the ongoing development of intercultural competence by its students and staff through meaningful engagement with cultural otherness and critical reflection on one's own culture.

4. Mindful of its Anglophone Caribbean context, the Spanish Section values the study of the Spanish language and the cultures of the Spanish-speaking world as a contribution to enhanced Global South solidarity toward the greater integration of Latin America and the Caribbean.

5. At the same time as it values and celebrates the manifold achievements of the Spanish-speaking world, the Spanish Section also values critical, decolonial and transformative approaches to the study of languages and cultures that entail active engagement with challenging aspects of the subject area such as colonialism in all its forms, social and political discord, or inequities around race, gender and class, among others.

A number of observations are relevant:

- The first bulleted item in the new Mission was proposed by me for inclusion in the "Expected Outcomes" of The UWI's new Language Policy. The decision of the primary drafters to incorporate it as the first such outcome, ahead of the more neoliberally oriented "create UWI students who are marketable," is arguably evidence that the revitalization of more radical and critical orientations in the institution at large is currently a key strategic priority and that language learning is seen as an arena in which this revitalization can be operationalized; these orientations are thus further reflected in Value no.4.

- While the framing of students as regionally and globally "marketable" in the second bulleted item in the new Mission would doubtless raise an eyebrow among orthodox critical pedagogues, it reflects understandably deep concerns around employment experienced by both students and educational strategists, particularly in light of the new anxieties generated by the current pandemic, heaped upon those already created by the financial crisis over the last decade.

- In Value 3, the inclusion of staff as members of a community of learners in the area of intercultural competence is intended to reflect the orientation towards co-construction of meaning between teachers/guides and learners in critical pedagogical approaches. It also derives from the reality of staffing volatility and necessarily foreign participation in the CHSS, described above.

5 Values-Based Innovation in the Caribbean Context... 95

- Value 4 is intended to root the CHSS firmly in its context, aligning its values statement with the geopolitical reality and developmental trajectory of its broader context. The explicit declaration of common cause with Latin America and the Global South is intended to serve as an overarching framework for strategic decision-making and a clear indicator of ideological affiliation to orient both new staff and students.
- In Value 5, the transformative approach was suggested as an addition to those listed by the Literature and Culture specialist in the CHSS. Though I was less familiar with this approach, associated with Mezirow (2000) and others, the emphasis on co-construction of meaning, a holistic conception of the educational experience and higher-order outcomes is clearly consonant with the goals of the project described herein. Equally, the acknowledgment of discomfort as a legitimate component of learning coheres with the general tenor of this value.

All four members of the CHSS responded positively and without reservation to the new statement of Mission and Values, as did the seven students who replied to a survey of the students in the program, providing initial confirmation that its content was fully compatible with the data gathered in the preparatory exercise.

An adapted version of the Mission and Values was then proposed for adoption by the broader CHDML and sent separately to the current head of the department, who is from the Discipline of Linguistics and has long experience in matters of institutional protocol. Several colleagues in the CHDML felt the text overall was too long and that "Vision" should replace "Mission" because the Department of Language, Linguistics and Literature already has a Mission, which is implicitly common to all of its disciplines. The head's advice agreed with the discipline's regarding the need to shorten the text but contradicted it regarding the headings: "Vision" should be retained, but "you should not limit it to the stated aims in The UWI Language policy since the discipline has been existence well before that. It should embody what ML see as their passion and goal (long term) so though it will relate to the Language Policy, I think it is also more personal." The Values, on the other hand, should be "restated as your Mission," because "Vision and Mission" are the headings

96   I. S. Craig

conventionally used in all units of the Institution since such statements have become part of its official discourse over the last five to ten years; the latest draft at time of writing is thus shown in Appendix 5.1.

In terms of innovation, these negotiations demonstrate the contextual forces bearing on any new intervention in a discursive field that has become more regimented as the twin imperatives of international accreditation and global branding have permeated The UWI over the last decade particularly, in common with higher education institutions worldwide. The language of the resulting text shown in Appendix 5.1 thus ends up combining, somewhat uneasily, the corporate terminology of the neoliberal provider in a marketplace and the values-driven, politically committed terrain I had intended to stake out—I lost my activist "Values" heading to the militaristic "Mission," but the "Vision" statement itself is arguably less constrained by a conformity to an institutional discursive hierarchy I had imagined was required, but turned out not to be in this instance. The competing and sometimes contradictory imperatives described above in "The Context" have thus inevitably molded the text as it has moved upward, but the values themselves are retained by some linguistic sleight of hand in the form of the head phrase "our mission is to cultivate" used to introduce them.

Evaluation

Given the nascent stage of this transformative project, evaluation of it focuses primarily on two principal strategic actions that derive logically from the new statement of Mission and Values and the orientation it imparts to the CHSS and the CHDML, by way of acknowledgment that localized adoption alone of such a statement proposed by the senior member of an academic unit hardly qualifies as innovation in itself, however new-in-context this move may be. It remains to be seen whether the sister units on the other UWI campuses will see fit to undertake a similar process of self-definition or prefer to define themselves implicitly under the terms of the new institution-wide Language Policy.

The following proposed innovations deriving from the new statement thus focus on the CHSS, showing how I as the senior member envision the possible and desirable expansion of this initial philosophical innovation into more concrete operational terrains, including an evaluation of chances of success. In doing so, I draw on Kirkland and Sutch's (2009) exposition of barriers to innovation using the Layers of Influence model, in which the perception of a given proposed innovation at different levels of proximity to its source—from students and peers (the micro level), through institutional structures (the meso level), up to national and wider stakeholders (the macro level)—is used to evaluate its possibilities of success and diffusion. Kirkland and Sutch also draw on Zhao and Frank (2003) to identify the three factors of longevity, fecundity and copy fidelity as core properties of successful innovations, designating respectively: the sustainability of the innovation over time; its applicability by different practitioners; its replicability in local conditions. Though both innovations discussed below form part of a longer list that emerged logically from the philosophical recalibration described above, I have deliberately selected one that seems highly attainable and another that seems less so, as a means of drawing out environmental affordances and constraints around innovation in The UWI context.

Area 1: Online Onboarding of New Staff and Students

One way of meaningfully instantiating a declaration of values is to embed it into onboarding processes for new students and staff. A fully online approach to these now appears much more feasible in light of the rapid acceleration in the development of online services and capacity in numerous areas of The UWI in the wake of the pandemic. This would entail crafting a modular series of online learning objects that inducts staff and students from a variety of backgrounds into the micro-culture of the CHSS or equivalent unit, with self-pacing capability to allow engagement from well before the beginning of the period of contract or course of study. The critical values orientation discussed above might be conveyed in several ways, such as screencasts giving concrete examples of contextually relevant pedagogy (and how it might differ from other contexts), videos of community-oriented engagements such as language tandems and buddy programs with visiting Latin American EFL students, or simply direct exposition of the Mission and Values themselves, explaining their rationale and relevance.

This innovation would be meaningful in the context of the CHSS without any need for diffusion to other levels or sister units on other campuses since the Section currently has no structured onboarding mechanism, relying purely on haphazard social interaction and a somewhat "sink or swim" approach to acclimatization. Nonetheless, if it proved successful, its replication would ideally add an explicit values dimension to the socializing processes of the units in question, possibly helping to mitigate clashes of expectations around values, which are not uncommon in highly diverse environments and especially in contexts characterized by "postcolonial ambivalence—a symptomatic condition of postcolonial societies in which they simultaneously embrace and reject the cultural, political and economic processes and expressions of the 'ex-colonizer'" (Sayed, 2016, p. 7).

The impediments to this innovation are relatively insignificant, given its demonstrable alignment with macro- and meso-level factors (that is, regional and institutional interests); the only micro-level requirements would seem to be consensus among CHSS staff and participating students, along with time for design, creation and implementation of the web resources. Though there would seem to be no significant impediments to its fecundity and copy fidelity across The UWI language programs, its adoption would naturally depend on sufficient demonstrable efficacy and added value through trial in the CHSS to motivate the initial investment by other units. Its longevity would also require sustained commitment to updating in order to avoid the pitfalls of alienation caused by outdated onboarding materials (Pappas, 2018).

Area 2: Caribbean Course Materials for Tertiary Spanish-language Teaching

The development and UWI-wide adoption of a coherent repertoire of regionally generated pedagogical materials for tertiary foreign language teaching is a natural corollary of an orientation that emphasizes the contextual specificity and developmental imperatives of a postcolonial region.

5 Values-Based Innovation in the Caribbean Context... 99

My own recent experience has confirmed this conviction. At the time of writing, I was in the process of teaching a final-year, B2-level "general" Spanish language course to which I was newly assigned only a year ago, using *Aula Internacional 5*, published in Spain by Editorial Difusión (Corpas et al., 2014). This textbook is part of a well-known series, adopted by CHSS throughout the Spanish Major and Minor to systematize progression through levels of competency, since the series is carefully benchmarked against the Common European Frame of Reference for Language Learning (CEFR); the character and implicit vision of this textbook series thus leave a significant imprint on the CHSS and perceptions of its pedagogy.

On first using *Aula 5* last year, I had felt uncomfortable both with the dissonance between the assumptions underpinning it and the new values orientation I was developing. This time round, therefore, I made a concerted effort to adapt to the materials offered in ways that were not merely cursory. For example, I worked up a mini-module on cultural appropriation to problematize the textbook's otherwise uncritical presentation of yoga and the popularity of flamenco in Japan, using it to contextualize an inquiry into regional examples such as the simultaneous harnessing and marginalization of Rastafarian identities. My conclusion was the same as following previous similar attempts at other levels of the Spanish program: the more genuinely critical and nonsuperficial the adaptation and exploration of the sociocultural topic, the greater my anxiety that progression through the language acquisition objectives was stalling. This trade-off is a common concern, as documented by Herman (2007, pp. 134–135), for example. Repeatedly, I found myself thinking: "this could only work if it were *fully integrated* into a new learning object, rather than tacked onto an existing one."

As desirable as it may be, however, the chances of success of a project of crafting an agreed repertoire of regionally customized tertiary foreign language-learning materials currently appear slim, mostly because of macro-level factors bearing on the process of textbook and course material production. A tertiary language textbook these days requires significant initial investments to attain the rigor and high production values expected by users, followed by sustained commitment to support the formidable array of ancillary online material required to compete with the products of the major publishers—who operate in large countries that can marshal the necessary economies of scale. However, new, disruptive models using open source and open licensing protocols such as OpenStax (Koenig, 2019; Rice University, n.d.) may have opened a path to circumvent these habitual strictures of small-island-developing-state dependency in the longer term, paving the way for creation of fully context-appropriate and sustainable pedagogical materials in smaller ecosystems such as ours.

If the emerging system evolves to be sufficiently flexible, threats to the fecundity and copy fidelity of any resulting resource corpus may also be mitigated by allowing appropriate contextually and personally motivated adaptation of specific materials around a robust disciplinary core. Such customizability would be essential to mitigating a number of meso-level impediments to the development and adoption of such a regional language-teaching resource bank for The UWI: considerable disparities in the content of the foreign language programs offered on each UWI campus, in spite of the common degree certificate attained; limited communication and collaboration between campuses; sense of rivalry and mutual suspicion between campuses (though far from universal, a not insignificant factor, rarely acknowledged openly); relatively high staff turnover in the area of language provision, with a preponderance of fixed-contract and nonlocal tutors, generating a consistently high burden of context-specific training and awareness-raising.

Implications

It is self-evident that an explicit statement of values, however sincere and carefully aligned to context, can only be meaningful if it acts as a driver for further innovation that materially enacts those values, deepening the integration of praxis with a conceptual framework that is now explicit and publicly visible. Clearly, for this symbiosis to remain effective, the values themselves must be allowed to evolve. One student-centered way of organically sustaining the relevance of the values formulated in this initial exercise would be to incorporate them into existing and new mechanisms of co-construction of meaning for the unit: as a community-building exercise at the beginning of their three-year degree cycle, students would be invited to reflect on the existing values statement and discuss how they expect their experience to be reflective of it; each year, they might revisit this exercise and report on how reality has measured up to these expectations. This regular cycle of revisitation would doubtless generate both refinements to the values themselves and new ideas on how they might be meaningfully embodied in the activities of the CHSS, in both academic and other dimensions.

This exercise would best be undertaken in a workshop format bringing together students from all levels of the program, as this would help to mitigate a deficit identified in a May 2021 Focus Group that I conducted with Modern Languages students: the lack of structured opportunities to interact with other students outside the immediate class cohort, to engage with the program itself (as against social interactions through the student-led Language Club, for example). A workshop around Vision and Mission might thus bookend a student-to-student mentoring cycle across levels one and two of the degree program, as well as allowing completing students to offer summative feedback on their experience of being part of the Section, measured against a specific self-definition. This exercise will continuously test the validity and reliability of the Vision and Mission: do they (still) accurately reflect the student experience, or have priorities changed? If they have changed, what does this mean for the values underpinning our work?

As a recommendation arising from the last Quality Assurance Review in 2019, the CHSS is also in the process of creating an Advisory Board of Key Stakeholders comprising representatives from the Barbados Community College, the secondary-school system, Spanish-speaking diplomatic missions and regional development bodies located in Barbados, together with regular employers of the Section's graduates. The new Vision and Mission will be a key text in locating the Section and its programs ideologically as this new consultant body is formally constituted from interlocutors with whom communication has thus far been on an occasional and "as necessary" basis only. The rationale for creating this body is, self-evidently, to connect the Section to the world beyond academia in a more intentional fashion, and it is likely that it will generate further momentum to modify our programs in a more vocational direction. This is a necessary evolution, which our students are also urging us to embrace. As we do so, it will be crucial to keep in mind the critical, decolonial and transformative perspectives that underpin an ethically conceived language education—as opposed to mere training—in order to retain the activist orientation that The UWI currently enjoins us to adopt.

Given the simple power of a statement of values that is carefully considered and aligned with context, rather than perfunctory and merely imitative of others, language units in postcolonial contexts have much to gain by taking this first step on the pathway toward a pedagogy that serves the developmental and emancipatory goals rendered necessary by ongoing dependency. By pinning our axiological colors to the mast, we clearly signal our intention to teach and learn languages in ways that serve the human interests of our nations and regions, rather than blindly following the market-driven imperatives that are passed off as *natural* and therefore value-free in the neoliberal vision. By keeping our values in proximal view, we moor our pedagogy and strategic thinking to firm ideological terrain, providing a solid basis for selecting and implementing other operational innovations—pedagogical, technological, curricular—in a manner that respects and celebrates the unique ecology of our institutions.

Appendix 5.1: Final Draft of Vision and Mission of CHDML

Vision

To empower students to engage meaningfully with other language communities and their cultures toward fulfilment of personal, professional and collective goals.

Mission

As a discipline, our mission is to cultivate the following:

- The capacity of language- and culture learning to foster a broad range of transferable skills that favor both gainful employment and solidary endeavors.

5 Values-Based Innovation in the Caribbean Context...

- The continuous development of intercultural competence by our students and staff through deep engagement with cultural otherness and critical reflection on one's own culture.
- The study of languages through decolonial and postcolonial lenses that actively counter inherited notions of linguistic privilege and bias, linguicism and cultural hegemony.
- Both celebratory and critical or transformative approaches to the study of languages that entail active engagement with challenging aspects of the subject area such as social and political struggle, or inequities around race, gender and class.

References

Abednia, A., & Crookes, G. V. (2019). Online language teacher education for a challenging innovation: Towards critical language pedagogy for Iran. In H. Reinders, C. Coombe, A. Littlejohn, & D. Tafazoli (Eds.), *Innovation in language learning and teaching: The case of the Middle East and North Africa* (pp. 241–261). Springer International Publishing. https://doi.org/10.1007/978-3-030-13413-6_12

Beckles, H. (2020, January 14). *Vice Chancellor's message | The new UWI: A global system for the future.* https://sta.uwi.edu/news/releases/release.asp?id=22036

Binyon, M. (2020, September 16). Barbados: Black Lives Matter and Windrush have changed the atmosphere. *The Times.* https://www.thetimes.co.uk/article/barbados-black-lives-matter-and-windrush-have-changed-the-atmosphere-g0cwkm67z

Block, D. (2009). *Second language identities.* Continuum.

Bori, P. (2018). *Language textbooks in the era of neoliberalism.* Routledge.

Canagarajah, A. S. (Ed.). (2005). *Reclaiming the local in language policy and practice* (1st ed.). Routledge.

CARICAD. (2014, January 24). *Vision of the ideal Caribbean person.* Caribbean Leadership Programme. https://www.caribbeanleadership.org/blog/posts/view/vision-of-the-ideal-caribbean-person

Carless, D. (2011). *From testing to productive student learning: Implementing formative assessment in Confucian-heritage settings.* Routledge.

Carless, D. (2012). Innovation in language teaching and learning. In C. A. Chapelle (Ed.), *The encyclopedia of applied linguistics*. Blackwell Publishing Ltd. https://doi.org/10.1002/9781405198431.wbeal0540

Contreras, E., Jr., López-McGee, L., Wick, D., & Willis, T. Y. (Eds.). (2020). Special issue on diversity, equity, and inclusion in education abroad. *Frontiers: The Interdisciplinary Journal of Study Abroad, 32*(1). https://doi.org/10.36366/frontiers.v32i1

Corpas, J., Garmendia, A., Sánchez, N., & Soriano, C. (2014). *Aula internacional 5: Libro del alumno* (Nueva edición). Difusión.

Craig, I. (2017). Traductología y pedagogía crítica para la ciudadanía global en la educación superior del Caribe anglófono contemporáneo. *Mutatis Mutandis. Revista Latinoamericana de Traducción, 10*(1), 19–45.

Craig, I. (2018). Student-centred second language study abroad for non-traditional sojourners: An anglophone caribbean example. In J. L. Plews & K. Misfeldt (Eds.), *Second language study abroad. Programming, pedagogy, and participant engagement* (pp. 83–121). Palgrave Macmillan. https://doi.org/10.1007/978-3-319-77134-2_4

Crossley, M. (2010). Context matters in educational research and international development: Learning from the small states experience. *Prospects, 40*(4), 421–429. https://doi.org/10.1007/s11125-010-9172-4

DeLano, L., Riley, L., & Crookes, G. (1994). The meaning of innovation for ESL teachers. *System, 22*(4), 487–496.

Freire, P. (1970). *Pedagogy of the oppressed*. The Seabury Press.

Herman, D. M. (2007). It's a small world after all: From stereotypes to invented worlds in secondary school Spanish textbooks. *Critical Inquiry in Language Studies, 4*(2–3), 117–150. https://doi.org/10.1080/15427580701389417

Humphrys, J. (2020, May 1). *After the lockdown is lifted: Back to the old ways?* YouGov. https://yougov.co.uk/topics/politics/articles-reports/2020/05/01/after-lockdown-lifted-back-old-ways

Kamasak, R., Ozbilgin, M., & Atay, D. (2020). The cultural impact of hidden curriculum on language learners: A review and some implications for curriculum design. In A. Slapac & S. A. Coppersmith (Eds.), *Beyond language learning instruction: Transformative supports for emergent bilinguals and educators* (pp. 104–125). IGI Global. https://doi.org/10.4018/978-1-7998-1962-2

Kirkland, K., & Sutch, D. (2009). *Overcoming the barriers to educational innovation: A literature review*. Futurelab. https://www.nfer.ac.uk/publications/futl61/futl61.pdf

5 Values-Based Innovation in the Caribbean Context... 105

Koenig, R. (2019, October 24). *How a university took on the textbook industry.* EdSurge. https://www.edsurge.com/news/2019-10-24-how-a-university-took-on-the-textbook-industry

la paperson. (2017). *A third university is possible.* University of Minnesota Press.

Macedo, D. (2019). *Decolonizing foreign language education: The misteaching of English and other imperial languages.* Routledge. https://ebookcentral.proquest.com/lib/qut/detail.action?docID=5630636

Marketing and Communications Department. (2019, May 21). *The UWI launches a transnational consortium agreement on critical thinking from the Global South.* https://sta.uwi.edu/news/releases/release.asp?id=21915

Mezirow, J., & Associates. (2000). *Learning as transformation: Critical perspectives on a theory in progress.* Wiley.

Morrissey, J. (2020, June 19). *COVID-19 and the neoliberal house of cards.* Transforming Society. http://www.transformingsociety.co.uk/2020/06/19/covid-19-and-the-neoliberal-house-of-cards/

Navarro, V. (2020). The consequences of neoliberalism in the current pandemic. *International Journal of Health Services, 50*(3), 271–275. https://doi.org/10.1177/0020731420925449

"Not enough to say sorry" for slavery links. (2020, June 19). BBC News. https://www.bbc.com/news/business-53102585

Pappas, C. (2018, February 25). *6 reasons why new hires dread onboarding online training.* ELearning Industry. https://elearningindustry.com/reasons-new-hires-dread-onboarding-online-training

Rice University. (n.d.). *About us—OpenStax.* OpenStax. Retrieved December 14, 2020, from https://openstax.org/about

Samuel, S. (2020, June 9). *Quarantine has changed us—And it's not all bad.* Vox. https://www.vox.com/future-perfect/2020/6/9/21279258/coronavirus-pandemic-new-quarantine-habits

Sayed, Z. (2016). *Postcolonial perspective on international knowledge transfer and spillover to Indian news media: From institutional duality to third space.* Jönköping University, Jönköping International Business School.

Strayhorn, T. L. (2019). *College students' sense of belonging: A key to educational success for all students* (2nd ed.). Routledge.

Tangney, S. (2014). Student-centred learning: A humanist perspective. *Teaching in Higher Education, 19*(3), 266–275. https://doi.org/10.1080/1356251 7.2013.860099

The University Office of Planning. (2017). *The UWI triple A strategy 2017–2022: Revitalizing Caribbean development.* The University of the West Indies. https://www.mona.uwi.edu/principal/departments/opair/uwi-strategic-plan

UWI and ACS through MOU commit to sustainable development, decolonisation and regionalism. (2020, October 31). UWI TV. https://uwitv.org/uwi-news/uwi-and-acs-through-mou-commit-to-sustainable-development-decolonisation-and-regionalism

Wedell, M. (2009). *Planning for educational change: Putting people and their contexts first*. Continuum.

Zhao, Y., & Frank, K. A. (2003). Factors affecting technology uses in schools: An ecological perspective. *American Educational Research Journal, 40*(4), 807–840. https://doi.org/10.3102/00028312040004807

6

Innovation in Language Education Partnerships: The Confucius Institute at The UWI, St Augustine

Beverly-Anne Carter

Introduction

Between 2010 and 2015, Confucius Institutes (CIs) were established on the islands of Jamaica, Trinidad and Barbados at The University of the West Indies (UWI) Mona, St Augustine and Cave Hill Campuses, respectively. The establishment of three CIs in the Anglophone Caribbean in such a short period of time reflects the growth and dynamism of China's Confucius Institute (CI), from the opening of the first CI in Seoul in 2004, to the current network of over 500 global CIs. The CI, like other international language organisations, for example France's Alliance Française, is a vehicle to promote language and culture, albeit one with "unique Chinese features" (Liu, 2019b, p. 256) (see also Danping & Adamson, 2015; Liu, 2019a; and Wang, 2020). But whereas

---

B.-A. Carter (✉)
Centre for Language Learning, The University of the West Indies, St Augustine, St. Augustine, Trinidad and Tobago
e-mail: Beverly-Anne.Carter@sta.uwi.edu

© The Author(s), under exclusive license to Springer Nature Switzerland AG 2023
D. Mideros et al. (eds.), *Innovation in Language Learning and Teaching*, New Language Learning and Teaching Environments, https://doi.org/10.1007/978-3-031-34182-3_6

the French alliance for the propagation of the national language in the colonies and abroad, more commonly known as L'Alliance Française, had over a century to evolve from its 1883 origin into a fit-for-purpose twenty-first-century organisation, the Beijing-based CI needed a strategic way to compensate for its late entry into the field and become an actor in foreign language education in the shortest possible time frame. Hanban, the CI Headquarters, did this chiefly via an innovative model, whereby a CI would be established as an academic partnership between a local higher education institution (HEI) and a Chinese HEI, with significant initial funding from Hanban. Another departure from earlier models of cultural cooperation was that Hanban, faithful to the Chinese win-win concept, recognised the need to create a truly *glocal* organisation, global in reach and scope, yet highly responsive to the institutional and national contexts where CIs are located. The premise was that establishing a CI would be of mutual benefit to China and the host community or country.

In keeping with the volume's theme on innovation in foreign language education, this chapter discusses the establishment of a CI at The UWI St Augustine Campus in Trinidad, aiming to show how it exemplifies the notion of innovation, in this case innovation in academic partnerships. The UWI is a multi-campus, multi-state federal university, so while the university has a single vision and mission and is driven by a common strategic plan, each campus is also shaped by and expected to be responsive to local needs. The chapter looks at why the CI at St Augustine began and grew in the way it did, as a member of the global network, bearing The UWI brand, yet in some ways distinct even from the other UWI CIs, because of its location. The chapter concludes by making some recommendations on how to keep innovation central to the development of the CI.

Background: Impetus for the Innovation

Collini (2012) notes that global knowledge sharing and communications is one of the hallmarks of globalisation in higher education. Transnational academic partnerships are an optimal way to foster and engage in educational globalisation and facilitate internationalisation. For much of

6 Innovation in Language Education Partnerships... 109

The UWI's early history, associations like the Association of Commonwealth Universities, the oldest global association of universities in higher education (Schreuder, 2013), would have been central to The UWI's internationalisation thrust. The CI is characteristic of The UWI's more recent academic partnerships and demonstrates its interest in moving beyond its traditional Western and Anglophone partners in forming strategic alliances. At a philosophical level, joining the CI network was testimony to The UWI's willingness to embrace global knowledge sharing and multilingual communication in languages other than English. The thinking at the Cave Hill Campus as expressed below was similar across all campuses as they pursued internationalisation by means of the CI:

> The CI was seen as a catalyst to help further the internationalization of the campus by including an additional world language, support the Government of Barbados in its bilateral links with China—(language facilitating culture and commerce)—and strengthening the role of the UWI in supporting regional development. (A. Fisher, personal communication, October 13, 2020)

From a disciplinary perspective, the St Augustine language centre and the modern language departments at Mona and Cave Hill were seeking to expand the teaching and learning of Chinese, and the establishment of a CI was a way to fulfil that goal. Thus, the CI, which sought to promote the teaching and learning of Chinese language and culture and promote international collaboration seemed in alignment with the thinking at The UWI on both philosophical and disciplinary grounds. But as stated earlier, each CI reflects a localisation of the CI "product" for the community and institutional context. Thus, to some extent, while the impetus across campuses might have been the same, implementation and operationalisation of the innovation were slightly different from campus to campus in reflection of the different country perspectives.

By 2013, when the CI was established at the St Augustine Campus, the CI network had been in existence for close to a decade. There was some early literature (e.g. Paradise, 2009; Starr, 2009; Zhao & Huang, 2010) that explored the operationalisation of CIs, including the tension arising from the formation of joint ventures between Chinese HEIs—seen as too closely linked to the central government—and HEIs, particularly those in the Global North, where institutional autonomy and academic freedom are cherished values. Moreover, Hanban is a unit of China's Ministry of Education, and therefore CI funding could be traced directly to the government and ultimately to the Chinese Communist Party (CCP).

While the CI is sometimes referred to as a Chinese soft power initiative, this chapter will adopt the term "cultural diplomacy" in the discussion of the CI. Hartig (2012) discusses the appropriacy of the term "cultural diplomacy" to describe the role played by CIs in China's foreign policy. Hartig (2015) develops his argument further, explaining how the CI is "one performing instrument of China's public diplomacy" (Hartig, 2015, p. 245). Liu (2019a) offers a detailed account of how the CI aligns with China's strategic planning, noting that in 2004 (significant as the year of the establishment of the first CI) culture was declared the third pillar of China's diplomacy, after politics and the economy. While soft power invariably brings to mind the notion of a power differential between the actors, cultural diplomacy tends to emphasise engagement and relationship among both state and non-state actors, as the following definition makes clear:

> Cultural Diplomacy may best be described as a course of actions, which are based on and utilize the exchange of ideas, values, traditions and other aspects of culture or identity, whether to strengthen relationships, enhance socio-cultural cooperation, promote national interests and beyond; Cultural diplomacy can be practiced by either the public sector, private sector or civil society. (Institute for Cultural Diplomacy, 2021)

The outcry against the impact of China's cultural diplomacy was most vociferous in the Global North leading eventually to the closure of some North American CIs (Peterson, 2017). Negative labels, such as "academic malware" (Sahlins, 2015), had become attached to the CI brand. Countries in the Global South were not unaware of the political and ideological issues surrounding the CI, nor the risks inherent in entering into a joint venture largely underwritten by the world's second largest economy. On the contrary, many of these former colonialised nations were cognisant of the dangers of (latter-day) imperialism, but lacking sinology departments in their universities and often lacking the funding to introduce new world languages, they grasped the opportunity to bring their language curricula into alignment with the political and economic realities of the twenty-first century, dubbed the Asian century. This was certainly the case at The UWI and arguably the case in other HEIs in developing countries. Academics working in the Global South generally expressed cautious optimism about the educational value of the CIs (see, for example, Theo & Leung, 2018; Wheeler, 2014) and were prepared to do a critical evaluation of the CI vis-à-vis their individual institutional and national contexts. This is the approach adopted in this chapter.

Context

From the beginning of the CI innovation at St Augustine, this academic partnership was materially different from previous academic partnerships. The Memorandum of Understanding (MOU) to promote foreign language education was not an inter-university agreement such as existing language-based MOUs, with the (then) Université des Antilles et de la Guyane, or Université de Bordeaux 3. Further, although The UWI was a signatory to other MOUs with state-supported organisations involved in international education cooperation like Colombia's *Instituto Colombiano de Crédito Educativo y Estudios Técnicos en el Exterior*, known by the acronym ICETEX, and *La Agencia Española de Cooperación Internacional para el Desarrollo* (AECID), Spain's development agency, the stakes seemed to be much higher with a CI and stakeholder involvement reflected this. As a prong of China's cultural diplomacy and evidence of China's engagement with a host country, witnesses to MOU signings were representatives at the highest level of government in China and the host country. Indeed, it was the scheduled arrival of President Xi Jinping on his first official visit to Latin America and the Caribbean that provided the impetus for the signing of the MOU between The UWI St Augustine and Hanban.

The initial discussions about the establishment of a CI were between The UWI St Augustine and the home institution of the language centre's overseas Chinese teacher. This was a natural outgrowth of the language centre's desire to expand its Chinese programme and to do so by drawing on the expertise of that HEI, which, as a normal university, was strongly focused on pedagogy and curriculum. The author, the then director of the language centre, was hosted for a weekend-long visit and meetings with senior academic administrators while attending a conference in China in August 2011. The university's vice president and the director of the Office of International Exchanges proposed a reciprocal visit the following year. Visa issues delayed the arrival of the Chinese academics, so it was not until early September 2012 that the second series of meetings between the two universities took place.

After fruitful face-to-face meetings, email and document exchanges, the two universities arrived at a draft proposal that was acceptable to both sides and likely to be approved by Hanban. As required, the proposal spoke of the strong demand for Chinese language instruction in the university and local community and The UWI's willingness to contribute to the CI operations. The proposal also reflected resolutions that had been arrived at concerning certain knotty issues, like the relationship between the language centre's existing Chinese programme and the eventual CI programme as discussed in the director's email of November 12 2012:

> I've attached a version with the changes I have made. In some cases, I rewrote the English to read more fluently. But in a few cases, I changed things that the Principal/the university will not want to agree to. For example, we are not going to get permission to offer credits through the CI. The credit courses will have to continue at the CLL and the CI will do the Chinese for specific purposes courses. We can't have both CLL and CI teaching the same courses. It would not make sense to duplicate our efforts, so my plan is to keep what we have now—general courses including the credit option and new offerings—Chinese for specific purposes, the programmes for the high school students etc. will be offered through the CI. (CI director, personal communication, November 12 2012)

The final proposal with all the necessary approvals on The UWI St Augustine side and the Chinese side (i.e. the HEI's and Education Bureau of the provincial government) was then sent to Hanban for approval. The proposal remained under review for several months, and with the passage of time fears grew on each side that the project would not receive Hanban's blessing.

Then in May 2013 it was announced that President Xi would pay a state visit to Trinidad and Tobago the following month. The visit would be the first to the English-speaking Caribbean by a Chinese president and part of President Xi's second overseas tour since assuming the presidency. As is the custom for a state visit, President Xi would be engaging with the most senior state representatives.

The stalled bottom-up initiative of the CI suddenly began to assume an unexpected level of importance. There is little doubt that Hanban saw merit in showcasing this powerful symbol of cultural diplomacy as one of the outputs of the state visit. And so, on June 1 2013, an MOU was signed by Hanban's executive director and the St Augustine principal, under the watchful eyes of the Chinese president and the Trinidad and Tobago prime minister. Just under five months later, on October 23, the CI was officially launched.

Key Stakeholders

A discussion of the key stakeholders in an innovation provides room to explore some of the affordances and constraints that could prove critical to the success or failure of the innovation. It is even more imperative to examine the range of interested parties in this case where stakeholders reside not only within the academic community, but other stakeholders have varying levels of involvement and influence in what is essentially an academic partnership.

Country Level

President Xi's state visit underscored Trinidad and Tobago's political and economic importance in the Caribbean and explained China's desire to exercise cultural diplomacy via the CI. For its part, the government of Trinidad and Tobago had long-standing friendly relations with the

People's Republic of China (PRC), having been among the countries to diplomatically recognise the PRC at the UN in 1971. The countries then entered into formal diplomatic relations in June 1974. There continues to be a solid relationship between the two countries, with Trinidad and Tobago being the first English-speaking Caribbean country to join the Belt and Road Initiative in May 2018. Yet, there exists strong criticism (see, for example, Tudoroiu & Ramlogan, 2021) of the link between the countries in certain quarters, and this would have shaped how some nationals viewed the establishment of a CI.

Local Chinese Community

The Chinese presence in Trinidad and Tobago is a long-standing one, and so an important stakeholder group is the approximately 1% of the population with ancestral ties to China (Johnson, 2006). The first Chinese migrants arrived in 1806, decades before the 1845 arrival of the largest ethnic group—the descendants of immigrants from India. A second wave of Chinese migrants arrived post-Emancipation in the 1850s and 1860s. A third wave coincided with the Chinese revolution from about the 1920s. A fourth wave, begun in the 1970s at the time of China's opening up, continues to date. Indeed, ethnic Chinese can be found in all spheres of the society: in the business and the private sector, generally; in the arts; in government; and in civil society.

An in-depth analysis of the attitudes of these different groups towards their ancestral land is beyond the scope of this chapter, but it is safe to say that in the local Chinese community attitudes range from those whose primary identity is Trinidadian—these are ethnic Chinese who identify as Trinidadian and have retained little of their linguistic and cultural heritage; through those first- and second-generation ethnic Chinese who are curious to discover more about their heritage and even revive ancestral ties; to recent immigrants who are Chinese citizens living and working abroad, forming a new category of entrepreneurial migrants, far removed from the older and well-established business class of Trinidadian Chinese. This diversity led to different levels of engagement with the Confucius Institute as a later discussion will show.

Academic Stakeholders

A Chinese HEI

The final MOU signed by Hanban included a curious detail that was originally thought to be an error in translation. The MOU stated that the implementation of the CI would be via a Memorandum of Agreement to be signed between The UWI St Augustine and "a" university. Given that the proposal had been prepared by The UWI St Augustine and a named Chinese HEI, the omission of that university, and the use of the indefinite "a" university was disconcerting. It soon became clear that Hanban had reservations about the Chinese academic partner with whom The UWI St Augustine had hoped to enter into agreement. The Hanban directorate felt that Trinidad and Tobago's regional importance and the strength of The UWI brand should result in an academic partnership with a higher-ranked Beijing-based university. A new academic partner was selected based on St Augustine's legacy as having grown out of the Imperial College of Tropical Agriculture. Hanban had perhaps made a valid assumption that a university whose roots were in agriculture would be best paired with a highly ranked Chinese university specialising in agriculture. But the reality is that in 2013 The UWI St Augustine was a comprehensive university and agriculture was no longer the leading discipline.

The Chinese Director

A unique characteristic of the CI academic partnership is the joint directorship, with each university partner naming a senior academic to perform this role. A senior Chinese academic was therefore selected to work alongside the local director. Each university selected the academic best placed to achieve the outputs and outcomes which it deemed critical to the success of the CI. However, where previously the two academic partners had engaged in long and productive exchanges and arrived at an understanding of the vision and mission of the CI, the academic eventually appointed as Chinese director arrived just a few short months after her university was selected as the Chinese partner institution. She had not had the benefit of a gradual introduction to the institutional and national context in which she would work and was perhaps less well equipped in terms of knowledge, skills and experience to negotiate the intricacies of this transnational and cross-cultural academic partnership.

The Local Director

As director of the Centre for Language Learning (CLL), the university language centre, I had been the academic to initiate the CI proposal and prepare it with our Chinese counterparts. But when it had seemed that the CI would not be established in 2013/2014, I decided to proceed on my already-approved sabbatical. Our new academic partner was somewhat unhappy that the assigned local director would not be in office during the first year of operations. However, an acting director had been selected and I was able to reassure our academic partner that my colleague would fulfil the role efficiently and effectively. As I anticipated, my colleague did an excellent job in managing the new project, but nevertheless there were certain tensions that could be attributed to both structural reasons (the double directorship) and individual (personal) reasons. Generally, the local director oversees all interactions at their home university, while their Chinese counterpart interfaces with Hanban. With the substantive local director away that first year and a Chinese director zealous to promote the CI and execute the authority she considered appropriate in a Chinese-financed project (albeit one to which The UWI had committed significant resources, including staff housing, and administrative space and support), she sometimes sought to leapfrog over the acting director and appeal directly to the university administration. Her attempts to exercise the levers of power on her own terms meant she quickly ran afoul of the institutional norms of the host university and found herself in a fractious relationship with some key internal stakeholders.

CLL Chinese Language Learners

Given that the rationale behind the CI was to enhance the learning experience in both quantitative and qualitative ways, mention must be made of the learners' expectations for the CI. Their language teacher, the overseas Chinese teacher, had told them of the many opportunities made possible by having a CI on campus, such as the Chinese Bridge programme; of the opportunities for immersion through study abroad and study tours; and of the opportunity to be exposed to tai chi, calligraphy and other traditional Chinese art forms. This stakeholder group was therefore among the most committed and excited to have a CI on campus. Their excitement was initially dampened when the Chinese director insisted that they would not be able to enjoy many of the benefits of the CI as they were not registered CI students. For example, they were told that they could not participate in the Chinese Bridge for university students unless they joined a CI programme. But Hanban soon clarified that this was not the case, and the students happily began to participate in the cultural and other activities sponsored by the CI.

The Faculty of Food and Agriculture

The selection of a Chinese university specialising in agriculture meant that an additional academic stakeholder was the faculty responsible for agriculture. The Faculty of Food and Agriculture (FFA) had no engagement with the CI proposal which was focused on language and culture collaboration. Moreover, the FFA already had an academic partner in China, the Crop Research Institute of Guangdong Academy of Agricultural Sciences (CRIGASS). Yet the faculty now found itself a participant in a second academic partnership with a Chinese university by virtue of the CI. The participation of the agriculture faculty also raised the issue of whether the mission and the vision of the CI might need to be recalibrated to be more inclusive of that faculty and its core business.

Students of the Chinese HEI

Student mobility is often a key objective of academic partnerships. The UWI students could be expected to go to China, but the proposal did not focus on student mobility from China as one of the outputs. The addition of the FFA as a stakeholder opened the possibility of bidirectional student mobility: students of language and agriculture could go to China and Chinese students in agriculture might in turn come to Trinidad. The initial response from the Chinese HEI to this possibility was non-committal. Instead, the university boasted of their existing academic partnerships with high-ranked US universities, the implication being that their students would prefer a US international educational experience to a Caribbean one. This caused some measure of discomfort on The UWI side, because it underscored the fact that the partner university had not sought to engage in a CI partnership with a Caribbean university, but had reputedly been directed to do so to further their university's internationalisation goals.

Other Important Stakeholders

One final stakeholder group merits discussion for the role they played in the context—the Chinese ambassadors. The Chinese ambassador in office during the period when the CI proposal was prepared and under review was on his second posting to Trinidad and Tobago, having served as a junior diplomat in an earlier posting. As the holder of an MPhil from Cambridge, he was clearly at ease in academic circles in the Anglophone world, and his fluency in English meant that he was a skilled interlocutor between his embassy and the host country. By happy coincidence, the ambassador had spent some time at the original Chinese partner university and felt that there was a good fit between the two institutions and that the new CI's mission could be achieved through this academic partnership. Unfortunately, the ambassador's term of office ended before the MOU with Hanban could be signed, bringing his involvement in the CI to a premature end. His successor was also a good friend of the campus and the CI. His arrival coincided with a very exciting and eventful period in the life of the embassy with the state visit by President Xi and the opening of the CI very early in his tenure.

Implementation Phase

The granular account of some of the principal stakeholders of the CI is intended to give a full account of the many factors and personalities at play in this transnational and cross-cultural academic partnership. The value of existing relationships, for example, with the home institution of the Chinese teacher and with the former Chinese ambassador, was an important element in bringing the academic partnership into being. But the driving force remained the importance of developing linguistic and cultural competence among the present generation of university students and through this the promotion of global knowledge sharing and communication. Having discussed the rationale and some aspects of the implementation of this innovation in academic partnerships, the chapter will now look specifically at how the innovation was implemented in terms of teaching and learning.

Implementation Phase: Teaching

The challenge in managing a transnational academic partnership often stems from both structural and interpersonal issues, and this was no less true in this instance. During the implementation of the CI, Hanban dispatched teachers through two separate Hanban Divisions, under the Chinese Overseas Teacher scheme and also through the CI as a distinct teaching entity. Although the teachers performed similar functions in teaching Chinese as a foreign language, their place in the host institution was slightly different, based on the different status of units in which they worked. The overseas teacher was attached to the language centre, which is an academic unit, whereas the CI did not enjoy the status of an academic unit, but was established as a special project. In terms of reporting lines, the overseas teacher reported to the director of the language centre, while the CI teachers reported to the Chinese director, and in academic matters, ultimately through her, to the local director. But the Chinese director quite early embarked on an aggressive drive to bring all Chinese teachers under her *wing*, trying to persuade the overseas teacher to be reassigned to the CI staff, attempting first to cajole and, when that failed, resorting to coercion, and eventually, in an egregious move, informing Hanban that there was no need to renew the contract of the overseas teacher, or make any further appointment to that position, since plans were afoot to bring all Chinese language teaching under the remit of the CI. No such plans had been made, or even discussed. Locating all teaching in the CI was in direct contradiction of the earlier agreement between The UWI St Augustine and the first HEI and indeed quite against both the spirit and the letter of the MOU signed between The UWI and Hanban. The tense situation between the Chinese director and the Chinese overseas teacher and by extension between the mission of the CI and the CLL only subsided when that Chinese director was recalled to China. Fortunately, since this implementation challenge was (inter-) personal rather than structural, the appointment of a new Chinese director who was much more adept at building a harmonious relationship brought this fraught situation to an end.

A far more persistent issue in terms of teaching is the sustainability of the CI programme because of the rotation of staff. The current staff complement is for two Chinese teachers with two-year contracts, renewable once, and up to three volunteers with nine-month contracts. It is well documented in the literature (Starr, 2009; Liu, 2019a) that staffing is one of the stress points in the CI enterprise. Hanban's ambitions for opening CIs have outstripped their capacity to deploy well-trained staff who can deliver good language pedagogy. The insufficiency of the teacher pool is even more pronounced, when, as in our case, the partner institution is not an HEI with a specialisation in language teaching, or teacher education, but one whose core mission revolves around agriculture.

In a typical academic partnership, there is a provision for staff mobility between partners. However, with the Chinese partner university being a specialist agriculture HEI with little in-house expertise in language pedagogy, the available pool of language specialists is small. The recourse is to unaffiliated Chinese language teachers, prepared to be recruited to work on behalf of the partner university; this results in a further layer of bureaucracy in the teacher recruitment exercise. Additionally, there are some recurring issues that stymie Hanban's efforts to dispatch language specialists, for example cultural maladjustment, personal challenges posed by the physical and emotional distance from family members, linguistic difficulties when teachers and volunteers are not proficient in the language of the host country, intra-community issues as discussed above and purely work-related issues. In the case of CIs operating in the Americas, there is also the recruitment constraint that locations in North America are more in demand, as seen as more attractive by Chinese nationals.

The St Augustine Campus conducts a programme to facilitate induction and orientation of new academic staff, but these are only available if a staff member arrives at the beginning of the academic year. More often than not, CI staff are unable to avail themselves of these opportunities, since the Hanban and UWI administrative calendars are not in sync and work permit processing adds to the time needed to onboard international staff. Our CI has therefore adopted internal measures like mentoring of new arrivals by those already in post, circulating a staff handbook with policy guidelines and advice, holding regular staff meetings and planning other strategies to build a team approach, and facilitating the staff's integration into the CI and the university at large. The role and personal management style of the Chinese director become tremendously important for staff wellbeing and productivity. The second Chinese director has displayed an empathetic leadership style, giving the Chinese staff a structure and framework they can look to for guidance and direction, but at the same time offering them the necessary scaffolding and care to counteract culture shock and feelings of homesickness. Her contribution to institution-building of the CI remains highly valued by all those who engage with her: students, local director, colleagues and other internal stakeholders, and the Chinese embassy staff.

Implementation Phase: Learning

Although the MOU assigned all CI language teaching to community language classes, there was an early attempt to cater to the staff and students in agriculture by offering them an in-faculty language course. That course was only offered once. The attrition rates were high, and there seemed to be little interest in further courses. On a more positive note, there has been a take-up of postgraduate study opportunities at the partner university in Beijing. Several students have earned graduate degrees and acquired some proficiency in Mandarin while doing so. The CI innovation *has* therefore resulted in educational opportunities for students of the university. A prestigious Agricultural Innovation Park, a joint venture with the Chinese university, is one of the outcomes of the CI innovation of which the university is most proud, since this presents an ongoing opportunity for knowledge sharing in the field of agriculture.

The community language courses have had a good measure of success in taking Chinese language learning closer to the population at large. For some time, the classes were offered in collaboration with the local ethnic Chinese community at the premises of the Chinese Association. But the venue was not ideal for language teaching, which drew heavily on the integration of technology, and other more appropriate teaching venues had to be found. Class numbers have fluctuated over time, but before the pandemic forced all teaching online, community language classes were offered in two venues in the north and south of the island. Discussions about offering a class in the sister isle of Tobago have been ongoing.

A collaboration with a private university affiliated with The UWI has led to a language programme with great potential for the students involved. The Ministry of Education has given its approval to Business Chinese as an alternative to Business Spanish in the Associate Degree in Business Management offered by this university. The programme, now in its third semester, has elicited very positive student feedback. This collaboration is a potential area of growth and development in Chinese for Specific Purposes, and to build on this initiative our CI applied for and was granted approval to establish an affiliated Confucius Classroom. The establishment of this Confucius Classroom is a measure of the growth and success of the CI's contribution to the field of tertiary-level education in Trinidad and Tobago.

The final example of the CI's success in promoting language learning comes from the thriving heritage language programme delivered to the children of Chinese citizens living and working in the country. Enrolment numbers in these Sunday classes (pre-pandemic) were approximately 100 per cohort. The parents of these children have sought out these classes, travelling in some cases from towns almost two hours away to give their children the opportunity to acquire literacy in their first language and guard against subtractive bilingualism.

As stated earlier, the glocal organisation, that is, the CI, has shown its innovativeness in adapting to the demands present in different local contexts and developing programmes in alignment with the needs of the stakeholder community. In the case of The UWI CIs, all three have promoted more adult language learning on the islands where they are located, with each CI developing programmes in response to societal needs. Similarly, in child language learning, provision is tailored to societal demand. Thus, the St Augustine CI has mainly worked with school-aged learners through its heritage classes, and in a few private primary schools. Barbados, on the other hand, has led a significant drive to integrate the CI into the public school sector. Unlike in Trinidad and Tobago, where Spanish and French remain the only languages available in the public school sector, in Barbados public policy has expanded to include a place for Chinese in the curriculum. As a result, the Barbados CI delivers very successful pilot programmes in four public schools, two at the secondary level and two at the primary level, in keeping with the national objective of giving persons under 18 the opportunity to acquire bilingual proficiency by 2030 (Austin, 2018).

All The UWI CIs have also made culture an intrinsic part of their programme offerings. Cultural activities like CI Day, Spring Festival celebrations, tea ceremonies, tai chi and calligraphy workshops are very important activities in the CIs in the Anglophone Caribbean. The St Augustine CI does no on-campus language teaching, so the CI's engagement with the student body is chiefly through tai chi, calligraphy and cultural workshops, for example on Chinese knots, in addition to more academic events like seminars on postgraduate study opportunities in China. This focus on culture is fairly typical in CI contexts where China is a little-known or -understood entity and cultural diplomacy becomes an important aspect of the work of the CI. This is in contrast to those countries where cultural and/or geographical proximity make China a familiar partner, and the academic and business opportunities afforded by the CI are an important selling point. Liu (2019a, p. 650), who has conducted empirical research into the CI with the study of five CIs from four continents, underscores how regional differences shape the focus of the CI:

> language teaching is the core function of the CIs in the East Asian cultural sphere...where traditional China enjoys a very respectable culture image and modern China offers new opportunities; while in Western countries...where vestiges of Orientalism and the Cold War mentality are amplified by distances in culture and space, Chinese cultural introduction and enhancing local people's understanding of contemporary China is given more weighting.

At the St Augustine Campus, interest in East Asian languages typically derives from interest in contemporary Asian culture. Thus manga, anime and other expressions of contemporary Japanese culture and K-Pop, Korean soaps and other expressions of contemporary Korean culture are the gateways to Japanese and Korean language learning. In the absence of a similar contemporary cultural magnet that would draw learners to Chinese language learning, one is faced with the paradox of using traditional artforms as a conduit to the discovery of contemporary China.

Conclusion

The chapter has sought to do a critical evaluation of the CI project at The UWI St Augustine Campus, using the lens of innovation. The CI is the product of an academic partnership between The UWI St Augustine on the one hand and Hanban and a Chinese HEI on the other. I first argued that the CI itself is an innovation, because although it drew on the models of other organisations, Hanban's decision to focus much of its efforts on establishing academic partnerships between Chinese and foreign universities to operationalise its language and culture organisation gave rise to a new entity, significantly different from the existing models of cultural organisations.

In assessing any kind of academic enterprise, pedagogical matters and their impact on academic quality is a primary concern. The problems identified, for example the availability and retention of qualified and competent teachers of Chinese as a foreign language, who are willing to engage in staff mobility in furtherance of an internationalisation agenda, are thus an important issue. (Hanban has been seeking to increase teacher training of L2 speakers of Chinese as one strategy to increase the numbers of trained teachers of Chinese, although in the absence of an established Chinese programme such persons may be rare. The St Augustine CI has identified just one former student of Chinese to engage in training.) In terms of institutional management, the role and position of the CI in the institution and the mechanism of the double directorship merit attention. From a cultural diplomacy perspective, the brand management and the attendant reputational risk to either party in the academic partnership are a significant matter. Moreover, since a CI links not only two universities, but, in the case of The UWI CIs, links two countries, a CI is indeed a high-stakes venture. Finally, the financial risks in a programme so dependent on external funding cannot be overlooked.

Each university needs to weigh the advantages and disadvantages before it makes the decision to establish a CI. From an institutional perspective, the CI innovation was linked to The UWI's internationalisation strategy, its strategic direction and its plans. But an important dimension of the success of the academic partnership must be how the individual partners are in alignment for their vision of the CI. In the case of the Chinese academic partner, their status as a specialist agriculture HEI means that all disciplines are valued for their contribution to the core discipline of agriculture. In the case of The UWI St Augustine, agriculture is no longer the central discipline of this comprehensive university. Ideally, a CI would serve as a platform for deeper engagement and collaboration in a specific discipline and ultimately for more collaboration over multiple disciplines. The CI at St Augustine cannot benefit from that disciplinary association which might give it a more solid anchoring in the institution. Conversely, one might argue that lacking that singular disciplinary focus, the CI can be a resource for any and all disciplines taught on campus.

The CI comes with some specification of responsibilities for programme management and delivery, namely the role of the local and Chinese directors. On the Chinese side, great care needs to be taken that the person selected has the skills, experience and personal characteristics to fulfil the demands of the role. The same also applies on The UWI side. The host university also needs to ensure that operationalisation and implementation of the CI are supported in a coherent and structured manner. This means that there must be a fully developed protocol for the intermeshing of the two directorates, as well as clear policy and procedures that would not be so dependent on the personal characteristics of the two academic administrators. Given the rotation of Chinese directors, the risk of the lack of continuity must be counterbalanced by appropriate succession planning to facilitate the sustainability of the programme.

Last, but by no means least, while the injection of external funds to meet budget shortfalls and introduce innovation could be a sufficient temporary fix, should a special project become linked to core teaching, the robustness of academic programmes is put at risk. In short, there must be a clear assessment of the academic, financial, reputational and other risks associated with an academic partnership such as the CI. An assessment strategy could include greater use of risk assessment guidelines, where available, in evaluating the feasibility of future projects. When one weighs the CI's strengths and weaknesses, I feel there is still more recommending the CI than militating against it. Performance of the CI will rely on the establishment of clear systems and structures, but to safeguard the innovative edge, a process approach which allows for a certain amount of flexibility and responsiveness is also crucial.

The challenges that arise during the implementation of an innovation from planned and unplanned absences of key stakeholders, possible mission shift, even the once-in-a-century occurrence of a pandemic mean that a core value in a CI must be flexibility and a willingness to adapt and to respond to circumstances. But a foundational principle of the CI was the very notion of innovation, namely how to take an existing language and culture model and shape it in a way to serve new audiences in the twenty-first century. In short, "innovation" is in the DNA of the CI and innovation must remain an adaptive strategy for the future. The global CI has once again demonstrated its potential to innovate with the introduction of two new entities: the Centre for Chinese Language Education and the Chinese International Education Foundation. These have been established as successor organisations to Hanban/CI HQ. These new entities seek to correct some of the organisational deficiencies identified in Hanban's earlier manifestation and retool a language and culture organisation for the future. The local CI must likewise remain wedded to innovation and committed to systematic review, so that the academic partnership, its outputs and its outcomes evolve to remain fit-for-purpose in the institutional and national contexts.

Acknowledgements I would like to thank my colleague Mr David Bulbulia, the co-director of the Confucius Institute at The University of the West Indies Cave Hill Campus, for the information provided on the CI in that island.

References

Austin, S. (2018, September 20). *Children to learn Mandarin*. Barbados Government Information Service. https://gisbarbados.gov.bb/blog/children-to-learn-mandarin-chinese/

Collini, S. (2012). *What are universities for?* Penguin Books.

Danping, W., & Adamson, B. (2015). War and peace: Perceptions of Confucius Institutes in China and USA. *The Asia-Pacific Education Researcher, 24*(1), 225–234. https://doi.org/10.1007/s40299-014-0174-5

Hartig, F. (2012). Confucius Institutes and the rise of China. *Journal of Chinese Political Science/Association of Chinese Political Studies, 17*, 53–76. https://doi.org/10.1007/s11366-011-9178-7

Hartig, F. (2015). Communicating China to the world: Confucius Institutes and China's strategic narratives. *Politics, 35*(3–4), 245–258. https://doi.org/10.1111/1467-9256.120

Institute for Cultural Diplomacy. (2021, April 27). What is cultural diplomacy. http://www.culturaldiplomacy.org/index.php?en_culturaldiplomacy

Johnson, K. (2006). *Descendants of the dragon: The Chinese in Trinidad 1806–2006*. Ian Randle.

Liu, X. (2019a). China's cultural diplomacy: A great leap outward with Chinese characteristics? Multiple comparative case studies of the Confucius Institutes. *Journal of Contemporary China, 28*(118), 646–661. https://doi.org/10.108 0/10670564.2018.1557951

Liu, X. (2019b). So similar, so different, so Chinese: Analytical comparisons of the Confucius Institute with its western counterparts. *Asian Studies Review, 43*(2), 256–275. https://doi.org/10.1080/10357823.2019.1584602

Paradise, J. F. (2009). China and international harmony: The role of Confucius Institutes in bolstering Beijing's soft power. *Asian Survey, 49*(4), 647–669. https://doi.org/10.1525/as.2009.49.4.647

Peterson, R. (2017). *Outsourced to China: Confucius Institutes and soft power in American higher education*. National Association of Scholars.

Sahlins, M. (2015). *Confucius Institutes: Academic malware*. Prickly Paradigm Press.

Schreuder, D. M. (2013). *Universities for a new world: Making a global network in higher education, 1913–2013*. Sage. The Association of Commonwealth Universities.

Starr, D. (2009). Chinese language education in Europe: The Confucius Institutes. *European Journal of Education, 44*(1), 65–82.

Theo, R., & Leung, M. W. H. (2018). China's Confucius Institute in Indonesia: Mobility, frictions and local surprises. *Sustainability, 10*(2), 530–545. https:// doi.org/10.3390/su10020530

Tudoroiu, T., with Ramlogan, A. (2021). Prestige projects: China and the elites of Trinidad and Tobago. In T. Tudoroiu with A. Ramlogan (Eds.), *China's international socialization of political elites in the Belt and Road Initiative* (pp. 116–145). Routledge.

Wang, X. (2020). *Winning American hearts and minds: China's image building efforts in the 21st century*. Springer Nature. https://doi.org/10.1007/ 978-981-15-3184-2_8

Wheeler, A. (2014). Cultural diplomacy, language planning, and the case of the University of Nairobi Confucius Institute. *Journal of Asian and African Studies, 49*(1), 49–63. https://doi.org/10.1177/0021909613477834

Zhao, H., & Huang, J. (2010). China's policy of Chinese as a foreign language and the use of overseas CIs. *Educational Research for Policy and Practice, 9*(2), 127–142.

7

Issues and Challenges of Continuing Education for Teachers of French as a Foreign Language in the English-Speaking Caribbean

Sabrina Lipoff

The Integrating French as a Language of Exchange (IFLE) Program

The Caribbean States share a certain geographical, historical, and cultural proximity, which may lead one to believe that strong relations and exchanges of all kinds exist between these countries. Indeed, there are several intergovernmental organizations such as the Organization of Eastern Caribbean States (OECS), Caribbean Community (CARICOM), and the Association of Caribbean States (ACS). These organizations all aim to strengthen regional cooperation on common issues such as tourism, trade, environment, or sustainable development. Mobility, at the heart of these issues and crucial in an insular context, is however hampered by the language barrier. The region is a mosaic where English, Spanish, French, Dutch and several forms of Creole coexist, but are not mastered by non-natives. We are therefore in a situation of

---

S. Lipoff (✉)
On Continue, Les Trois Ilets, Martinique
e-mail: sabrinalipoff@oncontinue.org

© The Author(s), under exclusive license to Springer Nature Switzerland AG 2023 **129**
D. Mideros et al. (eds.), *Innovation in Language Learning and Teaching*, New Language
Learning and Teaching Environments, https://doi.org/10.1007/978-3-031-34182-3_7

multilingualism, defined by the Common European Framework of Reference for Languages (CEFR) as "the coexistence of different languages in a given society" (Council of Europe, 2001, p. 4), whereas we should aim for plurilingualism, which is the ability to use languages for the purposes of communication and to take part in intercultural interaction, where a person, viewed as a social agent has proficiency, of varying degrees, in several languages and experience of several cultures (Council of Europe, 2001).

Plurilingualism thus appears as a vector of regional integration that could promote student, professional and cultural mobility. However, in order for language teaching and learning to be more effective, teachers of French as a foreign language (FFL) in the region need to be supported in a continuous training process. Thanks to the IFLE project, a training program adapted to their needs was designed and offered online and on a Caribbean-wide scale. In this chapter, we will illustrate how the continuing education of FFL teachers is one of the main issues for the success of learners, what training actions we have implemented, what were their successes and weaknesses, and what we can learn from them for the future.

The IFLE project came to life in March 2019 in St Lucia, after more than two years of work in the field. Financed by the French Ministry of Europe and Foreign Affairs through the Solidarity Fund for Innovative Projects, it was carried by the French Embassy in St Lucia and the *Alliance Française de Sainte Lucie*, general delegation of the network of *Alliances Françaises* in the Lesser Antilles. However, it was not limited to the Lesser Antilles and reached ten countries of the English-speaking Caribbean, namely Jamaica, Antigua and Barbuda, Saint Christopher and Nevis, Dominica, St Lucia, Barbados, Saint Vincent and the Grenadines, Grenada, Trinidad and Tobago, and Guyana. It had three main components: educational, cultural, and entrepreneurial. For each of them, the goal was to develop exchanges and mobility between English-speaking countries and French-speaking territories, using French as a communication tool for these exchanges. The "pedagogy" axis aimed to increase the competence of FFL teachers in order to develop the teaching and learning of French, and to integrate the DELF Junior exam (diploma in French language) in secondary schools, at different stages of learning. This exam

7 Issues and Challenges of Continuing Education for Teachers... 131

can be taken at each level of the CEFR, and we wanted to offer the DELF A1 (beginner) in the third year, A2 (elementary) in the fifth year, then B1 (intermediate) in the first year of CAPE, and B2 (upper-intermediate) in the second year. The DELF exam is widely recognized internationally and valid for life. Four skills are tested: listening, reading, writing and speaking, and there is a strong emphasis on communication. It is commonly required by French Universities (B2 level), or in order to obtain the French citizenship for example (B1 level). Introducing this exam in schools would enable the students to be more familiar with it, more interested in pursuing French, and more likely to further their studies in French territories. We counted on the fact that teachers' training would ensure greater motivation on the part of students, as well as a satisfactory success rate on the DELF exam (Timperley, 2011). In the long term, the goal was to allow students who had obtained the equivalent of the baccalaureate in an English-speaking Caribbean country to enter French universities (mainly in Guadeloupe and Martinique).

In addition to the opportunity to pursue their studies and gain a better command of the French language, foreign students in the French West Indies benefit from the experience of living in a French-speaking territory which allows them to better understand and integrate the similarities and cultural specificities of the region. They are thus better equipped to create an inclusive Caribbean community, to work together to preserve the gains of regional integration and to face the current challenges of economic recovery and sustainable human development, according to the CARICOM vision (CARICOM, 2020). The French universities in the region therefore offer an incomparable opportunity, especially since access to higher education is very limited in many Caribbean countries, either because they do not have a university or because the cost of enrolment is too high. French universities have the advantage of being less expensive while remaining fairly close to many English-speaking islands, but the disadvantage of requiring a B2 (upper-intermediate) level in French, as defined by the CEFR. Each year, a handful of candidates from the English-speaking Caribbean manage to get into our universities, but this remains largely insufficient compared to what our territories have to offer.

The IFLE project team therefore worked closely with the Ministries of Education to identify three to five "pilot" secondary schools in which to introduce the DELF exam officially, starting with the A2 level, in Form 3. This exam was to be taken on a voluntary basis, in addition to the regular exams. We also needed French teachers to ensure the success of candidates. It is in this particular field that the IFLE project has distinguished itself for its innovative training actions.

The Origin of the Project: Three Worrying Observations

The majority of the initiatives launched by the IFLE project for the "pedagogy" part are the result of several years of work and observations made by part of the IFLE project team. These observations are as follows:

Lack of Student Interest in Learning French

In most secondary schools in the English-speaking Caribbean, it is possible to drop French in the third grade in favour of Spanish or other subjects. As a result, very few students continue French into high school. Spanish is preferred because it is perceived as easier to learn and more intuitive. In fact, in a survey conducted by the Ministry of Education of St Lucia among students in the pilot schools and shared with the partners in their report of the project, those whose favourite subject was not French were asked why they were not interested in the language. The choice "spelling is difficult, there are too many accents" came first, selected by nearly 45% of respondents. If this prevalence of Spanish is understandable for the countries closest to South America such as Trinidad and Tobago, it is more surprising for the islands neighbouring French territories, such as Dominica or Saint Kitts and Nevis. Some islands such as St Lucia even have a Creole with a French lexical base (Alexander, 2014), which could encourage students to learn the language.

Yet, this linguistic proximity is seen more as an additional hurdle to overcome, for fear of confusing the two languages. On the contrary, some

7 Issues and Challenges of Continuing Education for Teachers...

believe that mastering Creole will allow them to express themselves without problems in the French-speaking islands and with any speaker, which is not the case. In fact, it is common to meet tourism or hotel professionals who speak Creole to French speakers and expect to be understood. Many parents also make this confusion and/or do not really pay attention to the learning of French, which they do not consider important for their child's future. At the beginning of the program, we held meetings with parents in the pilot schools in St Lucia to present various exchange opportunities in the French-speaking Caribbean, only a few parents attended. It was therefore crucial to make French language learning more attractive to both students and parents, by presenting the opportunities it offers, and in particular the possibility of pursuing a quality education at a lower cost.

The Lack of Training of Teachers in Teaching FFL

In the region, teachers with a university degree in FFL (or even in French) represent a very small minority. Indeed, Trinidad and Tobago is the only country in the region that requires a bachelor's degree to teach FFL. Jamaica also offers very good training for teachers of FFL, with an exchange program in France. However, in most cases the situations are variable, with some teachers having the equivalent of a baccalaureate, or others only having finished high school. We even had the case of a teacher who had never learned French before having to teach it to her students. In this context, it is understandable why teachers can only reproduce the way they themselves have learned French, generally very far from the action-oriented approach recommended by the CEFR. In the above-mentioned survey by the Ministry of Education in St Lucia, the reasons "concepts are not explained clearly," "activities do not interest me" and "lessons are boring" were selected, respectively, by 35%, 23% and 21% of the students surveyed. These results show that language instruction is not optimal. As Mr Robinson, curriculum officer for Modern Languages in St. Lucia, explains:

> Quite often the teaching of French remained at the exercise or activity level. Tasks are hardly used in assessment because of the structure of the

regional exam and the time teachers have to cover the curriculum. The integration of authentic materials is often limited to songs, videos, and recordings from the textbook. (Robinson, personal communication, October 28, 2020).

It is important to remind that inclusive and equitable quality education and life-long learning opportunities for all are among the Sustainable Development Goals (SDG 4), as defined by the United Nations in 2015. In fact, the participants in the World Education Forum "committed to ensure that teachers and educators are empowered, adequately recruited, well-trained, professionally qualified, motivated and supported within well-resourced, efficient and effectively governed systems" (UNESCO, 2019, p. 3).

This was clearly not the case for many French teachers in the region. To try to improve this, several actions were carried out by the *Alliance Française de Sainte Lucie* with the local teachers during the two years preceding the IFLE project. One of these was a monthly workshop to exchange best practices where teachers could meet to discuss their difficulties and receive or give advice. Discussions focused on the use of the mother tongue in the classroom, the teaching of culture and the difficulties it represents for teachers who do not have this knowledge, the modernization of textbooks, new technologies, as well as the creation of teaching sequences. As these issues are common to all teachers of FFL in the English-speaking Caribbean, the IFLE project sought to provide a basic understanding of FFL didactics to as many teachers in the region as possible, based on their difficulties, as observed in St Lucia.

The Lack of Mastery of the French Language (Real or Perceived) by the Teachers

Since many of the teachers did not have the benefit of real exposure to the language during their learning process, they did not feel comfortable with French and gave a predominant place to the mother tongue in their classes. This is also the reason why some of them did not dare to

7 Issues and Challenges of Continuing Education for Teachers... 135

participate in activities organized by the *Alliances françaises*, for fear of being judged by native French speakers or other teachers. We were faced with a vicious circle, since the fewer the teachers who practise the language, the less they would expose their students to it, and the less effective their teaching of French would be. The *Alliance Française de Sainte Lucie* had tried to set up conversation workshops for teachers only, but these were quickly discontinued due to lack of participants. This phenomenon called linguistic insecurity has been well documented for decades starting with Haugen (1972) and then Francard, Lambert and Berdal-Masuy (1993). Rincón Restrepo (2020) explains that French teachers who are non-native can have "a feeling of illegitimacy and vulnerability (…) They have the feeling, from their own perception and that of their entourage, that their competence will always be devalued in the face of the perfect image of the 'native'." In order to ensure effective teaching of the language, it was necessary to find a way to help the teachers progress in French without making them feel intimidated and/or judged.

Based on these observations, the pedagogical team of the IFLE project reflected on the best way to train teachers of FFL in the English-speaking Caribbean in both French language and pedagogy. Face-to-face training was quickly ruled out due to the number of countries involved, the cost of travel and the magnitude of the task. The idea of an asynchronous online training course lasting several weeks came up. This choice proved to be particularly wise as it allowed participants to familiarize themselves with distance learning and the tools available before having to use them for their own teaching in a pandemic context. Two tracks were identified: one on pedagogy and the other on French language. This made it possible to take into account the disparities in the level of language and training among the teachers and to offer them the choice of taking either the two courses or only the pedagogical course.

Implementing Continuous Training for FFL Teachers

Convincing Teachers to Participate and Assessing Their Level

In order to promote our training sessions to the teachers of FFL in the region, we started by contacting the representatives of the Ministries of Education to present our project. Most of them welcomed it with enthusiasm since nothing like this had ever been proposed. Indeed, some teachers had previously benefited from training grants in France or locally, but this had stopped at least ten years ago. A distance learning course, free of charge and open to all teachers in the region was therefore completely new. Some chose to communicate with all their teachers, others to target only the teachers of the "pilot" schools. Whatever the situation, teachers had to take an online placement test first, both to show their interest in the courses and so that the teaching team could better identify their needs and create an adapted course. Since the placement tests only evaluated written production, we supplemented them with a short oral interview to better understand not only the level of French of the future participants but also their background and expectations.

At the end of this process, 120 secondary school teachers from 9 countries were selected. The majority of the participants had a level of French between A2+ and B2, with a few teachers at A1 and C1 level (Council of Europe, 2001). For example, here are two excerpts from written productions (whose authors will not be cited for reasons of confidentiality), illustrating these differences in level:

> *En 2007, Je allé à Cuba. Ça était une expérience différent de tout J'eu avant. Tout le monde parlait Espagnol et ils étaient très gentilé. Les véhicules étaient très différents, ils étaient antiques. Je l'utilisais beaucoup pour aller au la ville.* (Anonymous, email, March 20, 2020)

And

7 Issues and Challenges of Continuing Education for Teachers...

Mon fils et moi sommes allés en Guadeloupe pour passer les fêtes de Noël avec notre famille. C'était un très beau moment de partage mais le seul bémol c'est que notre séjour était trop court. Nous aurions voulu rester beaucoup plus longtemps mais cela n'a pas été possible. (Anonymous, March 18, 2020)

The first text is representative of the A1 (beginner) level, and the second text corresponds to at least a B2 (upper-intermediate) level. Faced with such heterogeneity, we asked ourselves how to design a training program that would satisfy the greatest number of people. Rather than accepting only B1/B2 teachers, we chose to accept all volunteers. On the one hand, we did not want to risk discouraging them; on the other hand, we wanted to provide assistance to those teachers who needed it the most. In order not to put them in a situation of failure, we made ourselves available to them if they wished to stop during the training. On the other hand, we offered to exempt the few teachers who had a C1 (advanced) level from the language training, so that they would not have the impression that they were wasting their time. It is interesting to note that some of the Ministry of Education referents wished to register at the same time as their teachers, in order to better accompany them. This allowed us to have another look at these training sessions and other remarks to take into account to improve ourselves.

Creating an Adapted Training

In parallel to the identification of the participants, we had to choose an LMS and design these trainings. We chose to work with *Agora Learning Infinity*, and its creation tool *CreaLearning*. The team members followed a training to learn how to create the modules, upload them to the LMS and monitor the participants. This was one of the most complete LMS on the market, which made both the creation and the follow-up easier for us. We also had our first modules reviewed by a professional, and benefited from technical support when needed. Regarding the training itself, several questions arose, such as the following: "which linguistic/pedagogical points to address," "which documents to use or create," "how long to allocate to the complete training and to each module," "how to make

138 S. Lipoff

these trainings as interactive as possible," "how to evaluate the participants," and "how to work on oral production"? For each of these questions, we will explain the path we followed in order to provide a satisfactory answer.

In terms of the linguistic points addressed, we first tried to identify the recurrent errors in the placement tests. Then, we completed our selection with the aspects of the language that are generally problematic at the B1/B2 levels, namely the alternation of past tenses, the present and past conditional tenses, the different forms of hypotheses, and the articulation of the discourse (Chauvet, 2008). For the "pedagogy" part, we thought about the notions that would be most useful to teachers, both theoretical (the principles of the CEFR, the notion of task, etc.) and practical, such as the construction of a pedagogical sequence, the teaching of culture or phonetics, or the use of new technologies (Cuq & Gruca, 2002). The experience of the practice exchange workshops in St Lucia was very useful for the elaboration of this training plan since we had already identified certain needs of the teachers.

Regarding the choice of teaching materials used for language training, we quickly opted for authentic teaching materials for two reasons. The first is that this type of teaching materials allow us to work on written and oral reception by exposing participants to authentic language (Aslim-Yetis, 2010). The second is that these materials allow teachers to discover various sources of authentic teaching resources that they can use as inspiration for their own lessons. For example, we used videos from news reports or interviews, video clips, blog or newspaper articles, or excerpts from literary texts.

Integrating Interactivity

It is now widely known that interaction is critical in online learning. Woo and Reeves (2008) explain, "[o]ne of the key components of good teaching and learning, online or otherwise, is interaction. It has been argued that success or failure of online learning depends on the level of interaction that occurs." In order to make the modules as interactive as possible, and thus maintain the participants' attention and motivation until the

7 Issues and Challenges of Continuing Education for Teachers...

end, we decided to vary the learning experiences by alternating written or oral reception activities, quizzes, exercises, interactive images, or hypertext links. In this way, the learner becomes an actor in his or her learning, which ensures both greater participation and more effective learning (Pappas, 2015).

At the end of some of the modules, we asked the teachers to participate in the forum, through questions such as the following: "do you think it is useful and possible to implement a language portfolio in your school" and "how do you teach culture in your class: share one of your activities that your students enjoy"? These activities were very much appreciated by the teachers, and many got involved. This type of exchange contributed to the creation of a real community of French teachers (Lave & Wenger, 1991), as we had imagined it. At the end of each language training module, we proposed a written production activity to be sent back to us by email, so that the participants could reuse what they had just learned (or revised). As for the evaluation of the pedagogical training, it was done through final quizzes for each module, as well as the submission of a pedagogical sheet, also corrected and returned.

For the language training, we also needed to find a way to work on oral interaction, which is not easy in asynchronous online training. According to Rincón Restrepo (2020), the fact that teachers do not have the opportunity to practise the language outside of the classroom is one of the causes of their linguistic insecurity. We decided on weekly conversation classes, which would focus on the language point covered in the unit and allow participants to both practise speaking and interact with other teachers. We had to decide how long to run the classes, how many participants to accept, what topics to cover, and how to manage enrolment. We decided to offer several one-hour sessions that participants could sign up for themselves, with a maximum of eight people.

After the first session, we realized that not everyone could speak sufficiently, and we reduced the number of participants to six. Unfortunately, this limited us to about 20 participants per week, and some who were slow to sign up were frustrated that they could not participate. As such, we offered additional one-on-one conversation classes to teachers who wanted them. In total, 30 group conversation classes and 6 individual conversation classes were held. These classes, which were intended to work on specific linguistic points, soon presented other interests for the participants. Indeed, as our training took place partly during the confinement due to the pandemic, the teachers were able to use these moments of exchange to express their difficulties in this educational transition. They shared their tips for communicating with their students and ensuring pedagogical continuity despite the lack of access to technology and asked us for resources for their online courses. We were able to provide them with additional pedagogical support, while allowing them to practice the language. Through these conversation classes, teachers were able to meet colleagues from various countries, discuss their teaching practices and speak French regularly, which had never been possible before.

For the pedagogical training, we wanted to organize monthly gatherings in each *Alliance Française* (facilitated by the pedagogical coordinators in the Alliances) to allow participants to share their difficulties or to work on specific points discussed during the month. Indeed, according to DeMonte (2013, p. 8):

> [m]any of the professional-learning designs that show improvements in teaching and learning include some kind of regular collaboration among teachers in a school or across grade levels—sometimes with an instructional leader—to work on better strategies and practices for teaching.

Unfortunately, the health situation prevented us from doing so, and we did not have the time to replace these workshops with webinars or online meetings.

Managing the Pace

In order to organize the training plans, we had to choose a total duration as well as a distribution in modules and a work rhythm. We kept in mind that in order to be impactful, the training course had to last a certain number of hours. As DeMonte explains:

> It takes sustained investment of time into teacher training to change instruction and improve classroom outcomes. A review of research on the

effect of professional development on increased student learning found that programs had to include more than 14 hours of professional development for student learning to be affected. (DeMonte, 2013, p. 1)

At the very beginning, we asked the Ministries of Education if it were possible for them to give their teachers some time off during the week to follow the training course, but they all said it was not an option. This was one of the reasons why many teachers did not finish the training, as we will explain further. According to the *Teacher Policy Development Guide* "[e]mployers should provide a supportive environment for CPD, including ensuring that teachers are granted the necessary time and opportunities for professional development while in school" (UNESCO, 2019, p. 52). Since the teachers were taking the training on their own time, we decided to limit ourselves to ten weeks, with one module of about 1 hour per week for each training, for a total of 20 hours. Because of the written and oral production activities, it was necessary for everyone to progress at the same pace. This was to encourage teachers to be diligent and not fall too far behind, to avoid dropouts. We decided to open and close the modules one after the other each week. Unfortunately, we soon realized that the pace of work was too fast for the teachers, who asked us for extra time or even a week's break at the beginning of the school year in April. So we adjusted the pace by giving them more time to complete each module.

Once the trainings were ready and organized, we moved on to the facilitation and follow-up of the participants, which proved to be much more time-consuming than expected. On the one hand, the written productions proposed in the form of voluntary work were unexpectedly successful, with some teachers writing entire pages. In total, we corrected about 200 written productions and sent them back to the teachers, indicating the correct forms and sometimes reminding them of the grammar rules to use. In addition to this, the participants used the forum to report technical problems they encountered during the exercises or to ask additional questions on the theme of the module. On the other hand, we had to follow up with the participants a few days before the end of each unit to make sure that they finished on time. Despite this, many of them frequently asked us to give them access to the previous module again because they had not had time to complete it. We eventually created a "catch-up" session, in which we enrolled teachers who were consistently out of time or who could no longer keep up with the pace for personal reasons. In this session, modules were available without time limits, which allowed participants to move at their own pace, and also made it possible to add participants during the course. In order to facilitate communication and keep participants motivated, we created WhatsApp groups that brought together participants by country. We shared additional resources in these groups and used them as reminders of the closing of modules. Some teachers also used them to ask pedagogical or linguistic questions.

However, other participants who were less comfortable with new technologies were more difficult to contact. Some expressed difficulties in using the platform and navigating between modules, to the point that at the end of the training, they still did not understand that there were two different modules each week. We realized that we had not sufficiently taken into account the technical abilities of the participants, and that a video presentation of the interface would have been necessary at the beginning of the training. Nevertheless, the technical side of these trainings also helped some teachers, who were facing the challenge of using new technologies in the classroom. For example, we received this testimony, which we will keep anonymous:

> Today I am gradually embracing these modern times with great optimism. In fact I am proud to let everyone know, especially those who used to call me primitive, that I am doing this online training, something that would not have been possible a few decades ago. (Anonymous, email, April 1, 2020)

In the pedagogical training, we also had a module focusing on the new technologies that could be used to teach French, such as online games and quizzes like Kahoot or Socrative, apps like Duolingo for teachers, Apprendre TV5 Monde or even WhatsApp. This was also part of the innovative aspect of the training, since many teachers did not use these tools in the classroom, often due to the lack of equipment. They mainly used textbooks and the audio materials that came with it. A few teachers brought their own laptop and speakers to their classroom, but it was only a minority. Thanks to our training, when classes had to be held online,

Evaluation

Feedback from Teachers and Members of the Ministries

Halfway through the course, we carried out an initial consultation with the participants, with the aim of rectifying any problems and promoting our courses. The first feedback was very positive, as can be seen in this example:

> …in my opinion this training is very timely, informative and beneficial. … In this training, we get the opportunity to improve the use of the French language and teaching techniques that will definitely help us as teachers to give lessons to our students in a more practical and innovative way. I have learned so much so far. I can't wait every week to face a new challenge and learn interesting points about the language that I didn't know. For me this course is really useful and to the organizers of this course I say a thousand thanks. It's a real pleasure to participate. (Anonymous, personal communication, March 2020)

Once the training sessions were over, we asked the participants to answer an anonymous satisfaction questionnaire (see Appendix). The results were very satisfactory, as 100% of the respondents said they were satisfied with the trainings and found the content useful. Both courses also scored very well, with 3.55/4 for the language course and 3.73/4 for the pedagogical course. The content was also appreciated, with a score of 3.69/4. Finally, 86% of respondents said they would be willing to take a second course of this type if it were offered to them.

Participants were able to share their impressions and comments on these trainings, most of which were positive. Here are some examples, all anonymous: "It was very well organized. Thank you very much for the courses because I am already passing on what I learned in the teachings for my students on Google Classroom and there are positive results." "Just to say that I am looking forward to another course next year.

Continue with the same courses, French language and pedagogy. Thank you very much." "Well designed courses. Very good training, to be recommended without moderation. Thank you again for this gift," or "The information received was very useful and very well presented." (Anonymous, personal communication, May 17, 2020)

Areas for Improvement

As we feared, however, the majority of comments that suggested improvements were related to the workload of these trainings in the time available. Comments from participants on this issue included:

> "To start with, it was a little too much, but throughout the training, it improved a lot" and "I suggest that next year's training be on a vacation where we have enough time to study it and in a shorter period of time." (Anonymous, personal communication, May 17, 2020)

The organization of the conversation classes also received some remarks:

> The conversation classes could have been offered after the two trainings or maybe during the summer, ... it takes more time for the conversation classes if the number of participants is more than 3. (Anonymous, personal communication, May 17, 2020)

Finally, several suggestions for a possible second training focused on the practical exercises of the "pedagogy" course, and in particular the construction of a sequence. Here are some of them:

> Practicing this aspect of teaching: Optimizing resources or building pedagogical, methodological and raw sequences to make them more effective. I'll need to get better at this. So if I'm not the only one asking, it would be nice to have more practice on this. Thank you. (Anonymous, personal communication, May 17, 2020)

7 Issues and Challenges of Continuing Education for Teachers... 145

We can get more examples of courses that are tailored to the length of courses in this area, or maybe we can create some team-based lesson plans. (Anonymous, personal communication, May 17, 2020)

In grading the instructional sequences submitted by participants, we did find that the proposed modules were not sufficiently developed to allow for proper mastery, and that more time should have been spent on them, with more hands-on activities. Even after completing the modules in question, the teaching materials used by the participants were not always authentic and/or adapted; some instructions and exercises were still written in their mother tongue, and some tasks had no connection with real life. By confronting this exercise and following our remarks, the teachers became aware of their difficulties. In fact, we received several comments expressing their doubts about this, such as the following:

I also think I know where to start and finish but it's the middle that I have trouble with. I don't know if you'd be interested in looking at what I did even if it's not complete to see if I even have an idea of what to do. (Anonymous, email, May 12, 2020)

I want to say thank you for this module. For the first time ever I have prepared a class in French from start to finish. I hope I did what was asked. (Anonymous, email, June 30, 2020)

It is therefore an interesting theme for future training and will allow teachers to build more motivating and effective courses for students.

A similar problem occurred with the language training. We noticed that the participants were not able to correct their recurrent mistakes, despite our explanations, the proposed activities, the complementary resources, and our corrections. A good example is the module on past tenses. Here is an excerpt from the written work of one of the participants:

Pendant l'été j'ai marché dans les parcs après les cours ou le travail, et je suis allée a Dairy Queen à huit heures du soir parce qu'il y a eu toujours le soleil. Pendant l'automne j'ai fait des excursions pour faire la cueillette de pommes et

146   S. Lipoff

> *de framboises. Pendant l'hiver j'ai fait du ski une fois.* (Anonymous, email, March 19, 2020)

It is noticeable that some confusion between the *imparfait* and the *passé composé* persists. The author uses the *passé composé* in "*j'ai marché*," "*je suis allée*," or "*il y a eu*," whereas they should use the *imparfait* since they are speaking about recurring actions or habits, and a description. However, the last two sentences are correct. This type of confusion is not surprising since the more complex the rules, the more difficult it is to correct them (Guénette & Jean, 2012). One might therefore wonder about the usefulness of this training, which seems to be very short to overcome errors that have sometimes been ingrained for years. However, we have received several pieces of feedback from teachers for whom the training was beneficial and gave rise to a desire to go further. Here is an example:

> Thank you for your comments last week. It's true that I was starting to feel confused about the tenses. I'll have to review and internalize a bit more. I have to admit that the practice helps me a lot to understand better why and how to use time in French. Through the training you get into more detail and it makes it much easier to understand. (Anonymous, email, May 12, 2020).

Thus, it can be said that this training is useful, even if the progress is not immediately visible.

Overall, participants recognized the value of these trainings, which had never been offered in the region, as this teacher testified:

> The course gave me the opportunity to refresh this level of French in a way that there is no such opportunity in an English-speaking country. It's been more than ten years since I had the opportunity to study French in college, so I really appreciated it. (Anonymous, personal communication, May 17, 2020)

Or, as Leonard Robinson, Modern Languages curriculum officer from St. Lucia, stated:

7 Issues and Challenges of Continuing Education for Teachers...

I must admit that both trainings were very timely. The pedagogy training allowed teachers to discover their weaknesses. ... I believe that teachers who have taken the pedagogy training are now well equipped to make French learning more authentic and lively. As for the French language training, whose objective was to bring the participants to a level equivalent to DELF B1/B2, it was very well structured and addressed the aspects of the language that were problematic for them. The addition of conversation, in my opinion, was a strong point of the training because it allowed the participants to practice what they learned in the different modules. From the feedback, the training was very well received. Although some of them did not manage to complete the training due to time constraints, they learned a lot. (Robinson, personal communication, October 28, 2020)

Ideas for the Future

One might wonder about the sustainability of these one-time, fully subsidized actions. Were the pedagogical innovations implemented by the IFLE project sufficient to make a lasting impression on the region's teaching staff? Given the enthusiasm generated by this training and the excellent feedback from teachers and representatives of the Ministries of Education, it is obvious that they will bear fruit. Through them, we have succeeded in creating a community of teachers who are better trained, motivated, and ready to transmit their passion to their students in a more effective way. In a practical way, we have been able to identify the strong points of these actions, such as the distance learning which allows us to reach teachers from different countries, the interactivity of the contents, the possibility of exchanging with the other participants, or the complementarity of the two courses. We have also become aware of their weaknesses, such as the pedagogical techniques that require further study, the need for synchronous exchange moments in the pedagogical training, the distribution of the workload in the modules, or the number of participants in the conversation classes. The constant contact with the teachers and all the exchanges we have had with them during this period of educational transition have also allowed us to better understand their needs

148 S. Lipoff

and expectations in terms of continuing education. We now have all the cards in hand to develop other types of actions, reach more teachers, and continue to innovate.

Appendix: Satisfaction Survey Sent to the Participants

Are you globally satisfied with the training (French language and/or pedagogy) offered by IFLE?
On a scale of 0 (not at all satisfied) to 4 (fully satisfied), how would you rate the trainings? Langue française
- language
- pedagogy

Were the contents of the French Language training useful to you?
Were the contents of the **Pedagogy** course useful to you?
Were the conversation classes useful to you?
How would you evaluate the overall content of the courses (quizzes, geniuses, images, exercises, etc.)?
Do you have any comments about the content of the two courses?
Regarding the training, was it:
- too long
- not too long nor too short (taking into account the extensions given by the team)
- too short

Did the COVID-19 crisis prevent you from taking the training as you would have liked?
If a new training was offered next year, would you like to take it?
Do you have any suggestions/comments/feedback to help us improve and offer another training next year?

References

Alexander, L-A. (2014). État des lieux de l'enseignement du créole à Sainte-Lucie. *Contextes et Didactiques* [Online]. https://doi.org/10.4000/ced.332

Aslim-Yetis, V. (2010). Le document authentique: un exemple d'exploitation en classe de FLE. *Synergies Canada*, (2). https://doi.org/10.21083/synergies.v0i2.1173

CARICOM. (2020). *Vision, mission and core values.* https://caricom.org/vision-mission-and-core-values/

7 Issues and Challenges of Continuing Education for Teachers... 149

Chauvet, A. (2008). *Référentiel de l'Alliance française pour le Cadre européen commun.* CLE International.

Council of Europe. (2001). *Common European framework of reference for languages: Learning, teaching, assessment.* Press Syndicate of the University of Cambridge. https://www.coe.int/en/web/common-european-framework-reference-languages

Cuq, J. P., & Gruca, I. (2002). *Cours de didactique du français langue étrangère et seconde.* PUG.

DeMonte, J. (2013). *High-quality professional development for teachers: Supporting teacher training to improve student learning.* Center for American Progress.

Francard, M., Lambert, J., & Berdal-Masuy, F. (1993). *L'insécurité linguistique en Communauté française de Belgique.* Service de la langue française de la Communauté française Wallonie-Bruxelles.

Guénette, D., & Jean, G. (2012). Les erreurs linguistiques des apprenants en langue seconde: Quoi corriger, et comment le faire? *Correspondance, 18*(1). https://correspo.ccdmd.qc.ca/index.php/document/cinq-pistes-pour-favoriser-le-developpement-des-competences-a-lecrit/les-erreurs-linguistiques-des-apprenants-en-langue-seconde-quoi-corriger-et-comment-le-faire/

Haugen, E. (1972). Schizoglossia and the linguistic norm. In E. Firchow (Ed.), *Studies by Einar Haugen: Presented on the occasion of his 65th birthday, April 19, 1971* (pp. 441–445). De Gruyter Mouton. https://doi.org/10.1515/9783110879124.441

Lave, J., & Wenger, E. (1991). *Situated learning: Legitimate peripheral participation.* Cambridge University Press. https://doi.org/10.1017/CBO9780511815355

Pappas, C. (2015, April 18). *eLearning interactivity: The ultimate guide for elearning professionals.* eLearning Industry. https://elearningindustry.com/elearning-interactivity-the-ultimate-guide-for-elearning-professionals

Rincón Restrepo, C. (2020). Insécurité linguistique chez les enseignants non natifs de FLE: Le cas des Colombiens. *Circula,* (12), 177–196. https://doi.org/10.17118/11143/18448

Timperley, H. (2011). Le développement professionnel des enseignants et ses effets positifs sur les apprentissages des élèves. *Revue Française de Pédagogie, 174,* 31–40. https://doi.org/10.4000/rfp.2910

UNESCO. (2019). *Teacher policy development guide.* Paris. https://unesdoc.unesco.org/ark:/48223/pf0000370966

Woo, Y., & Reeves, T. C. (2008). Interaction in asynchronous web-based learning environments. *Journal of Asynchronous Learning Networks, 12*(3), 179–194.

8

Learning Spanish Beyond the Classroom in a Corporate Setting

Diego Mideros and Paola Palma

Introduction and Description of the Area of Innovation

The area of innovation explored in this chapter is learning beyond the classroom (LBC) in a corporate setting. LBC is a field of research linked to autonomous learning, independent learning, self-instructed learning, and self-access learning (Benson, 2017; Benson & Reinders, 2011; Murray

---

D. Mideros (✉)
Centre for Language Learning, The University of the West Indies,
St. Augustine, Trinidad and Tobago
e-mail: Diego.Mideros@sta.uwi.edu

P. Palma
Centre for Language Learning, The University of the West Indies,
St. Augustine, Trinidad and Tobago

Department of Modern Languages and Linguistics, The University of the
West Indies, St. Augustine, Trinidad and Tobago
e-mail: Paola.Palma@sta.uwi.edu

© The Author(s), under exclusive license to Springer Nature Switzerland AG 2023
D. Mideros et al. (eds.), *Innovation in Language Learning and Teaching*, New Language
Learning and Teaching Environments, https://doi.org/10.1007/978-3-031-34182-3_8

& Lamb, 2017; Nunan & Richards, 2015; Reinders, 2014, 2020; Reinders & Benson, 2017). LBC refers to any kind of language learning that takes place outside the classroom. In this chapter, we illustrate how we attempted to incorporate LBC in a blended course designed for a company in the aviation industry in Trinidad and Tobago. We also evaluate the affordances and constraints we encountered during the process. We shall begin by situating our innovation within the LBC literature.

More than a decade ago, Benson (2011a) proposed an LBC model that encompasses four dimensions: (i) location, (ii) formality, (iii) pedagogy, and (iv) locus of control. Each dimension is conceptualised on a continuum of seemingly opposites. The location dimension looks at whether learning takes place in the classroom or outside of it, and it is also concerned with the social and pedagogical factors inherent in a physical or a virtual space. The formality dimension considers whether learning is formal or informal. The pedagogy dimension is concerned with whether there is instruction or no instruction. The locus of control dimension looks at the decision-making process and whether decisions are made for the learner by others or by the learner. This framework has evolved throughout the years, and recently Reinders (2020, p. 68) argued that Benson's framework can be better understood in practical terms seeking to answer questions related to each dimension:

Location: In what physical and/or virtual space(s) does the learning take place?
Formality: To what extent is the learning linked to qualifications?
Pedagogy: To what extent is instruction involved?
Control: How much choice do the learners exert?

As a research construct, LBC is complex because it can take different forms. The studies featured in the literature provide a wide spectrum of LBC possibilities, as researchers have explored an array of LBC-related topics and activities. LBC has been used to get learners involved and to encourage them to further practise extensive reading (Day & Robb, 2015), extensive listening (Gilliland, 2015), vocabulary (Walters, 2015), and pronunciation (Long & Huang, 2015) and to reflect about learning through journaling (Chiesa & Bailey, 2015). Computer-mediated learning and the rapid changes that digital technologies and tools have made

8 Learning Spanish Beyond the Classroom in a Corporate Setting

available to enhance teaching and learning have been widely used to promote LBC (Reinders & White, 2017). Examples of the use of technology for LBC include the use of online resources to learn vocabulary (Coxhead & Bytheway, 2015), digital games (Reinhardt, 2019), social media, social networks and exchange websites (Kozar, 2015; Righini, 2015), and tandem learning (González & Nagao, 2018), among others.

Another area in LBC studies has been out-of-class social interaction with native speakers, friends, relatives, tutors, and so on (Sundqvist & Sylvén, 2016). Several dimensions of social interaction have been explored in LBC studies such as culture (Arnold & Fonseca-Mora, 2015), study abroad (Kinginger, 2019), communities of practice (Thomson & Mori, 2015), home tutoring (Barkhuizen, 2015), learner-learner interactions (Zimmerman, 2011), and social learning spaces (Murray & Fujishima, 2016). Television and popular culture are considered good LBC tools for learners to access authentic language (Hanf, 2015), learn vocabulary (Lin & Siyanova-Chanturia, 2015), or simply engage in extensive viewing (Webb, 2015). The use of popular culture has also been considered to study LBC among teenagers (Bailly, 2011).

A promising area of research and practice seeks to combine classroom learning with out-of-class learning. Projects that students complete outside the classroom represent a worthwhile effort to encourage learners to engage with the language (Grode & Stacy, 2015; Miller & Hafner, 2015; Toffoli, 2020). Interestingly, these studies sought to promote autonomy through the completion of LBC projects. Some of those projects encouraged learners to find authentic materials to improve accuracy, or to learn how to learn independently using technology.

Promoting LBC from the classroom is an exciting area of research for learner autonomy enthusiasts. However, this was not always the case. Years ago, when discussing "out-of-class learning" Benson (2011b) argued that the term was reserved "for activities that have no direct relationship to schooling... out-of-class learning is typically initiated by the learner, makes use of authentic resources and involves pleasure and interest, as well as language learning" (p. 139). Undoubtedly, the classroom and teachers play a role in promoting autonomy *and* LBC. Cotterall's (2017) pedagogical model stresses five affordances to foster learner autonomy from the classroom that include engagement, exploration, personalisation, reflection, and support. Such affordances also seem appropriate for learners to engage in LBC activities in settings of formal instruction.

The variety of LBC studies found in the literature suggests that this area is by no means a homogenous one, and serves as evidence of the four dimensions of Benson's (2011a) model. Based on previous studies employing or advocating LBC, Reinders and Benson (2017) added more layers to Benson's LBC model. Those layers include trajectory, variety of activities, mediation, sociality, modality, and a linguistic dimension. They also added three specific characteristics of the learning process that might be helpful in analysing LBC activities: (i) intentional or incidental learning, (ii) explicit or implicit learning, and (iii) inductive and deductive learning. In their effort to make LBC a well-established field of inquiry, they propose an agenda to consider when conducting LBC studies. Their agenda encourages research in different settings where LBC might take place, be it virtually, in the classroom, or in naturalistic settings such as study abroad. They also encourage researching how learners learn beyond the classroom to explore and document their experiences, the strategies they use, and the role of technology to enhance learning. Last, but not least, is researching the role that teachers play in supporting LBC by exploring teachers' beliefs about LBC, how teachers promote LBC from the classroom, and how they prepare learners for LBC.

More recently, Reinders (2020) proposes a framework where getting students involved lies in the middle of the intersection between class and beyond the classroom learning. His framework encompasses four stages: encouraging, preparing, supporting, and offering learning opportunities. Teachers should first *encourage* learners through raising awareness and motivating them to engage in LBC. Second, teachers should *prepare* students for LBC through controlled practice. Third, teachers should *support* LBC by providing assistance in the form of feedback or guided activities. And fourth, teachers should *offer learning opportunities* for LBC where minimal teacher assistance is required.

The process of innovation we describe in this chapter is informed by the dimensions presented by Benson's (2011a) and Reinders' (2020) framework for LBC. In relation to the LBC model, our study stands as follows:

Location: mixture of in-class and virtual learning
Formality: formal as required by the company

Pedagogy: mixture of other-instructed and self-instructed pedagogy
Control: mixture of other and self-regulated locus of control.

The evaluation of our implementation will take into consideration the affordances that teachers identified to promote LBC (Menezes, 2011; Murray, 2017). It will take into account Diego's teacher narrative, the main author of the chapter, as the academic leader and designer of the implementation; and Paola's teacher narrative, the co-author of this chapter, as one of the tutors who delivered the course. In-depth interviews with two more tutors complement the evaluation from the teachers' perspective. Of prime importance is to look at how the teachers supported and promoted LBC from the classroom. We will also report on how some learners (51) perceived the implementation.

Context and Impetus

The Centre for Language Learning (CLL) at The University of the West Indies, St Augustine Campus, in Trinidad and Tobago offers non-specialist language courses in 12 different languages to the university community and the general public. It also offers language training in Spanish, French, and English as a second language to organisations based in Trinidad. Spanish courses are the most popular at the centre, and the demand for Spanish is the highest nationwide. When public and private companies approach us seeking language training, they mainly look for courses with a business focus. Therefore, we are always willing to customise the content of our courses to suit the needs of any company. We usually use or adapt the content of our courses from Business Spanish textbooks, which follow the Common European Framework of Reference for Languages (CEFR) (Council of Europe, 2001). Corporate courses are generally for beginner learners; therefore, they start at level A1. For these courses, tutors often teach in situ, as this is a more convenient arrangement for companies.

Moodle is the learning management system (LMS) employed by the university for registered students in degree programmes. Since the CLL caters to both the university community and the general public, and our courses do not fall under any particular degree programme, not all CLL students have access to Moodle. The reason for this lack of access is that members of the public do not have the status of registered university students. To compensate for this lack of an LMS, we encourage tutors at the centre to use free alternatives such as Edmodo or Google Classroom to engage students in the use of technology and to upload additional materials.

The impetus for this innovation came from an external pressure. A regional airline approached the CLL seeking a proposal for a 45-hour online conversational Spanish course for 293 flight attendants. The airline had recently begun operations to a Spanish-speaking island in the Caribbean. Therefore, they sought training in the language for the in-flight crew to be able to function in Spanish during the flight. Diego, the main author of this chapter and the academic coordinator of the Spanish courses at the CLL, met with the CLL's director and a group of administrators at the centre to evaluate the feasibility of the project. We had a number of concerns because we had not had a request of such magnitude in the past, and we had no experience designing and delivering fully online courses. The specificity of the course required some research before the design stage. The next concern was the absence of an LMS platform to deliver the course. The major concern was the readiness of the flight attendants to successfully pursue a fully online language course and to meet the learning outcomes independently. Last, but not least, Diego is the only full-time academic in Spanish at the centre; all tutors work on a part-time basis, and this meant designing the course by himself and also finding suitable tutors to deliver the course.

We understood the airline's inclination to have a fully online course given the seemingly flexibility it offers, especially for flight attendants with unfixed schedules. However, based on the experience of teaching courses with online components and even being enrolled in online courses, we knew that learning online requires serious commitment and learner training, or else work can easily pile up. Also, our lack of practical experience designing and delivering fully online courses led us to reject the idea of designing a fully online course. We proposed instead a blended course with a focus on speaking and listening only. The 45-hour course was divided into 30 hours of face-to-face instruction with a tutor, and 15

8 Learning Spanish Beyond the Classroom in a Corporate Setting 157

hours of independent study where students would engage with an online platform with the contents of the course for self-paced learning. When all details were finalised, a Memorandum of Understanding was signed between the airline and the university for the creation and delivery of the course with a slight modification: the course would no longer be for flight attendants only, but for staff of different offices and divisions. This modification changed the initial plan and the emphasis on in-flight crew.

The CLL's director assigned Diego as the academic leader of the project and brought in an instructional designer with experience in designing online courses to team with Diego in the creation of the online segment of the course. Another tutor was hired to assist Diego in the lesson planning process. The project also had administrative support to liaise with the university to gain access to the university's Moodle platform. It was decided that the course would be delivered in three cohorts of 100 learners each. Groups of 20 learners would meet face to face with a tutor on a weekly basis for 2.5 hours for a period of 12 weeks. The face-to-face sessions would be complemented by weekly independent work on the platform where students would find explanations and exercises directly related to the weekly content of the lessons. Suitable and available tutors were selected to deliver the courses. Preference was given to selecting native-speaker teachers over non-native speakers.

In sum, our innovation was a response to an external request that encouraged us to move out of our comfort zone when teaching language courses to organisations outside of the university. Used to teaching solely face to face, the challenge was to create and incorporate an online component of a course for a client. However, apart from the online component, we also had to adapt the contents of our traditional Business Spanish courses to suit the needs of an airline. Our innovation fits the definition provided by O'Sullivan and Dooley (2009) as "the process of making changes to something established by introducing something new" (p. 3). As a process, Brewer and Tierney (2012) describe three things necessary for an innovation plan for education: "an idea, its implementation, and the outcome that results from the execution of the idea and produces a change" (p. 5). In our case, more than an original idea, our innovation resulted from the need to respond to a particular teaching request that we had not considered before and which forced us to come up with a solution to address such request.

Design and Implementation

In this section, we shall present a brief description of the process of creating the course with a focus on the academic side of the implementation. Although many administrative challenges occurred, they are beyond the scope of this chapter. We will also introduce the first set of data for the study, which is a "teacher narrative" (Barkhuizen et al., 2014, p. 40) produced by Diego as the academic leader of the project. Diego's narrative captures what happened during the planning phase of the course and its implementation and certain difficulties that took place while preparing the course and the online segment of it.

Course Outline

Together with the part-time tutor hired to assist with the creation of the modules, we drafted a course outline with ten lessons to be delivered in 12 weeks with oral and listening assessments halfway through the course and at the end of it. We adapted the course based on the Business Spanish textbook used for all other corporate clients. We decided to design the course using a flipped classroom approach (Adnan, 2017; Huang, 2020), where learners would have access to the materials and explanations on the platform prior to the face-to-face sessions. Learners were expected to familiarise themselves with the contents first and then attend class. This was clearly stated in the course outline students received before the beginning of the course. The decision to use the flipped classroom approach was twofold. On the one hand, we sought to meet the expectations of the airline, as they envisioned an online component for their staff to learn independently. On the other hand, we designed the course to explore how learners would respond to the flipped approach in a corporate teaching context.

8 Learning Spanish Beyond the Classroom in a Corporate Setting

Online Platform

When drafting the course outline, we kept in mind the recommendations received from the instructional designer. Each lesson had to present a "scenario" for the instructional designer to create a Sharable Content Object Reference Model (SCORM), which had a fixed structure and an instructional narrative. The instructional designer insisted on having "scenarios" with protagonists and a conflict to resolve. It was important to produce original materials to avoid facing copyright issues. Each lesson had the following structure:

(i)   title (usually a scenario),
(ii)   objectives,
(iii)   scenario 1 (input),
(iv)   knowledge check 1 (an explanation of a particular item or items presented in scenario 1)
(v)   scenario 2 (input)
(vi)   knowledge check 2
(vii)   checkpoint (assessment with 3 to 5 multiple choice or matching items)

The following are the lessons and in brackets the objectives for each of them:

Lesson 1:   At the Airport (To introduce oneself)
Lesson 2:   We are Caribbean (To get to know others)
Lesson 3:   Personal information (To ask for and provide personal information 1)
Lesson 4:   At immigration (To ask for and provide personal information 2)
Lesson 5:   Welcome to the airline (To give information about a company)
Lesson 6:   At a conference (To introduce someone. To ask for and provide work-related information about someone. To describe someone in a business setting)

160   D. Mideros and P. Palma

Lesson 7:   Arrivals and departures (To express obligation and needs. To talk about location. To talk about the time. To inquire about products and services)
Lesson 8:   Just do it! (To give *usted* commands)
Lesson 9:   Let's eat! (To express likes, dislikes)
Lesson 10:   At a hotel (To express preference)

Adapting the content of the textbook to make it relevant to the target audience did not represent a major challenge. Since the knowledge that learners should acquire at an A1 level seems standard, we focused on modifying and incorporating vocabulary related to the airport, flying, and travelling. However, creating scenarios as required by the instructional designer proved difficult. The following is Diego's account on this:

> …*my director hired an instructional designer who sold us an online course that we found attractive at first sight. The programme seemed interactive and contained animations created by the instructional designer. The final product had interactive dialogues undoubtedly appealing to the eye.*
>
> *In a first meeting with the designer, she explained to us the kinds of contents we had to prepare. She asked us to prepare word documents with 2 or 3 scenarios to explain vocabulary and structures. We also had to prepare practice exercises and assessment exercises for what was presented in each scenario.*
>
> *Scenarios had to have characters, a main event, and a problem to resolve. This was difficult because it was easier for me to think in terms of situations rather than scenarios. In any case, my colleague and I attempted as much as we could to produce rich input with the vocabulary and structures that each lesson would cover. However, the comments we got from the instructional designer indicated that the input we prepared was too long. She literally said that she was expecting 3-line dialogues, which made me wonder: "how can I produce rich input in only 3 lines?" Furthermore, the more the course progresses, the more input is needed, which means richer input. That to me was a major difficulty.*
>
> *Another difficulty was the assessment exercises for the platform. My colleague and I designed various multiple choice, true/false, fill in the gap exercises, exercises like the ones we would use in class, and exercises that we often see on different websites. But again, for the instructional designer those exercises were too complicated. At the end, she reduced the exercises to a minimum, which from*

my point of view, seemed too simplistic, and required no major effort from learners.

Undoubtedly, Diego felt frustrated during the planning phase as he had to share control of the decisions that he would normally make by himself for his own teaching and curriculum design. To an extent, what presented itself as an affordance at the beginning of the project, that is, having an instructional designer to assist him with designing the platform, soon became a limitation for him. However, as he started to see the drafts of the SCORMs, he began to understand the complexities of transferring activities that could usually be conducted in the classroom to an LMS. Later in his narrative, he reflected:

> *...perhaps I was trying too hard to transfer to the platform activities that I would normally have in the classroom and perhaps not all the activities and rich input were appropriate for an online environment. Even if I still believe that the activities were too simplistic in most cases, it might also be true that very complex activities may be difficult for learners who might feel intimidated to see big loads of information. But I also believe there should be some middle ground between too complex and too simple.*
>
> *I also managed to learn that for the instructional designer transforming all the information we sent her into the scenarios in the platform was a lot of work, especially the animations. Perhaps something important when designing activities for online environments is to keep things simple and manageable to avoid intimidating the learners.*

Selection of Tutors and Course Delivery

Once the course outline and the platform were ready, the next step was to find tutors who were qualified and available to teach this course. Up to the moment when this chapter was being prepared, we had delivered two of the three cohorts that had been initially agreed. The first cohort was delivered by the part-time tutor who assisted Diego in the planning phase and Paola, the second author of this chapter. The part-time tutor did not need much prior guidance to teach the course because she had taken part in its planning. Paola received the documentation for the course and access to the platform. Paola works full-time teaching university students, and she has vast experience using Moodle and teaching blended courses. The second cohort was taught by two different tutors. In order to protect their identities, we will refer to them as tutor A and tutor B. Both tutors work at the CLL on a part-time basis, and both are native speakers of Spanish.

All tutors received the course documentation, access to the platform and the Business Spanish textbook. Students also received the textbook. Diego explained to the tutors the idea behind the flipped classroom and how students were expected to study the content of the platform and to complete the activities prior to the face-to-face sessions.

While the course had an online component to it, no explicit online teaching was required from the tutors. The platform contained animations with dialogues, explanations, and self-corrected exercises so that learners could navigate intuitively. Teachers did not even have to monitor learners' activity reports because this was an administrative task conducted by the centre's contract officer. Therefore, teachers' sole responsibility was to encourage students to actively use the platform so that they could engage and participate in the classroom activities. At the same time, tutors had to familiarise themselves with the platform to understand that the content of the textbook had been adapted for the online content.

The textbook was a tool for the tutors to choose activities to engage students in the classroom and motivate them to practise what they had learned *before* the session. Diego attempted to design the course in a way that tutors would not need to source additional materials. The textbook had sufficient activities and listening exercises to practise speaking and listening, the two main skills of the course. The platform had explanations in English and exercises that tutors could also use in class to address learners' questions or difficulties.

An aspect worth mentioning is that the company insisted that we monitor learners' participation and completion of the course. Because of the big financial investment that the company made to bring the course free of charge to its staff, the company required accountability from those enrolled. We therefore had to monitor learners' attendance and the

8 Learning Spanish Beyond the Classroom in a Corporate Setting

completion of online activities, but as mentioned above, the latter task was carried out by the centre's contract officer and not by the teachers.

Evaluation

In this section we evaluate the implementation, paying particular attention to the role that the tutors played in promoting LBC. Diego interviewed each tutor separately to explore the ways in which they promoted the use of the platform. We will present excerpts of the interviews in Spanish. In the interest of time and space, we will discuss the excerpts attempting to provide the reader with the main idea and interpretation of the excerpt instead of providing a direct translation.

In the following excerpts, tutors explain how they and their learners approached the use of the online platform:

> *Los que ya tenían conocimiento básico de español, ellos eran los que iban a la plataforma. Eso era como refrescarles la memoria y para ellos hacer los ejercicios era muy rápido, pero para la mayoría no… ellos aprovecharon más el curso, pero [ellos] eran una minoría… 5 o 6. (Tutor 1)*

Above, Tutor 1 explains that only those learners with some knowledge of Spanish made use of the platform. For those learners, the explanations served as a refresher, and they were able to complete the activities quickly. However, this was a minority, five or six of them. When Diego asked Tutor 1 about the activities to promote the use of the platform, the following was the response:

> *Yo entraba en la plataforma y miraba en general lo que había allí. Yo no me ponía a hacer todos los ejercicios, sino que miraba lo que tenía que enseñar. Miraba los objetivos generales, lo principal y ya. Te mentiría si te dijera que yo entré y miré todos los ejercicios… tampoco manejo muy bien la plataforma.*
>
> *WhatsApp era mi herramienta principal, por ahí yo les mandaba ejercicios adicionales para que trabajaran, preguntas para que practicaran, tomaba fotos de actividades y les decía que eso era lo que tenían que hacer. (Tutor 1)*

Tutor 1 admitted a scarce use of the platform that was limited to having a quick look at the objectives and the main topic for the session. However, this tutor did not spend much time looking at the exercises and completing them. In fact, this tutor admits to not knowing well how to navigate the platform. Instead, Tutor 1 made avid use of WhatsApp to send learners additional materials and pictures of activities. In light of what the literature says about affordances (Menezes, 2011; Murray, 2017), this tutor's response suggests that she may not have perceived the platform as an affordance to teach because her efforts to incorporate the platform in the classroom seemed minimal. Tutors do have the responsibility to engage (Cotterall, 2017), encourage, and prepare (Reinders, 2020) students for LBC.

We now turn to Tutor 2 and how learners in his group approached the use of the platform:

> *No sé si a los estudiantes les gustaba el componente online porque ellos lo hacían en la casa y cuando venían a clase hablábamos del contenido de las actividades... Ellos sabían que tenían que cumplir con sus actividades online para no tener problemas con Recursos Humanos.* (Tutor 2)

Tutor 2 mentions an external circumstance that seemed to have influenced that group of learners to use the platform: learners were aware that they had to complete all activities because Human Resources monitored their records. According to Tutor 2, this group used the platform and attended the sessions having completed the online activities. This is what Tutor 2 said about promoting the use of the platform among his students:

> *Yo usaba la plataforma en clase, especialmente cuando* [los estudiantes] *llegaban con dudas. Y para evitar tener que explicar lo mismo varias veces, lo hacía para toda la clase.... No soy un fan de las cosas online, en general prefiero las clases presenciales. La utilicé* [la plataforma] *porque me tocó utilizarla. Con mis conocimientos, el libro y las presentaciones fue suficiente para poder dar una clase exitosa.* (Tutor 2)

8 Learning Spanish Beyond the Classroom in a Corporate Setting 165

Tutor 2 used the platform in class whenever students had questions. He addressed concerns about content from the platform to the entire class to avoid having to repeat the same explanation several times. Interestingly, Tutor 2 admitted not being a fan of technology and recognised using the platform because it was required; other than that Tutor's 2 knowledge, the textbook and slides would have been good enough to deliver a successful class. Tutor's 2 comments remind us of the importance of teachers' beliefs about LBC (Reinders & Benson, 2017), and something that emerges in this study is the importance of teachers' perceptions of LBC tools and activities. Tutor 2 is not keen on technology and may have not fully promoted the use of the platform outside of class. However, external circumstances—human resources monitoring students' participation records—played in Tutor's 2 favour for learners to use the platform.

Paola's interview serves as evidence of the kind of teaching Diego had envisioned when he designed the course:

Al principio fue difícil que [los estudiantes] *se acostrumbraran a hacer las actividades de la plataforma antes de la clase, solamente pocos las hacían... Algunos llegaban a clase sin hacer ninguna actividad, esperaban que se les explicara en la clase para luego hacer las actividades como práctica o refuerzo... Desde la primera clase yo les insistía que era importante hacer las actividades antes de la clase para ahorrar tiempo y que como ellos podían hacer las actividades tantas veces como quisieran, iba a ser más beneficioso para ellos. Como en la cuarta semana ya todos hacían las actividades en línea antes de la clase.*

Paola describes a process that went from having a hard time getting students to complete the activities before class, to having students complete the activities before class by week four. At the beginning, some students attended class without having completed the activities and expecting an explanation to then go home and practise. However, from day one, Paola stressed the importance of completing the activities prior to the session to save class time.

Paola's Teacher Narrative

Intrigued by what sounded like a success story, Diego invited Paola to co-author the chapter and to produce a "teacher narrative" (Barkhuizen et al., 2014, p. 40) in English where she could explain her approach to promoting LBC:

> As I had previous experience using Moodle, I expected common problems for the first class: student's not having access to the platform... not being familiar with the use of it... or technical difficulties that are common in these learning environments. I also knew that my students were adult learners, and I expected many of them not to be tech savvy. So I didn't expect them to do the online activities before the first F2F session.
>
> I used the opportunity of having access to the internet and a laptop with a projector to show the entire class how to access Moodle, and how to access and complete the weekly activities.
>
> Preparing for each class was not time consuming because most of the work was already done [all explanations were readily available on the platform], but it did require organized planning. I began by watching the videos and doing the activities on the platform myself, this way I could see the input that the students were supposed to look at before the F2F session. That way I could predict possible difficulties that they may have encountered.
>
> In the PowerPoint presentations I prepared for my classes, I included screenshots from the online videos of the scenarios to recreate the context, revise vocabulary, or present (again) a grammatical explanation. This way, if the students completed the activities before class, I would activate previous knowledge. If they didn't, then whenever they attempted the online activities, they would be activating that previous knowledge and the students would be able to remember more easily.

Paola's narrative illustrates the role she played in promoting the use of the platform. Her previous experience working with Moodle and delivering blended courses enabled her to foresee difficulties. If we go back to affordances (Menezes, 2011; Murray, 2017), Paola's narrative serves as evidence that "affordances depend on learners' perceptions. Learners have to be able to see the potential in the environment. Affordances also rely on the discourses surrounding an environment" (Murray, 2017, p. 122).

8 Learning Spanish Beyond the Classroom in a Corporate Setting 167

Paola, through her constant reinforcement of the importance of the platform and its active use in the classroom, helped her students to see its potential. This was not the case with Tutors 1 and 2, who did not seem to have perceived the platform as an affordance for their own teaching and expressed it explicitly in the interviews. Thus, they were also unable to show their learners the platform's potential.

Learners' Engagement and Responses to the Course

Although this chapter has focused mostly on the role teachers play in promoting LBC, we would also like to feature some of the perceptions we gathered from some of the learners who took the course. In this section, we will briefly discuss two question items from the course evaluation survey. A total of 51 learners voluntarily and anonymously completed the survey, which can be accessed on (https://forms.gle/fZubfAiPLgZbX-E5PA). This instrument is merely descriptive, and it sought to compare both modes of delivery. We would have liked to record more responses from learners from both cohorts, but only 51 responded to our call.

For the first question (see Fig. 8.1) we wish to discuss here, we asked learners which of the following did they find more helpful: (a) the online explanations, (b) the face-to-face session, or (c) both? The majority of respondents (N = 30) perceived (c), both face-to-face sessions and online explanations, helpful, followed by (N = 14), who perceived (b), the face-to-face sessions alone, as helpful. The least-favoured option was (a), the online explanations, with only (N = 7) respondents choosing this option. This suggests that a combination of both online explanations and face-to-face sessions can be more beneficial than an online delivery alone. It is worth noting that the perception of the face-to-face mode of delivery is still high compared to online delivery.

The second and last question (see Fig. 8.2) was, "Which did you enjoy more?"; this item compared again (a) the online explanations, (b) the face-to-face session, and (c) both. Technically, for this item there was a tie between (c), both the online platform and the face-to-face session (N = 22), and (b), the face-to-face sessions alone (N = 21), which suggests that students still feel more comfortable learning in the classroom

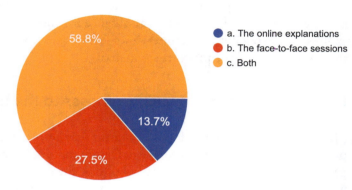

Fig. 8.1 Which did you find more helpful?

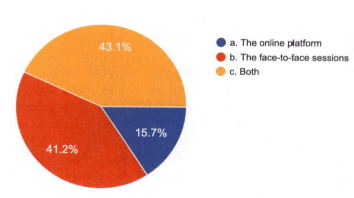

Fig. 8.2 Which did you enjoy more?

with a teacher. Option (c), the online platform, got the lowest number of responses ($N = 8$), which leads us to wonder about the learners' readiness for a fully independent course as initially suggested by the airline.

Concluding Remarks and Implications

Our implementation explored how LBC was promoted as part of a blended Spanish course designed for an airline in Trinidad and Tobago. Through a qualitative analysis of three interviews with the tutors who delivered the course, and the narratives of one of the tutors and the academic leader of the project, we found that the role of the teacher in promoting LBC from the classroom is pivotal. Paola identified affordances for teaching and learning in the online platform. Using the platform as a teaching resource in her face-to-face classes enabled her to link both modes of delivery, online and face to face. By actively using the platform in class, she was able to show her students how to navigate the platform and benefit from it. Murray reminds us that "affordances depend on learners' perceptions. Learners have to be able to see the potential in the environment. Affordances also rely on the discourses surrounding an environment" (2017, p. 122). But we should also add that teachers must see LBC resources as affordances in order to encourage students to use such resources. Teachers often help create the discourses that surround the environment, and through those discourses teachers can help students see affordances more easily instead of hoping that learners discover those affordances on their own.

While Paola saw those affordances and helped her students see them as well, the other two tutors did not see the same potential and were unable to help their learners see the benefits they could get from engaging with the platform. The main implication of this finding is a reminder that in formal settings teachers play a role in preparing learners for LBC (Reinders & Benson, 2017). Teachers have the responsibility to create conditions to help learners see the potential of different materials and resources that could enable them to exercise responsibility as learners.

The most importance lesson from this innovative exercise is the need to sensitise teachers to their role in encouraging, preparing, supporting, and offering learning opportunities for LBC (Reinders, 2020). While great efforts were devoted to adapting the course and designing the activities for the platform, more time and effort should have been devoted to training teachers. We must admit that Paola was successful in promoting LBC as a result of her vast experience in teaching blended courses.

However, the same was not the case with the other two teachers, which leads us to believe that for future implementations like this, careful sensitisation and guidance are necessary to ensure that less experienced teachers are in a good position to promote LBC. After all, if teachers do not believe in online delivery or any other LBC tools, they will not be able to promote LBC among the learners. For an innovation to be truly innovative, the change that it brings about should be perceived as an affordance by those who make use of it, and by those who will eventually benefit from it.

References

Adnan, M. (2017). Perceptions of senior-year ELT students for flipped classroom: A materials development course. *Computer Assisted Language Learning, 30*(3–4), 204–222. https://doi.org/10.1080/09588221.2017.1301958

Arnold, J., & Fonseca-Mora, C. (2015). Language and cultural encounters: Opportunities for interaction with native speakers. In D. Nunan & J. C. Richards (Eds.), *Language learning beyond the classroom* (pp. 225–234). Routledge.

Bailly, S. (2011). Teenagers learning languages out of school: What, why and how do they learn? How can school help them? In P. Benson & H. Reinders (Eds.), *Beyond the language classroom* (pp. 119–131). Palgrave Macmillan. https://doi.org/10.1057/9780230306790_10

Barkhuizen, G. (2015). Learning English with a home tutor: Meeting the needs of migrant learners. In D. Nunan & J. C. Richards (Eds.), *Language learning beyond the classroom* (pp. 282–291). Routledge.

Barkhuizen, G., Benson, P., & Chik, A. (2014). *Narrative inquiry in language teaching and learning research*. Routledge.

Benson, P. (2011a). Language learning and teaching beyond the classroom: An introduction to the field. In P. Benson & H. Reinders (Eds.), *Beyond the Language Classroom* (pp. 7–16). Palgrave Macmillan. https://doi.org/10.1057/9780230306790_2

Benson, P. (2011b). *Teaching and researching autonomy* (2nd ed.). Longman Pearson.

8 Learning Spanish Beyond the Classroom in a Corporate Setting 171

Benson, P. (2017). Language learning beyond the classroom: Access all areas. *Studies in Self-Access Learning Journal, 8*(2), 135–146. https://doi.org/10.37237/080206

Benson, P., & Reinders, H. (Eds.). (2011). *Beyond the language classroom. The theory and practice of informal language learning and teaching.* Palgrave Macmillan.

Brewer, D., & Tierney, W. (2012). Barriers to innovation in US education. In B. Wildavsky, A. P. Kelly, & K. Carey (Eds.), *Reinventing higher education: The promise of innovation* (pp. 11–40). Harvard Education Press.

Chiesa, D. L., & Bailey, K. M. (2015). Dialogue journals: Learning for a lifetime. In D. Nunan & J. C. Richards (Eds.), *Language learning beyond the classroom* (pp. 53–62). Routledge.

Cotterall, S. (2017). The pedagogy of learner autonomy: Lessons from the classroom. *Studies in Self-Access Learning Journal, 8*(2), 102–115. https://doi.org/10.37237/080204

Council of Europe. (2001). *Common European framework of reference for languages: Learning, teaching, assessment.* Press Syndicate of the University of Cambridge. https://www.coe.int/en/web/common-european-framework-reference-languages

Coxhead, A., & Bytheway, J. (2015). Learning vocabulary using two massive online resources: You will not blink. In D. Nunan & J. C. Richards (Eds.), *Language learning beyond the classroom* (pp. 65–74). Routledge.

Day, R., & Robb, T. (2015). Extensive reading. In D. Nunan & J. C. Richards (Eds.), *Language learning beyond the classroom* (pp. 3–12). Routledge.

Gilliland, B. (2015). Listening logs for extensive listening practice. In D. Nunan & J. C. Richards (Eds.), *Language learning beyond the classroom* (pp. 13–22). Routledge.

González, S., & Nagao, K. (2018). Collaborative learning through Japanese-Spanish teletandem. *Studies in Self-Access Learning Journal, 9*(2), 196–216. https://doi.org/10.37237/090210

Grode, J., & Stacy, A. (2015). Authentic materials and project-based learning: In pursuit of accuracy. In D. Nunan & J. C. Richards (Eds.), *Language learning beyond the classroom* (pp. 171–179). Routledge.

Hanf, A. (2015). Resourcing authentic language in television series. In D. Nunan & J. C. Richards (Eds.), *Language learning beyond the classroom* (pp. 138–148). Routledge.

Huang, H. (2020). Learner autonomy and responsibility: Self-learning through a flipped online EFL course. In M. Freiermuth & N. Zarrinabadi (Eds.),

Technology and the psychology of second language learners and users. New language learning and teaching environments (pp. 203–223). Palgrave Macmillan. https://doi.org/10.1007/978-3-030-34212-8_8

Kinginger, C. (2019). Four questions for the next generation of study abroad researchers. In M. Howard (Ed.), *Study abroad, second language acquisition, and interculturality: Contemporary perspectives* (pp. 263–278). Multilingual Matters.

Kozar, O. (2015). Language exchange websites for independent learning. In D. Nunan & J. C. Richards (Eds.), *Language learning beyond the classroom* (pp. 105–114). Routledge.

Lin, P. M. S., & Siyanova-Chanturia, A. (2015). Internet television for L2 learning. In D. Nunan & J. C. Richards (Eds.), *Language learning beyond the classroom* (pp. 149–150). Routledge.

Long, N., & Huang, J. (2015). Out-of-class pronunciation learning: Are EFL learners ready in China? In D. Nunan & J. C. Richards (Eds.), *Language learning beyond the classroom* (pp. 43–52). Routledge.

Menezes, V. (2011). Affordances for language learning beyond the classroom. In P. Benson & H. Reinders (Eds.), *Beyond the Language Classroom* (pp. 59–71). Palgrave Macmillan. https://doi.org/10.1057/9780230306790_6

Miller, L., & Hafner, C. A. (2015). Taking control: A digital video project for English for Science students. In D. Nunan & J. C. Richards (Eds.), *Language learning beyond the classroom* (pp. 212–222). Routledge.

Murray, G. (2017). Autonomy in the time of complexity: Lessons from beyond the classroom. *Studies in Self-Access Learning Journal, 8*(2), 116–134. https://doi.org/10.37237/080205

Murray, G., & Fujishima, N. (2016). *Social spaces for language learning: Stories from the L-café.* Palgrave Pivot. https://doi.org/10.1007/978-1-137-53010-3_18

Murray, G., & Lamb, T. (Eds.). (2017). *Space, place and autonomy in language learning.* Routledge.

Nunan, D., & Richards, J. C. (2015). *Language learning beyond the classroom.* Routledge.

O'Sullivan, D., & Dooley, L. (2009). *Applying innovation. SAGE Publications.* https://doi.org/10.4135/9781452274898

Reinders, H. (2014). Personal learning environments for supporting out-of-class language learning. *ELT Forum, 52*(4), 14–19.

Reinders, H. (2020). A framework for learning beyond the classroom. In M. Jiménez Raya & F. Vieira (Eds.), *Autonomy in language education: Theory, research and practice* (pp. 63–73). Routledge.

Reinders, H., & Benson, P. (2017). Language learning beyond the classroom: A research agenda. *Language Teaching, 50*(4), 561–578. https://doi.org/10.1017/S0261444817000192

Reinders, H., & White, C. (2017). Re-imagining the margins: Exploring the transformative potential of technology and out-of-class learning. In C. Nicolaides & W. Magno (Eds.), *Innovations and challenges in applied linguistics and learner autonomy* (pp. 167–179). Pontes Editores.

Reinhardt, J. (2019). *Gameful second and foreign language teaching and learning: Theory, research, and practice*. Palgrave Macmillan.

Righini, M. (2015). The use of social media resources in advanced level classes. In D. Nunan & J. C. Richards (Eds.), *Language learning beyond the classroom* (pp. 85–94). Routledge.

Sundqvist, P., & Sylvén, L. K. (2016). *Extramural English in teaching and learning: From theory and research practice*. Palgrave Macmillan.

Thomson, C. K., & Mori, T. (2015). Japanese communities of practice: Creating opportunities for out-of-class learning. In D. Nunan & J. C. Richards (Eds.), *Language learning beyond the classroom* (pp. 272–281). Routledge.

Toffoli, D. (2020). *Informal learning and institution-wide language provision: University language learners in the 21st century*. Palgrave Macmillan.

Walters, J. (2015). Carrying vocabulary learning outside the classroom. In D. Nunan & J. C. Richards (Eds.), *Language learning beyond the classroom* (pp. 23–32). Routledge.

Webb, S. (2015). Extensive viewing: Language learning through watching television. In D. Nunan & J. C. Richards (Eds.), *Language learning beyond the classroom* (pp. 159–168). Routledge.

Zimmerman, E. (2011). Talk about language use: 'I know a little about your language'. In P. Benson & H. Reinders (Eds.), *Beyond the Language Classroom* (pp. 88–105). Palgrave Macmillan. https://doi.org/10.1057/9780230306790_8

9

"Guess I have no choice but to do the e-book": Non-specialist Learners' Perceptions in Spanish and Other Languages during the Pandemic

Beverly-Anne Carter, Avian Daly, and Mathilde Dallier

Introduction

In one higher education (HE) context, at The University of the West Indies (UWI), St Augustine Campus, in Trinidad and Tobago, March 13, 2020, marked the last day of full in-person teaching in the 2019/2020 academic year. When classes resumed one or more weeks later, all in-person teaching had been suspended and delivery in all disciplines was solely online. In content-based courses with considerable online materials in UWI's Learning Management System (LMS), classes resumed in a relatively short period, typically in the week it took to enhance the existing content with additional recorded lectures and podcasts. That quick pivot to ERT proved more challenging in programmes such as the one

---

B.-A. Carter (✉) • A. Daly • M. Dallier
Centre for Language Learning, Department of Modern Languages and Linguistics, The University of the West Indies,
St. Augustine, Trinidad and Tobago
e-mail: Beverly-Anne.Carter@sta.uwi.edu; Avian.Daly@sta.uwi.edu;
Mathilde.Dallier@sta.uwi.edu

© The Author(s), under exclusive license to Springer Nature Switzerland AG 2023   **175**
D. Mideros et al. (eds.), *Innovation in Language Learning and Teaching*, New Language Learning and Teaching Environments, https://doi.org/10.1007/978-3-031-34182-3_9

176   B.-A. Carter et al.

discussed here, a foreign language (L2) programme for non-specialist learners, with a pedagogical focus on skill gaining and using, on communication and interaction in the L2 and, importantly, without online resources in the LMS. (It should be noted that although some courses had online content in Edmodo, not all did. Furthermore, since only enrolled students could log in to the university LMS, materials uploaded there would have been inaccessible to all but the programme's university students.)

Notwithstanding the curriculum deficiencies of ERT compared to carefully designed online learning, we thought it important to capture the learners' perception, since, for many of them, it was their first experience of language learning outside of a face-to-face (F2F) mode. Learners were therefore asked to complete a short reflective task as one of the final course activities. This chapter looks at learner perception in a foreign language programme following the move to emergency remote teaching (ERT) arising out of the Covid-19 pandemic. Drawing on data from the learners' responses, the chapter will look at this case study of learning during the pandemic through the lens of innovation in teaching and learning, the theme of this volume.

Context

The Centre for Language Learning (CLL) is the university language centre at the St Augustine Campus. In Semester 2, 2019/2020, when this study was conducted, courses were offered at varying levels, from CEFR A1 to approximately CEFR B1+, in eight languages: Mandarin Chinese, French, German, Hindi, Japanese, Korean, Spanish, and Yoruba. That semester, just under 900 learners enrolled in courses with the majority registering for Spanish, French (both taught at the secondary level of education), and Japanese, in that order. As is the norm, the enrolled learners were a mixed population of university students, faculty, and staff, and members of the public.

Learners in less commonly taught languages like Mandarin Chinese, Japanese, and Korean may have had some prior exposure to these languages and cultures through television and social media, but their classes at the language centre were their first introduction to classroom-based acquisition. Because of the heterogeneity of the learners' academic and professional backgrounds and the varying languages being learnt, the learning cohort might be defined more by their differences than their similarities. Yet, their shared experience of the pandemic and the pivot to remote learning gave them a unique and research-worthy perspective on learning a language online.

Literature Review: From CALL to ERT

A copious literature on the integration of computers to promote effective language learning, under such labels as computer-assisted language learning (CALL) and computer-mediated communication (CMC) extends back several decades. Some early work can be found in Garrett (1988), Hoven (1992), Levy (1997), Marsh (1997), and Warschauer (1997). Another body of work relevant to this study is the literature on (language) learning in distance education, such as White (2003, 2006) and Veletsianos and Houlden (2019). As blended learning has grown in popularity in technology-rich contexts, the research has kept pace, for example Garrison et al. (2002), Marsh (2012), Mizza and Rubio (2020), and Neumeier (2005). While this latter research is very appropriate to inform future curriculum design, these pre-pandemic courses were designed as F2F courses, not for delivery as blended learning or in a dual mode.

Intentional and systematic online curriculum design has always given primacy to the theory of online pedagogy and underscored student engagement in online learning. Despite this, there is a generalised feeling that online learning is a poor substitute for F2F instruction, whether it is in terms of learner satisfaction or learning achievement, as noted by Hodges et al. (2020) and Van Wart et al. (2020), among others. With the shift to ERT, there is likely to be heightened scepticism about the effectiveness and efficacy of learning online, making it all the more critical not to conflate the two and to distinguish between the pandemic-induced ERT and online learning grounded in detailed and thoughtful curriculum planning, to wit:

Online learning carries a stigma of being lower quality than face-to-face learning, despite research showing otherwise. These hurried moves online by so many institutions at once could seal the perception of online learning as a weak option, when in truth nobody making the transition to online teaching under these circumstances will truly be designing to take full advantage of the affordances and possibilities of the online format. (Hodges et al., 2020)

And again:

Well-planned online learning experiences are meaningfully different from courses offered online in response to a crisis or disaster. Colleges and universities working to maintain instruction during the COVID-19 pandemic should understand those differences when evaluating this emergency remote teaching. (Hodges et al., 2020)

Hodges et al. provide a definition of emergency remote teaching which emphasises this and which is well worth quoting in full:

emergency remote teaching (ERT) is a temporary shift of instructional delivery to an alternate delivery mode due to crisis circumstances. It involves the use of fully remote teaching solutions for instruction or education that would otherwise be delivered face-to-face or as blended or hybrid courses and that will return to that format once the crisis or emergency has abated. The primary objective in these circumstances is not to re-create a robust educational ecosystem but rather to provide temporary access to instruction and instructional supports in a manner that is quick to set up and is reliably available during an emergency or crisis. (Hodges et al., 2020)

Having established a clear definition of emergency remote teaching, we now discuss a few examples relevant to this emerging genre.

Emergency Remote Teaching Measures and Strategies: A Short Review

According to the United Nations Educational, Scientific and Cultural Organization (UNESCO), 69.3% of enrolled students from early childhood to tertiary levels in 163 countries or regions were affected by the pandemic. The global effect of the pandemic on the entire educational sector was such that it compelled an urgent response on the part of UNESCO, leading to the publication of a 2020 report entitled "COVID-19 Educational Disruption and Response." Subsequently, UNESCO working with a coalition of UN agencies, civil society, academia, and the private sector established the Global Education Coalition, adopting a strategy resting on three pillars: Connectivity, Teachers, and Gender Equality and using the hashtag #learningneverstops. The UNESCO model is laudable, not only because of the integrated approach it deploys, but also because it attempts to use the pandemic "opportunity" to address chronic issues like gender equality, and connectivity in technology-poor contexts.

Two studies of ERT early in the pandemic are reviewed, here, providing examples of how teachers and learners responded to the closing of their HE institutions and the move to remote teaching. In their study of 19 English as a Foreign Language (EFL) students in an undergraduate Management of Tourism degree in the Czech Republic, Klimova (2021) explored the students' attitudes to learning online. These students were in their third year of English language studies having followed a blended curriculum with considerable e-learning materials. The homogeneity of the group also allowed the researcher to probe students' perceptions of the gains made or losses suffered in their language skills during the pandemic and to suggest which skills are best supported in the online environment.

Despite their familiarity with the online medium, students expressed a clear preference for their F2F learning which they felt boosted them both emotionally and cognitively. They missed the socialisation of F2F learning, feeling less engaged in the virtual environment, especially since many students kept their cameras off during class sessions. They felt less comfortable cognitively without hard copy documents on which to take notes, highlight information, and practise other cognitive strategies to support learning, and, generally, less motivated to remain engaged in learning that was solely online. The author was careful not to make generalisations given the small sample size, but the students' perceptions provide an interesting contrast with the learners in our study given the formers' familiarity with an online environment, their technological competence, and the likely importance of their English courses in a tourism degree.

Another study (Zhang & Wu, 2022) of a small group of EFL learners in a comprehensive university, in a coastal city in southern China, looked at students' perceptions of synchronous learning in the initial stage of the pandemic, in the period March 9 to June 26. The participants were selected by purposeful sampling to arrive at a group representative of the gender distribution, year of study, and place of origin. Like the students in Klimova's (2021) study, a major challenge arose in the socio-cognitive domain.

The students missed the emotional support of their peers. They found their home environment more unsettling and distracting than on-campus attendance. Learning online thus proved to be a metacognitive challenge for many students. Like the students in Klimova's (2021) study, the absence, both of hard copy materials to write on and of a calm space to engage in learning, was a cause for concern to learners whose academic success mattered greatly. Teacher-scaffolding and the development of learner autonomy appeared as both positive and negative factors. While most students initially missed the support of their teachers since the customary out-of-class interaction was no longer possible, many soon began to develop the capacity (Holec, 1979) for autonomy and became more self-directed in seeking out Internet-based materials to promote their learning. In terms of developing language skills, many students felt that the lack of F2F interaction affected their oral skills as the amount of corrective feedback was less than in the F2F environment. The final challenge identified in the study related to assessment. The students' level of study and the curriculum focus at that level were factors that affected their perception of the assessment changes made during ERT.

9 "Guess I have no choice but to do the e-book": Non-specialist...   181

In these two studies, despite the move from the physical to the virtual world, students still craved the degree of interaction with their peers and teachers to which they were accustomed. Furthermore, the perceived link between emotional wellbeing and academic performance clearly emerges in the learners' accounts. Students who feel less supported emotionally are more likely to feel their academic performance affected. At issue here is the very different climate of learning that prevailed in ERT. Seif et al.'s (2012) definition of the climate of learning, as cited in Zhang and Wu (2022, p. 4), namely, "The social, emotional, and physical conditions under which one acquires knowledge," is useful to retain. It has become almost a truism to state that the pandemic was very deleterious to the climate of learning.

An interesting note is the role of technology in these two studies. Klimova (2021) felt that the teachers and students had a level of mastery of technology which was not a factor in their perception of online learning. Zhang and Wu (2022) did not discuss in any detail whether students were hampered by their or their teachers' technology deficits during their synchronous learning. They did, however, recommend that teachers needed to strengthen their ability to integrate technology into their teaching.

The final section of the literature review examines Moore et al.'s (2021) "One year later and counting: Reflections on emergency remote teaching and online learning," in which they suggest that instead of being a past crisis, the pandemic and its disruptive effects are ongoing and recurring. Meadows' (2008) typology of a feedback loop as cited in Moore et al. (2021) is used by the authors to describe how different educational institutions have weathered the disruptive effects of the pandemic. The first type of feedback loop described as "stabilizing (balancing)" maintains steadiness, with variation occurring within a range. The second type of feedback loop labelled "runaway or reinforcing" can be imagined more as a spiral, leading to a vicious or virtuous circle according to the outcome. Meadows further contends that "The primary symptom of a balancing feedback loop structure is that not much changes, despite outside forces pushing the system" (p. 112). Stabilising then far from being a positive quality, points to a degree of stasis and resistance to change. Runaway or reinforcing feedback loops entail greater possibilities for movement and forward trajectory. Feedback loops that restore or rebuild, that aim to revert to a notional pre-pandemic "normal" while seeming to imply more positivity, are less to be valued than those that learn and evolve.

Moore et al. (2021) suggest, however, that investment in and commitment to online learning pre-pandemic should be seen as the starting point for the feedback loop. Institutions that resisted the push to integrate technology via online learning pre-pandemic and continue to do so post-ERT are likely to be operating in a balancing feedback loop. Institutions that were forced to innovate during ERT but want to restore and rebuild in order to return to their pre-pandemic "normal" are unlikely to maximise the opportunities created by the pandemic. On the other hand, institutions that integrate the lessons and best practices of ERT would be operating in a feedback loop that evolves with a snowballing effect on their future operations. Those institutions with the most forward-looking feedback loops (whether they have always shown a commitment to different learning modalities or have been impelled to adopt that stance post-ERT) are more agile and more intent on "creating learning modalities and technologies that [form] a rich learning ecosystem to afford flexibility, access, continuity, and resilience" (Moore et al. 2021). It is our contention that the optimum conditions for innovation in teaching and learning exist where the best of ERT infuses the post-ERT curriculum.

Methodology

The research sought to capture the learners' perception of (1) their initial response and feedback to learning a language online; (2) factors that affected the experience; (3) the lessons learnt; (4) the degree of fulfilment of their expectations; and (5) their willingness to continue learning remotely. The research was therefore guided by three research questions, namely:

1. What did learners think about online learning made necessary by the pandemic and online learning generally?

9 "Guess I have no choice but to do the e-book": Non-specialist... 183

2. What were some of the opportunities presented and challenges endured in the move to emergency remote teaching?
3. What did the learners' experience imply for the future of online learning in our programmes?

In keeping with the focus of this volume, a more global question posed by the researchers was whether the move to remote teaching represented an innovation in learning and teaching.

It was decided that a short piece of reflective writing would gather the learners' feedback better than the customary questionnaire. Teachers and programme administrators sought to gain as full an understanding as possible of the learners' experience of online learning, given that in past surveys and discussions learners had always expressed a clear preference for F2F learning and a reluctance for any kind of computer-mediated learning. Some learners were even reluctant to use e-textbooks when these replaced hard copy textbooks. The article's title is based on an email from a learner in which she reluctantly agrees to the purchase of an e-book.

Conduct of the Survey

Although research on the mental health effects of the pandemic on students (e.g. Son et al., 2020) was still in its infancy, anecdotal evidence suggested that greater care needed to be taken in managing our demands on and expectations of the learners. A reflective writing task seemed well suited to give the learners a safe space to express themselves while giving the researchers enough insight into their thoughts. The final instrument was modelled on the guidelines in the Skills you need website (n.d.) and took the learners through a four-stage process of describing the experience, reflection, theorising, and experimentation. Learners were asked to respond to the writing prompts in a Google form (see Appendix 9.1) entitled "Learning a foreign language online—my experience." The reflective writing was done in their final class, on or circa April 29, approximately one month after the resumption of classes on March 31. Learners were given 30 minutes to respond and submit their feedback.

Overall, 419 reflective pieces were submitted out of a total enrolled population of 874 learners, or approximately 48% of those enrolled.

Constraints/Limitations

Both the title of the document and the instructions sought to make clear that we were seeking very personal, individual feedback from the respondents. They were told, however, that the answers could inform our future curriculum development and be used for research purposes. Given the way in which the data were elicited via a classroom-based writing task, we did not need to obtain permission from the Campus' Ethics Committee for the survey. The research team's decision to exclude any identifier and request no demographic information meant that no correlation could be made between sex/age/language studied and learner perspective. Yet the anonymity of their responses and the convenience of submitting their feedback within the classroom session were no doubt factors that facilitated increased learner participation in the survey.

Data Analysis Procedures

The data were analysed at two intervals by two different researchers using QDA Miner, versions 5.0.34 and 6.0.11, respectively. Both researchers followed the same process of importing the data into the qualitative software and using the keyword retrieval feature to identify frequently recurring themes. A written report was then generated to reflect the content and thematic analysis obtained. Illustrative samples of the respondents' feedback were included in each report.

The first report focused on the first two writing prompts, namely:

1. In your own words, what happened and when? What was your initial response/what were your initial thoughts? How did you behave during the online sessions? How did learning a language online make you feel?
2. What challenges/benefits can you identify from your online language learning experience? What factors influenced (positively and/or nega-

9 "Guess I have no choice but to do the e-book": Non-specialist... 185

tively) your experience? What have you learned from the experience? Did you learn anything about yourself as a language learner that you did not know before?

An in-depth report was completed in February 2022 and confirmed an earlier quick review of the data which showed an overwhelmingly positive response to the courses delivered remotely. Indeed, 72% of the learners judged their classes positively.

The second round of data analysis was done in June 2022. This time the thematic and content analysis included the following questions:

1. Was the experience as you initially expected? How does it relate to what you might have experienced using a language learning app? If you have never used a language learning app, how do you think your experience compares to other online language learning courses?
2. If online language were to become the norm in the future, what would you do differently/the same? What strategies might you try out?

While this analysis of the data once again showed an overwhelmingly positive response to doing their courses online, the most frequently mentioned theme pertained to the challenges and benefits of online learning. The second analysis added a quantitative dimension to the qualitative analysis as it calculated the percentage of the respondents who held certain perceptions.

Data Analysis and Findings

The February 2022 data analysis showed that the convenience of continuing their language classes from home and being able to complete the course despite the country's lockdown contributed greatly to learner satisfaction. The majority of learners seemed to have approached remote learning with a level of apprehension, but in many cases this eventually subsided with some learners even coming to prefer remote learning. Some learners felt less anxiety in the online environment since they felt less judged and were more willing to participate. Others noted their easy access to online resources which was not always possible in the classroom since not all classrooms were connected to the Internet. They also appreciated the utility of recordings which allowed them to review the classes at their leisure. One learner commended a better fit with their learning style and the teacher's style in the online environment, since the teacher, who previously seldom wrote on the whiteboard, made greater use of visual resources:

> *It was a bit strange to be in an online class initially. After the first session I settled down well…It helps a lot to only do audio and not video for me at least because I find video of the other students can be very distracting. I love however seeing video of my Professor because that way it becomes a bit more personal.* **(Respondent (R)13)**
>
> *I was uncertain about learning online. I felt it strange at first but as I became accustomed, I felt free to participate in activities since I felt less judged when I gave responses. I enjoyed it very much.* **(R41)**
>
> *The benefits are tremendous:*
>
> *a) A tremendous amount of time is saved by not having to travel to and from the physical class. The time saved can be used to review materials.*
>
> *b) Our lecturer records and posts the recording of the class. I am able to review in detail. This helps my learning process.*
>
> *c) The above benefits assume that the lecturer is organised and effective as ours.* **(R16)**
>
> *At first it felt a little weird but at the end of the first class I became more comfortable. The classes were very interactive and I was able to ask my questions and get them answered…One benefit was that I felt more comfortable asking and answering questions. This was caused by my lecturer (XX), attempts to make the classes as comfortable and interactive as possible.* **(R66)**
>
> *At first it was glitchy (the vibe, not the program used), but as we all got more accustomed, and as the teacher included more and more interactive activities it grew quite fun! In person classes are still preferred but this is a much welcomed close second!* **(R129)**

This positive experience did not extend to all learners, some of whom remained less satisfied with the online experience than they had been with the F2F course.

> *All in all, the experience was a new one and everyone tried their best to accommodate the issues as we did not really have much of a choice. The lack of intimacy found in a conventional class room however, was missed. Online learning was a bit more stressful mentally and I would prefer to not have the experience again specifically for learning languages. (R15)*

In contrast to the earlier learner, who found the teacher's changed teaching style a better fit with their learning style, was the learner who found just the opposite. For this learner, it was more than a simple style clash. The learner felt the need to fundamentally rethink their metacognitive strategies to accommodate the demands placed on them by remote teaching:

> *Learning it online made me feel somewhat strange and frustrated as I had to readjust my learning pattern that I was accustomed to for multiple years. (R05)*

Yet, on the whole, the largely positive experience of the learners is well summed up in the following extract:

> *I previously was not a fan of online classes as I preferred face to face sessions. As we eventually transitioned to the online classes I grew very comfortable as the platform was easy to access and the lecturer was excellent in his delivery. It felt as if I was still in the physical classroom. I even think that I participated more.*
>
> *As a result of this experience I realized that learning a language online is possible with proper delivery of the course content by the lecturer. Throughout this, I confirmed my passion for learning the language. The experience was not as I initially expected. It surpassed my expectations. It was very interactive and delivery was excellent. (R20)*

Learner satisfaction was also derived from the teaching approach adopted. Many learners missed the physical interaction with the teacher and peers, the sense of community experienced in the traditional classroom, and this coloured the learning experience. The majority of learners (university students and others) in the CLL's programme are doing a language on an extracurricular basis or for leisure. So their motivation is not mainly extrinsic, or linked to academic or professional success. On the contrary, for many of these learners their prime motivation is linked to sociocultural aspects of language learning and the opportunity to engage in multilingual and multicultural interaction in the learning space. There was, however, even among those who were less positive about the online experience, a high degree of praise for the pedagogical approaches adopted. Learners attributed their overall satisfaction to the teachers' pedagogy: facilitating a supportive learning climate, making even greater efforts to facilitate interaction, provide feedback, integrate online resources, and so on:

> *I think genuine interest in learning the language I am studying helped me to overcome several negative reactions I had in the latter part of my language course. The wholehearted effort of the lecturer, the clarity of the explanations and the ongoing feedback also helped. (R07)*

ERT in the early days of the pandemic often amounted to F2F classes delivered remotely. To the great credit of the teachers, it seemed that they were able to recreate a very convivial and highly engaging environment, which is one of the most attractive features of our language centre's F2F classes. For many learners, their satisfaction was not diminished by the online learning experience as their teachers tried their utmost to promote communication and interaction in the virtual space.

The second in-depth analysis confirmed and supplemented the February analysis. This time, responses to all four reflective prompts were analysed. While this report underscored that the vast majority of learners seemed receptive to remote teaching, which allowed them to continue learning despite the national lockdown, there were some negative attitudes, ranging from reluctance to concern. Figure 9.1 shows that while the majority of learners were open to the forced move to the online environment, over a third expressed reluctance or concern.

> *My first thoughts were how? It was unimaginable how we could have moved from face to face having no real experience or point of reference of an online class. (R126)*

Yet, the overwhelmingly positive reaction to the online experience, after the initial apprehension, revealed that learners were clear-sighted about the logistical, affective, and cognitive benefits they derived from learning

9 "Guess I have no choice but to do the e-book": Non-specialist...

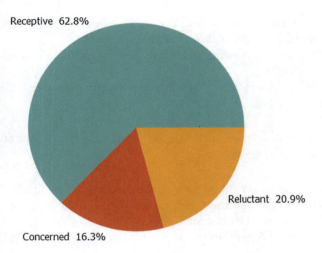

Fig. 9.1 The learners' initial responses/thoughts

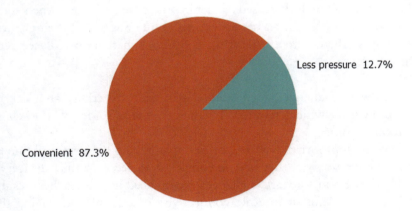

Fig. 9.2 Benefits of the online experience

in the online space. Figure 9.2 gives further insight into what made the online experience a positive and beneficial one.

"Online classes are convenient and the application was easy to understand." (**R31**)

"I found it convenient, and I was glad to be able to complete the course in spite of the circumstances." **(R203)**

"One of the benefits of online learning is that it is more convenient." **(R210)**

"Online classes are a lot more convenient than physically going to class…" **(R312)**

Some learners felt less pressure in terms of general anxiety, classroom learning, and assessment:

"Less pressure for final exams by having an assignment." **(R5)**
"Online sessions helped with my anxiety…" **(R1)**
"Less stress and distractions." **(R12)**
"It didn't feel so pressuring to grasp the audios played." **(R42)**

While technology did not prove to be a barrier in the two studies reviewed above, it was a much-discussed barrier in our context. Some learners indicated that access to the classes or sessions online was one of their greatest challenges. There were three distinct conditions that hampered access for the learners:

- Hardware challenges, for example Internet connectivity and lack of bandwidth, which resulted in their missing some of the classroom sessions;
- Lack of appropriate devices, for example relying on a smartphone to attend classes since they had no computer, tablet, or similar device;
- Hardware and software challenges experienced by the teachers resulting in problems of Internet connectivity or difficulty managing the campus' Blackboard Collaborate.

Figure 9.3 shows what learners found especially challenging. Technological obstacles and digital fatigue topped the list. The complaints about digital fatigue were somewhat surprising because teachers had been advised to introduce more frequent breaks into their online classes. It seems, however, that in the early days of EMT not all the teachers had shifted their perspective on the differences between in-person and online learning

9 "Guess I have no choice but to do the e-book": Non-specialist… 191

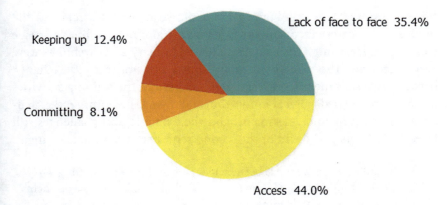

Fig. 9.3 Challenges

with regards to learners' attention span and engagement. This suggests the need for teacher training for online delivery, as advocated by Kebritchi et al. (2017, p. 21) and cited in Bruce and Stakounis (2021, p. 72).

> "If a student has a connectivity issue then it would be difficult for them to attend classes." *(R24)*
> "Connectivity issues sometimes lead towards missing content / explanations during class." *(R29)*
> "One challenge is that interaction is not the same due to internet connectivity issues faced by my classmates." *(R141)*
> "It was pretty difficult given the fact that my device wasn't compatible with the app being used for classes…" *(R30)*
> "I had a lot of audio issues and had to eventually run the class from my mobile device as opposed to my laptop because of said problems." *(R409)*
> "…difficult to look at a computer screen straight for 2 hrs." *(R5)*
> "Shorten the classes, with an increased number of classes per week as staring at a computer screen for 4 hours can be really painful." *(R407)*

The St Augustine Centre for Excellence in Teaching and Learning (CETL) posted teaching tips and links to useful resources to support the move from in-person learning to remote delivery on March 16, 23, and 30. But it is unlikely that all the teachers, the majority of whom were part-time tutors, would have paid heed to the guidance on remote teaching. As

EMT continued in the following academic year, the CLL retained the services of an external consultant to do staff training in online language teaching and learning. The August 2020 and January 2021 webinars were very successful. The following extract from a December 2020 exchange between two staff members gives a good account of the training activities undertaken, the pedagogical innovations following the training, the challenges in teaching and assessment, and the technological challenges still faced by learners at the end of the second semester of remote teaching:

> Yes, the online assessment has been challenging and time consuming lately but I'm glad I have acquired so many new skills!!! Thank you for your help with creating videos, uploading on youtube etc!
>
> I am looking forward to another webinar of course, it is always informative and welcome, in order to improve classes and motivate students. I used the same activities as (Colleague) D. I also used word wall in class, spinning the wheel activity, which was quite successful. The challenge though and the reason why I mainly used PowerPoint presentations in my classes with activities on them/ pictures etc. is that many students have technological issues, whether it's the internet, their device, they are only using a phone, some did not have a working camera and even microphone for almost the whole semester...So, offering activities that require a good device and good internet would have been too challenging sometimes for a few students. I was going to use Kahoot for example (I think (Trainer) J showed a platform that is similar to this one) when (Colleague) Y mentioned that he did and the students using their phone were unable to navigate between the game and the main screen with questions on the phone itself, so I decided against using it. I did use some French websites with self-correcting exercises for grammar, and this worked well, as students could work at their own pace. I also used google slides as a collaborative exercise in order to practice writing skills, where all students could write, sometimes in pairs, sometimes individually, and it was easy for me to point out errors and they could correct themselves immediately. I also used Google maps to practice the city vocabulary, similar to something J had shown. If I remember well, he had used Google Earth. I took them to my hometown and went through the city centre showing the stores and buildings we had learnt in the lesson, and after this, they had to list all the words that they heard and use them. Also, because I am doing research on mobile assisted language learning, I

used WhatsApp to get them to practice speaking (and also writing) where they had to leave voice notes on a specific topic. They also had to write a few sentences sometimes. So, I am giving you these details to show you how I practiced all skills with various activities that allowed all students to take part, even from a phone. It was really trial and error.

I am looking forward to discovering new tools again and putting them into practice during the webinar, as it would be most beneficial for all of us, but for the students who only use their phones, I would like if he could also recommend activities that don't need too much technology/internet to be used.

Figure 9.4 sought to capture what self-knowledge learners gained during their language course delivered remotely.

"…personally I would try to practise more on my own since online classes can often allow a laid back approach." *(R348)*

"…I learned that I need to practise speaking to persons who speak the language…" *(R298)*

"This experience helped me not to only improve my language skills but also my tech skills and it helped me develop the knowledge of the language as keys to navigate through the text and follow without being in a face to face environment…" *(R37)*

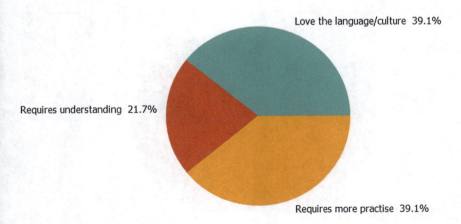

Fig. 9.4 Lessons learnt/takeaways

"I learnt that learning a language you have to saturate yourself in order to grasp a new language." *(R38)*

"...I learned that I really love Chinese culture." *(R1)*

In Fig. 9.5, we see that the vast majority of learners felt that their expectations for doing a language online were met or exceeded.

"All my expectations from the beginning of the course were met. The switch to an online medium did not hinder any of my expectations..." *(R29)*

"Better than I expected..." *(R84)*

"...the course exceeded my expectations..." *(R24)*

"The experience was not as I initially expected. It surpassed my expectations..." *(R20)*

Finally, in Fig. 9.6, half of the respondents were highly receptive to doing a future blended language course.

"I hope CLL can offer a combination of both face to face and online learning..." *(R115)*

"I personally feel like both can work hand in hand..." *(R52)*

"I would rather a mixed approach..." *(R71)*

"It would be nice to use a mixture of both online and in class sessions. There are advantages to both and a mixture can achieve such." *(R3)*

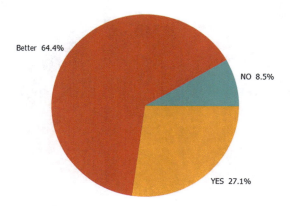

Fig. 9.5 Fulfilment of initial expectations about ERT

9 "Guess I have no choice but to do the e-book": Non-specialist...

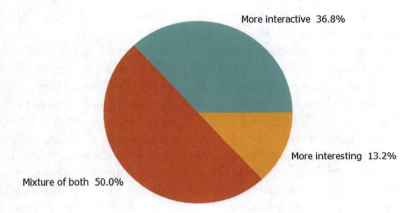

Fig. 9.6 Going forward

Discussion

The findings above are based on the qualitative data collected from 419 learners at the end of four weeks of remote teaching that had been preceded by eight weeks of F2F teaching. Although there was a relatively high response rate, our understanding of learner perceptions is limited by the absence of feedback from the non-respondents and the fact that the qualitative data came from a single source and was not triangulated. Nonetheless, the number and richness of the learner accounts was important to provide a timely exploration of learner perceptions at the very onset of ERT.

As novel as was the coronavirus in March 2020, so too was most educators' understanding of teaching in a crisis. As researchers committed to effective student learning, we could not ignore the opportunity to better understand the learning environment from the student perspective. Yet, operating at a time when we were all struggling with the first impact of the pandemic and enormous disruption in our personal and professional lives, we felt the need to proceed with care and manage the demands placed on others. We are extremely grateful to the learners who did not abandon their classes, to the teachers who made the learning experience such that the learners were prepared to continue, and to those learners who took the time to respond to the survey.

The pandemic's effect on teaching and learning was experienced globally: suspension and disruption of F2F classes in all education sectors in most countries, student attrition, teacher fatigue, and mental health challenges for teachers and students. The scenarios seemed similar in the Global North and South. Additional challenges were posed around connectivity that were more sharply felt in the Global South. Yet, without the pandemic, many contexts that have now embraced elements of online learning would have continued their neutrality and even hostility to online learning. Most contexts are now poised to do more technology, not less than in the pre-pandemic days. The potential is there for positive reinforcing feedback loops across a large swath of HE institutions.

While ERT is of itself an innovation in teaching and learning as it represented a radical change from F2F teaching, embedding innovation into the curriculum would require the adoption of some of the most positive aspects of pandemic teaching and learning. This must be done creatively and with intentionality since successful innovation would require a shift in mentality. A retreat to a teaching approach that does not integrate technology—whether it be through more e-learning content, blended, or fully online learning—will be unsustainable in a post-pandemic world. The aim then should not be simply for a stabilising feedback loop, as described by Meadows (2008).

Both the students in the review articles cited and the learners in our context, having become more familiar with the affordances of technology, would no doubt seek more technology both in their in-class and out-of-class learning. A feedback loop aiming to restore and rebuild would not move the integration of technology far enough along. What is needed is the type of feedback loop that learns and evolves and informs an online curriculum grounded in best practice and the latest research. That is how innovation will infuse the curriculum.

A new learner expectation is certain to be the flexibility and access which ERT allowed. ERT in the pandemic enabled continuity; this too is likely to shape the adult learner's expectations around (language) learning in the future. Although professional and personal constraints might make traditional classroom-based learning difficult at times, learners could expect institutions to provide dual modes allowing them to move seamlessly between full in-person and remotely delivered teaching so that there is no disruption to the continuity of their learning project. It has too often been the case that education lags in adapting technologies that are part of the learner's daily life. As more and more businesses grapple with concepts like a four-day work week and partial- to full remote work, learners will probably bring the same expectations to their lifelong learning. Educators and higher education would need to think creatively to accommodate the digital natives and the digital immigrants (Prensky, 2001) whose migration to a more digital space was forced upon them by the pandemic.

Conclusion

Despite the many challenges endured, the resilience of teachers and learners and the resilience of the supporting infrastructure (e.g. via the teaching and learning centre and the campus' technology infrastructure) staved off a collapse in the crisis situation of the pandemic. Teachers must be continually recycled through training for online learning in order to keep their pedagogy fresh and innovative. Learner satisfaction and student success require no less. Thus, one condition of innovation in the teaching and learning context discussed here, as elsewhere, must be continuous work on encoding resilience into the DNA of our curriculum design and our pedagogical approaches. Doing so requires constructing a robust educational ecosystem, open and responsive to change. Our programme must lean on the research and our learners' feedback to craft new strategies for a post-ERT world that will keep innovation at the heart of teaching and learning.

Appendix 9.1: Google Form "Learning a Foreign Language Online—My Experience"

Dear Students,

The move from face-to-face classes to online classes was an exciting new challenge for all of us. As we prepare for the new academic year and the possibility of more online classes, we really would like to hear about your experience of learning a language online. Was this the first time you did an online language class? How was it? If it was not the first time, how does this experience compare with your previous experience? Please take some time and answer the questions that follow.

As we here at the CLL are all keen researchers, your answers may be used in research publications. But there is no risk involved; your identity will not be revealed or disclosed in any way. The responses are anonymous. We hope you will use the opportunity to help us and guide us as we strive to give you the best online experience that we can.

B. Carter
Director
The Centre for Language Learning

Section 2

So tell us, what happened?

Take a few minutes to reflect on your experience of moving from learning your foreign language in the classroom to the online environment. Some questions are provided for guidance, but whatever you write should be your personal reflection, summarised in a few paragraphs.

In your own words, what happened and when? What was your initial response/what were your initial thoughts? How did you behave during the online sessions? How did learning a language online make you feel?

What challenges/benefits can you identify from your online language learning experience? What factors influenced (positively and/or negatively) your experience?

What have you learned from the experience? Did you learn anything about yourself as a language learner that you did not know before?

Section 3

Was it what you expected?

Take a few minutes to think about how attending your language classes online compared with your initial expectations.

Was the experience as you initially expected? How does it relate to what you might have experienced using a language learning app? If you have never used a language learning app, how do you think your experience compares to other online language learning courses?

If online language were to become the norm in the future, what would you do differently/the same? What strategies might you try out?

References

Bruce, E., & Stakounis, H. (2021). *The impact of Covid-19 on the UK EAP sector during the initial six months of the pandemic.* BALEAP-funded Report.

Garrett, N. (1988). Computers in foreign language education: Teaching, learning, and language-acquisition research. *ADFL Bulletin, 19*(3), 6–12.

Garrison, R., Kanuka, H., & Hawes, D. (2002). *Blended learning: Archetypes for more effective undergraduate learning experiences.* University of Calgary: Learning Commons.

Hodges, C.B., Moore, S.L., Lockee, B.B., Trust, T. & Bond, M.A. (2020, March 27). The difference between emergency remote teaching and online learning. *EDUCAUSE Review.* https://tinyurl.com/rekxcrq

Holec, H. (1979). *Autonomy and foreign language learning.* Pergamon Press.

Hoven, D. (1992). CALL in a language learning environment. *CÆLL Journal, 3*(2), 19–27.

Kebritchi, M., Lipschuetz, A., & Santiague, L. (2017). Issues and challenges for teaching successful online courses in higher education: A literature review. *Journal of Educational Technology Systems, 46*(1), 4–29.

Klimova, B. (2021). An insight into online foreign language learning and teaching in the era of COVID-19 pandemic. *Procedia Computer Science, 192,* 1787–1794. https://doi.org/10.1016/j.procs.2021.08.183

Levy, M. (1997). *Computer-assisted language learning. Context and conceptualization.* Clarendon Press.

Marsh, D. (1997). Computer conferencing: Taking the loneliness out of independent learning. *The Language Learning Journal, 15*(1), 21–25. https://doi.org/10.1080/09571739785200051

Marsh, D. (2012). *Blended learning. Creating learning opportunities for language learners.* Cambridge University Press.

Meadows, D. H. (2008). *Thinking in systems: A primer.* Chelsea Green Publishing.

Mizza, D., & Rubio, F. (2020). *Creating effective blended language learning courses. A research-based guide from planning to evaluation.* Cambridge University Press.

Moore S., Trust T., Lockee B., Bond A. & Hodges C., (2021, November 10). One year later… and counting: Reflections on emergency remote teaching and online learning. *EDUCAUSE Review.* One Year Later … and Counting: Reflections on Emergency Remote Teaching and Online Learning | EDUCAUSE.

Neumeier, P. (2005). A closer look at blended learning—Parameters for designing a blended learning environment for language teaching and learning. *ReCALL, 17*(2), 163–178. https://doi.org/10.1017/S0958344005000224

Prensky, M. (2001). Digital natives, digital immigrants part 1. *On the Horizon, 9*(5), 1–6. https://doi.org/10.1108/10748120110424816

Seif, E., Tableman, B., & Carlson, J. S. (2012). Climate of learning. In N. M. Seel (Ed.), *Encyclopedia of the sciences of learning* (pp. 554–557). Springer.

Skills you need. (n.d.). *Reflective practice.* https://www.skillsyouneed.com/ps/reflective-practice.html

Son, C., Hegde, S., Smith, A., Wang, X., & Sasangohar, F. (2020). Effects of COVID-19 on college students' mental health in the United States: Interview survey study. *Journal of Medical Internet Research, 22*(9), e21279. https://doi.org/10.2196/21279

UNESCO. (2020). *COVID-19 Educational disruption and response.* https://en.unesco.org/covid19/educationresponse/

Van Wart, M., Ni, A., Medina, P., Canelon, J., Kordrostami, M., Zhang, J., & Liu, Y. (2020). Integrating students' perspectives about online learning: A hierarchy of factors. *International Journal of Educational Technology in Higher Education, 17*(1), 53. https://doi.org/10.1186/s41239-020-00229-8

Veletsianos, G., & Houlden, S. (2019). An analysis of flexible learning and flexibility over the last 40 years of Distance Education. *Distance Education, 40*(4), 454–468.

Warschauer, M. (1997). Computer-mediated collaborative learning: Theory and practice. *The Modern Language Journal, 81*(4), 470–481.

White, C. (2003). *Language learning in distance education*. Cambridge Language Teaching Library. CUP.

White, C. (2006). Distance learning of foreign languages. *Language Teaching, 39*(04), 247–264.

Zhang, K., & Wu, H. (2022). Synchronous online learning during COVID-19: Chinese university EFL students' perspectives. *SAGE Open*. https://doi.org/10.1177/21582440221094821

10

Foreign/Second Language Learning and Teaching in the Southern Caribbean: Future Directions

Diego Mideros, Nicole Roberts, Beverly-Anne Carter, and Hayo Reinders

Introduction

Originally, we visualised this volume as one which would include all of the Caribbean. However, this was scaled back to centre on our area of the Southern Caribbean because we recognised how necessary the volume was to showcase the work being done on L2 learning and teaching among our small-island states. In this chapter, we discuss innovation as presented in the chapters of the volume, the challenges faced and the takeaways,

---

D. Mideros • N. Roberts (✉) • B.-A. Carter
Centre for Language Learning, Department of Modern Languages and Linguistics, The University of the West Indies,
St. Augustine, Trinidad and Tobago
e-mail: diego.mideros@sta.uwi.edu; nicole.roberts@sta.uwi.edu

H. Reinders
King Mongkut's University of Technology Thonburi—KMUTT,
Bangkok, Thailand

© The Author(s), under exclusive license to Springer Nature Switzerland AG 2023
D. Mideros et al. (eds.), *Innovation in Language Learning and Teaching*, New Language Learning and Teaching Environments, https://doi.org/10.1007/978-3-031-34182-3_10

Innovation in Foreign/Second Language Learning and Teaching in the Southern Caribbean

In this section, we will discuss what innovation looks like in light of the chapters of the volume. All the innovations presented in the previous chapters proved to be systematic and carefully thought out, with the exception of Chap. 9, where Carter et al. illustrated what we could perhaps term as "forced" innovation, as remote emergency teaching resulted from the emergence of the novel coronavirus. As such, it is pertinent to analyse what prompted the different innovations and what innovation in language learning and teaching looks like in the Southern Caribbean.

The impetus for the different innovations is derived from both external forces and personal concerns from the teacher-researchers in this volume. In some cases, the innovations appeared more top-down, and in other cases they appeared more bottom-up. In Chap. 6, Carter describes the establishment of a Confucius Institute to enhance the language centre's Mandarin Chinese programme. Unlike earlier international language and culture organisation, the Confucius Institute's inherent strength was the collaboration it facilitated between two academic institutions, one Chinese and the other in the host country, with major funding from and under the aegis of Hanban. But both cross-cultural factors and factors intrinsic to each institution could determine the success of the Confucius Institute's innovation. In this case, the replacement of the original provincial university by a more prestigious Beijing-based institution, but one less focused on the teaching of Chinese, meant that the initial objective of establishing the Confucius Institute became secondary to fulfilling the strategic and institutional goals of both Hanban and the two academic institutions. In Chap. 5, Craig describes his personal account of rethinking the mission and values of the Modern Languages department in his institution as a result of a university-wide new foreign language policy that was in the approval stages, which motivated him to re-evaluate the role of a programme where he is the most senior staff member. Mideros and Palma in Chap. 8 present an innovation that came from the request of an external client who sought a fully online Spanish course for all members of staff of an airline in Trinidad and Tobago. Such an ambitious request took place at a time when the institution and staff had no experience in designing and delivering fully online courses, but it represented an excellent opportunity given the importance of the client and the money involved if they got the contract to deliver the course. In these cases, although at obvious varying scales, innovation looks in a way like what Hyland and Wong describe, "from above by policy-makers in government offices" (2013, p. 2) or external agencies that give language practitioners imperatives to which they must respond to the best of their ability and with the resources available to them (or not).

The other chapters illustrate innovations that resulted from more personal concerns and observations, which look like the other side of the coin; that is, innovations that result from "classroom practitioners trying to make their students more active or their lessons more effective" (Hyland & Wong, 2013, p. 2). Céspedes Suárez in Chap. 2 illustrates exemplarily the need to explicitly teach and promote intercultural communicative competence paying attention to both "lowbrow" (habits, traditions, behaviours, etc.) and "highbrow" (politics, geography, or history) elements of Hispanic culture to advanced learners of Spanish. Given that her study is located in Cave Hill, Barbados, she also connects her innovation with the language policy discussed by Craig in Chap. 5. In Chap. 3, Bardol's innovation seeks to improve Martinican university students' pronunciation and English language level. Learners in Bardol's implementation are French university students from different disciplines who are required to graduate with a B2 CEFR level of competence in the English language, and this innovation is an effort to respond to this imperative. Although it was not explicitly discussed in his chapter, we can probably assume that students being required to achieve a B2 CEFR level in English is perhaps a language policy or directive from Bardol's institution, a directive that he and his colleagues should try to achieve. As such, we can probably interpret that Bardol's impetus has both extrinsic and personal elements.

In Chap. 4, Rose presents an innovation that sought to promote collective teacher efficacy through project-based learning and course-based undergraduate research (CURE). What makes Rose's innovation fascinating is the fact that it originated from a mixture of her own concerns to make her "Teaching of Language Arts at the Primary Level" course more authentic and relevant, *and* the students in her class who came up with the idea of promoting reading for pleasure among primary school students in Guyana. In one class presentation, students discussed the issue of declining literacy rates in primary schools and proposed the idea. In Chap. 7, Lipoff describes a large-scale and ambitious innovation that sought to strengthen French teachers' level of French as well as to provide them with better teaching tools and strategies to teach the language in the English-speaking Caribbean. This innovation is an initiative of the Integrating French as a Language of Exchange (IFLE) programme, which, as its name indicates, aims to integrate Caribbean countries by means of promoting the French language and thus facilitate academic mobility. Students in the English-speaking Caribbean can benefit from academic opportunities in universities in Guadeloupe or Martinique, which fall under the French academic system, as long as they are competent in the French language. Lipoff's innovation is a concrete effort to strengthen the teaching of French in the English-speaking Caribbean. Finally, Carter et al. describe how students responded to emergency remote teaching at the beginning of the pandemic, illustrating how in most cases learners in their context went from reluctant to satisfied and highlighting the innovations that emerged from the emergency response to the Covid-19 pandemic.

Invariably, the different chapters respond to a variety of contextual demands or concerns. In most cases, the innovations featured in this volume highlight truly human capital represented by teacher-researchers-practitioners attempting to improve or enhance elements of learning among their learners; that is the case of Céspedes Suárez in Chap. 2, Bardol in Chap. 3, Rose in Chap. 4, and Mideros and Palma in Chap. 8. Carter et al. in Chap. 9 feature students' voices and perceptions to present their experience in going from in-person learning to emergency remote learning/teaching; they indirectly capture aspects of teaching, but the key element is highlighting the learners' experience and engagement under new and unprecedented circumstances. To a lesser extent, Mideros and Palma in Chap. 8 also feature the responses of a group of students to a blended course that incorporated learning beyond the classroom. Rose's Chap. 4 and Lipoff's Chap. 7 are both devoted to teachers and teacher education. The former is a formal course for primary school teachers, while the latter is a large-scale workshop for teachers of French as a foreign language. Innovation at institutional levels is presented by Craig in Chap. 5 and Carter in Chap. 6. Interestingly, in both cases their accounts are personal as they describe in first person their experiences. In Craig's case, his role, as the most senior member of staff in his section with seniority and experience, is to lead the process of reflecting, reviewing, rethinking, and drafting important mission and value statements for his academic section. In Carter's case, her role as director of the Centre for Language Learning who experienced first-hand all the intricacies and hoops of establishing a transnational and cross cultural academic partnership that resulted in the launch of a Confucius Institute at her university. These chapters illustrate vehemently the importance of human capital in innovation.

In Chap. 1, we set out to assess innovation as a sociocultural enterprise under the umbrella of agency (Ahearn, 2001; Deters et al., 2015; Huang & Benson, 2013; Kayi-Aydar et al., 2019; Lantolf & Pavlenko, 2001; Larsen-Freeman, 2019; van Lier, 2008). As such, it is in our best interest to evaluate the affordances and constraints that teacher-researchers-practitioners had in their contexts during the different phases of their implementations. In this section, we pay particular attention to the resources available for each of the innovations and other contextual elements presented in each of the chapters. Specific challenges, however, will be addressed in the next section of this chapter.

Those innovations whose focus was learning and teaching required concrete resources for the design and implementation phases. Céspedes Suárez (Chap. 2), Bardol (Chap. 3), Rose (Chap. 4), Lipoff (Chap. 7), Mideros and Palma (Chap. 8), and Carter et al. (Chap. 9), all referred to the active use of technology and digital resources for their innovations. In all cases, numerous mentions of learning management systems (LMS) were made. With the exception of Carter et al. (Chap. 9), these innovations began before the pandemic, and in all cases the authors claimed having access to LMS for teaching and learning in their contexts. Mideros and Palma (Chap. 8) described a situation where they had to create a new blended course, a first in their context and with some access challenges—since the course was for a corporate client and not a course for university students, they had to jump through some hoops to get access to an LMS platform exclusive to university students, which was the same case as Carter et al. (Chap. 9). Nonetheless, they received sufficient human and capital support to be able to create and deliver the course for the paying corporate client. Bardol (Chap. 3) described a smooth experience where the technology unit of his university was of great support. In Bardol's case, it is worth remembering—as he also described in his chapter—that his university is a French university and is guided by the regulations and perks of belonging to the French system. Lipoff's (Chap. 7) innovation was completely online for which she also mentioned the successful use of an LMS. Finally, Carter et al. (Chap. 9) described the difficulties experienced by some of their learners as in some cases they did not have good connectivity or appropriate devices to make the sudden transition to emergency remote learning/teaching. Yet, they described more successes than difficulties and a seemingly rapid adaptation to what back then was known as "the new normal", remote teaching and learning.

The issue of access to resources was different for Rose (Chap. 4). While her course made use of a flipped approach, students in her class were to gain skills that would enable them to solve problems through service-based learning to develop collective teacher efficacy. Her innovation took place outside the classroom, and students were required to engage in a plethora of activities in order to acquire reading materials that they would donate to primary schools to promote literacy.

The notion of agency is more intricate at the institutional level. A salient theme in both Craig (Chap. 5) and Carter's (Chap. 6) reflections is the issue of hierarchy as a component of innovation. In both cases, Craig and Carter describe contextual elements that are beyond their control and which at times served to hinder their action. Craig carefully described the process of drafting the Mission and Values for the Modern Languages section in consultation with colleagues of Spanish and students of his final-year course. By the time he presented the draft to his colleagues in other languages of the Modern Languages department, no consensus was reached. What complicated matters even more is the fact that he is outranked by two professors of another language. In his chapter, Craig explains in detail his choice of values over vision, as values better represent a student-centred philosophy and an emphasis on deep learning. Yet, when the draft reached his head of department, he was asked to retain both "Vision" and "Mission," as those are the conventional headings used by the institution. Carter provides a detailed account of what she calls "cultural diplomacy" instead of "soft power." One of the most compelling examples of a contextual constraint beyond her control as director of the Centre for Language Learning at her institution, was the signing of the MOU with an agricultural university in China, a university which had no faculty of humanities and no specialists in Chinese as a foreign language. This was something that happened after she had engaged in talks and made progress with another potential university before the official MOU was signed. This is just one example that Carter provides to illustrate hierarchy and how our hands can be tied after decisions that are beyond our control are taken, decisions that may affect us directly or indirectly.

Outcomes, Challenges, and Lessons Learned

Besides presenting us with examples of innovation, the teacher-researcher-practitioners of this volume proved that their innovations were successful for the most part. In this section, we discuss the successes of each innovation, the challenges experienced by the different actors of the different implementations, and the lessons learned. In the interest of clarity, each chapter will be discussed separately. At the end of the section, we provide a general reflection.

Céspedes Suárez's (Chap. 2) attempt to promote intercultural communicative competence resulted in her students—most of them from Barbados—questioning their own beliefs and identities. Her implementation encouraged her students to look at different cultural products from Latin America and Spain and contrast those with their own culture and to find similarities and ideas to reflect on. Challenges reported in this chapter include the difficulty to objectively assess intercultural communicative competence. Another challenge is the kinds of materials used in Céspedes Suárez's class and the materials she analysed for this innovation. She found that most materials for Spanish as a foreign language tend to be Eurocentric in nature without appropriately representing more diversity and particularly Caribbean students. Undoubtedly, the main lesson is the importance of assigning culture the place it deserves in the language classroom. Céspedes Suárez provides ideas that can be replicated by Spanish teachers across the region and other latitudes to raise students' awareness of different cultural elements that will enrich their language learning.

Bardol's (Chap. 3) blended implementation sought to improve students' English pronunciation at a university in Martinique. Students in this innovation come from varied disciplines and different levels of English. What was truly innovative about this implementation was the attempt to teach pronunciation through what Bardol calls a multisensoriality and reflexivity approach, which means that students can have the opportunity to "feel," "see," and hear the sounds of the English language. Students were exposed to a four-step approach that comprised (i) perceiving, (ii) (auditory) discrimination, (iii) appropriation, and (iv) expression. The project also implemented formative assessment tasks and the use of digital tools. According to the multiple sources of data collected for this study, students did improve their English pronunciation as a result of this implementation. The challenges that Bardol encountered included the heterogeneity of the learners, in other words learners from varying levels of English; some students lacked motivation and felt discouraged from the beginning and thus did not achieve the learning outcomes of the course. A valuable element of this implementation was the attempt to use journals for students to reflect on their pronunciation and as a means to help them gain more confidence in their speaking and pronunciation.

Rose's (Chap. 4) implementation combined project-based learning, service-based learning, and course-based undergraduate research to promote collective teacher efficacy. The main outcome was that by means of active student collaboration and integration with the community, the project successfully managed to develop collective teacher efficacy for problem-solving. Another key outcome was the positive impact that the implementation had on primary students' literacy as reported by teachers. The creation of reading spaces in primary schools had a positive

10 Foreign/Second Language Learning and Teaching...   211

impact on students. The challenges found have to do with the workload of projects of this nature together with assessment. While collaboration is powerful, group work often presents challenges as not all group members contribute equally. Furthermore, implementations like this are undoubtedly time consuming and require a high level of investment. Perhaps the main lesson that we can take from this innovation is the pivotal role that authentic tasks have for learning.

Craig's (Chap. 5) attempt to rethink the Mission Mssio and values of the Spanish section in his university resulted in a revised Mission that integrates critical elements seeking to foster critical global citizenship skills together with producing Spanish graduates who possess the necessary skills for the job market. To achieve this mission, he proposes explicit values that stress language and culture learning, academic rigour, vocational and social relevance, intercultural competence with mindfulness of the values of the Spanish-speaking countries, and an appreciation for decolonial and transformative approaches to the study of language and culture. The main challenge was to get colleagues from other languages and disciplines to reach a consensus and buy into the notion of values over vision. The main lesson is the need to translate Mission and values statements into tangible and coherent action that guide the practices of the Spanish section at his institution and positively impact student performance.

Carter's (Chap. 6) main outcome is the obvious launch and establishment of a Confucius Institute and the promotion of Chinese language learning, particularly among the Chinese heritage community of Trinidad, together with the few students who have learned Mandarin and graduated from Chinese universities. The main challenge is the availability and retention of *qualified* Chinese teachers willing to teach in Trinidad and Tobago. As discussed in the previous section, Carter's home university ended up signing an MOU with a university whose focus is agriculture, and which does not produce Chinese language teachers. Hence, this presented a difficulty in easily identifying and appointing qualified Chinese teachers capable of teaching Chinese as a foreign language. The main lesson from Carter's experience is probably the difficulty in managing to achieve truly *glocal* goals that benefit both parties. It seems as though things may have been lost in translation giving room to both linguistic and intercultural misunderstandings, which framed under the legal terms of an MOU quite probably leave little room for flexibility.

Lipoff's (Chap. 7) innovation sought to deliver two courses for French teachers in the English-speaking Caribbean. One course was a French language course to strengthen the participants' linguistic skills. The other course was a teaching course that provided participants with tools and strategies to improve their teaching of French. The main outcome of this innovation was the participants' positive response expressing gratitude for how productive and informative the course had been. The main challenge that we identified does not have to do with the implementation itself but with the background information that justified the need for these workshops: the lack of truly qualified teachers of French in some English-speaking Caribbean countries. Lipoff provides a picture of the current situation that the teaching of French faces in the region, and it is truly a disheartening picture. This is the only chapter in the volume that speaks about the teaching of French, and it raises a number of red flags. Probably the main lesson that we can take from Lipoff's innovation is the need to find ways to revitalise the teaching of one of the main languages spoken in the region. Efforts like the one reported by Lipoff are invaluable but more needs to happen to raise students' interest in the learning of French.

Mideros and Palma (Chap. 8) sought to promote learning beyond the classroom in a Spanish course designed for an airline in Trinidad and Tobago. The main outcome of their innovation was identifying the key role that teachers have in modelling and showing students how to go about learning beyond the classroom. Since this was a blended course, students had to engage with an online platform designed to complement the face-to-face classes they had as part of their training. Only one of the three teachers interviewed for this study actively modelled in class what students had to do outside of the classroom. The main challenge reported in this innovation was the urge to transfer content and activities that usually take place in a face-to-face environment in the classroom to an online platform to design asynchronous online activities. The tension described by Mideros' account with the instructional designer simply points to an urge to mimic face-to-face classroom activities to online activities in a blended environment. It is worth noting that this innovation took place before the pandemic. The main lesson that we can take from this chapter is the need for teacher training when new materials or teaching resources are going to be incorporated by teachers who did not create or choose such materials or resources. Teachers need as much training and modelling as do students.

Carter et al. (Chap. 9) provide insights on students' responses to emergency remote teaching at the beginning of the pandemic. The main outcome they found in their report was that students went from initially reluctant to satisfied with remote teaching and learning as a result of the convenience of attending classes from any location and avoiding traffic. Forced to move to remote delivery, uncertainty was the main feeling shared by both teachers and learners and the move to remote delivery was a jump into something unknown for most. However, Carter et al. capture and document nicely the impressions and emotions students felt at the time. The main challenge or challenges have to do with connectivity and the quality and/or capacity of the devices to connect to a synchronous online session together with digital fatigue experienced by both teachers and learners. The main lesson from this chapter is the reflection Carter et al. leave us with. While this was not a planned and systematic innovation, these teacher-researcher-practitioners do stress the need to embed innovation into the curriculum. Undoubtedly, all teachers were forced to acquire skills they did not previously have in order to make remote delivery work during lockdown months. This chapter highlights the lessons learned from having to move to remote teaching and how such lessons should be reflected on, researched, and embedded in the curriculum with a deep sense of purpose.

Generally speaking, the innovations in all chapters accomplished what they set out to achieve. The challenges encountered revolve around issues of assessment in the case of Céspedes Suárez (Chap. 2) and Rose (Chap. 4), possible misunderstandings or lack of clear consensus (Craig, Chap. 5; Carter, Chap. 6; Mideros and Palma, Chap. 8), varying language levels among students and workshop participants (Bardol, Chap. 3; Lipoff, Chap. 7), and technological difficulties (Carter et al., Chap. 9). The main lessons are specific to the nature of the individual innovations in each chapter. However, reflection is the key lesson in all cases. Reflections about the importance of intercultural competence are presented explicitly in

214   D. Mideros et al.

Céspedes Suárez's work (Chap. 2) and implicitly in Carter's experience (Chap. 6). Craig (Chap. 5) leaves us with an important reflection on the role of Mission and values or Vision and the deep meaning that those statements should carry for the philosophy and practices of any given academic unit. We are also left with reflections about:

- the nature of academic endeavours and activities and their authenticity (Rose, Chap. 4),
- tools such as journals (Bardol, Chap. 3),
- the role that teachers play in promoting certain materials or activities for students to engage in out-of-class learning (Mideros and Palma, Chap. 8),
- teaching and how to keep or make language teaching innovative (Carter et al., Chap. 9), and
- how to revitalise a language like French (Lipoff, Chap. 7).

Foreign/Second Language Learning in the Southern Caribbean: Pedagogical Implications

In the previous sections of this chapter, we looked at innovation and what innovation looks like in the chapters of this volume. We also looked at the outcomes, challenges, and lessons learned from each particular implementation. In this section, we look specifically at language learning and what we can learn about language learning in the Southern Caribbean in light of the content presented by all the teacher-researcher-practitioners who accepted our invitation to participate in this project.

We must start by acknowledging one of the limitations of this volume: the absence of information or innovations on primary or secondary schools in the region. All the chapters in this book explored language learning with adult learners in university settings with the exception of Lipoff's (Chap. 7) project. The only mention about primary school children is made by Rose (Chap. 4) and the literacy project to promote reading in primary schools. Only tangentially, Lipoff mentions secondary school teachers of French and their need for training in cases where they could not really speak the language. Our call for proposals for this project was open to all levels of language learning and teaching, but we received no proposals from practitioners in these levels.

The languages covered in this volume are Chinese, French, English, and Spanish (English as a foreign language in the context of Martinique, and Chinese in the context of Trinidad and Tobago, although Carter also mentions Barbados in her chapter). The chapter that covers the teaching of French in the volume (Chap. 7) provides us with a picture of the efforts that exist to promote the use of French language in the region and the possibilities that students with a good command of French could have to access educational opportunities in the French Caribbean or even France. Undoubtedly, more academic mobility and exchange could take place if more students engaged in learning the language early on in school. However, Lipoff in her chapter echoes an idea that Jennings (2001) had expressed over two decades ago: parents discourage their children from studying languages. In her discussion and in the rationale of her project, Lipoff highlights once again that parents appear as a factor for students choosing not to do French. French has traditionally been the second language most studied in the English-speaking Caribbean after Spanish. However, we are disheartened to see that French is not better represented in this volume in the form of more innovations and chapters discussing issues affecting the learning and teaching of French. While Lipoff's innovation is truly innovative and it reached a large number of participants, the background behind that implementation clearly shows the need to promote the study of French more strongly through regional efforts.

The case of Spanish is the opposite of French; Spanish is represented in this volume in three chapters fully devoted to Spanish and prepared by Spanish teachers (Céspedes Suárez, Chap. 2; Craig, Chap. 5; Mideros and Palma, Chap. 8). Chapter 9, by Carter et al., includes Spanish in its title, although it also mentions other languages. Factors for the strong presence of Spanish as a foreign language could be historical and geographical. Historically, Spanish has been a language in the curriculum in the English-speaking Caribbean together with French; however, the perception that Spanish is easier than French (Carter, 2006) is possibly a key factor in students choosing Spanish over French. Neighbouring countries in the Spanish-speaking Caribbean also have a strong cultural influence in the form of popular art, more specifically reggaeton music, which has attracted massive attention in recent years. In Chap. 6, Carter speaks about K-pop, K-drama, anime, and manga as gateways to Korean and Japanese language learning. The strong presence of Spanish-speaking products in platforms such as Amazon Prime, Disney+, HBO Max, or Netflix could also serve as gateways to Hispanic language and culture learning that makes students prefer Spanish.

The recent influx of migration from Venezuelan nationals in the region makes it more tangible for the population to see that the Spanish language is now close to them and coexists in the same environment. In fact, both Céspedes Suárez (Chap. 2) and Craig (Chap. 5) mention migration as a phenomenon that should lead students to be more understanding and empathetic and display solidarity with vulnerable populations of migrants. Intercultural communicative competence is explicit in both Chaps. 2 and 5. Céspedes Suárez provides clear and concrete examples illustrating how to go about promoting such competence, and Craig makes it one of the explicit values in his statements. Furthermore, these chapters' positioning of culture and intercultural communicative competence as central in their teaching and curriculum clearly shows a different view of language learning and teaching. By positioning language and culture learning together, language learning moves away from the mere and traditional acquisition of linguistic forms, which Céspedes Suárez exemplifies well in her innovation.

In Chap. 1, we viewed Jennings' (2001) findings and claims as a historical piece that we could use to contrast how things have evolved over the past 20 years:

> ...the teaching and learning tradition in the Caribbean has entrenched didactic classroom practices which support teacher dominance while a shortage of material resources tends to bolster passivity on the part of the learner. What in the longer term may bring about a shift in this pedagogical mode are the application and use of new technology. (Jennings, 2001, p. 131)

10 Foreign/Second Language Learning and Teaching... 217

Although we cannot speak for sure about learning and teaching in primary and secondary schools, all chapters in this volume show an evolution from what Jennings described above. In fact, many of the chapters display student-centred approaches that promote reflection, autonomy, and independent learning (Céspedes Suárez, Chap. 2; Bardol, Chap. 3; Rose, Chap. 4; Craig, Chap. 5; Mideros and Palma, Chap. 8; Carter et al., Chap. 9). The use of technology and digital resources now seems the norm, a factor which was heightened during the pandemic. But even before the pandemic, at least in university settings, technology played a key role in language learning and teaching.

Chapters 3 (Bardol) and 8 (Mideros and Palma) illustrate how more responsibilities are now given to the student. The expectation that students engage in more language learning practices outside of the classroom are now more common than before. But this does not mean that one should assume that students are going to accept such responsibility simply by telling them they have to. Teachers do have the responsibility of guiding students and clearly explaining what is expected of them and providing examples or models of what students are supposed to do on their own. In Chap. 8, Mideros and Palma discuss the role that teachers play in promoting learning beyond the classroom or out-of-class learning. The role is one of actively and frequently providing meaningful examples that students can transfer to their independent study time. Bardol in his chapter found that a majority of the participants in his study rejected the use of journals as a way of reflecting on their progress. In cases like this, it can be useful to show students examples of journals for them to see that they can follow those examples.

A salient theme in various chapters, particularly those dealing with learning and teaching, was time. Bardol (Chap. 3) expressed that one of the main constraints for his implementation is the limited amount of time he has for his course: a total of 24 hours per semester. Céspedes Suárez (Chap. 2) expressed that she only had one hour for the delivery of her cultural modules. Lipoff (Chap. 7) mentioned the limited amount of time she had for the delivery of conversation sessions. Mideros and Palma (Chap. 8) described a situation where their client was seeking a fully online asynchronous course, and after some negotiation they settled for a 45-hour course with 30-hour face-to-face and 15 hours of online independent asynchronous work. It seems that time is becoming more and more scarce, and with the advent of technology, especially after the pandemic, hours of language learning are slowly moving to online asynchronous delivery and language teachers are not getting sufficient time for real-time interaction with students. This is not an ideal situation and policymakers and administrators should be guided by language teachers and applied linguists at the time of proposing policies that assume that language learning can take place in isolation in front of a screen for short periods of time. In fact, it is the opposite, language learning is a human enterprise that requires time, dedication, effort, and active interaction with other human beings.

The issue of ensuring L2 teaching quality by means of qualified language teachers is an issue salient in Carter (Chap. 6) and Lipoff (Chap. 7). Although both contexts are radically different, the underlying issue seems the same. Lipoff discusses cases where teachers who are supposed to teach French have never even studied the language or who did some French in the past and are not adequately qualified to teach. Carter describes a situation where identifying qualified Chinese teachers is tremendously difficult because they are non-existent at the institution which is the signatory of the MOU with her home university. Furthermore, she also spoke about situations where qualified teachers in China often opt to go to countries in the Global North as countries in the Global South do not appear as appealing or developed as in the north. The salient issue is that language teaching requires proper, comprehensive, extensive, and solid training, and must be looked at as a serious profession and not a simple enterprise that can take place downloading an app on a smartphone. A great example of the importance of good and experienced language teachers is reported in Chap. 9 by Carter et al., teachers who managed to ease up the anxieties students felt at first when remote emergency teaching began and made students so comfortable that they did not stop seeing the value of classroom language learning while learning from home during lockdown.

Future Directions

In closing, we underscore the notion that language is fundamental to all of the Caribbean, not only because of its impact on identity but rather because the thrust for unification depends on L2 learning and teaching. This means that L2 learning and teaching continues to be of importance across the countries of the Southern Caribbean. In this volume, we have seen the importance of English and Spanish. English's international role continues to hold sway today. But the new developments surrounding migrants and refugees dictate that Spanish also holds a pivotal role in many of the countries in the region. Across our contemporary Caribbean societies, we have come to understand the realities of global competitiveness. Confucius Institutes in Barbados and Trinidad and Tobago demonstrate the diversification of culture. These factors all impact foreign language learning. Moreover, the Covid-19 pandemic left an indelible mark on the small-island states, the implications of which we may see in decades to come. We end the chapter by reiterating the suggested recommendations which we see as invaluable to the Southern Caribbean region. First, the need to promote more the learning and teaching of French; however, the same applies to the teaching and learning of other languages in today's globalised world. Second, future projects should look at L2 learning and teaching in primary and secondary schools, a necessary obligation as primary and secondary students today are future university students. Finally, a recommendation that follows from Chaps. 2 and 5 is the central need to address the issue of materials which are relevant to Caribbean students, which accurately portrays them and their culture and thus impacts their identities.

The chapters featured in this volume are all great examples of the key role that the human capital plays in innovation. The human element is the main element present in all the innovations that participated in this project. There is no innovation without human capital and human efforts. The efforts to promote and innovate L2 learning and to improve L2 learning and teaching have the human capital element at the very core, since, after all, L2 learning is a human endeavour. It is our hope that research in foreign/second language learning and teaching continues to grow and impact regional efforts to promote the study of many other global languages and cultures.

References

Ahearn, L. (2001). Language and agency. *Annual Review of Anthropology, 30,* 109–137.

Carter, B. (2006). *Teacher/student responsibility in foreign language learning.* Peter Lang.

Deters, P., Gao, X., Miller, E., & Vitanova, G. (Eds.). (2015). *Theorizing and analyzing agency in second language learning.* Multilingual Matters.

Huang, J., & Benson, P. (2013). Autonomy, Agency and Identity in Foreign and Second Language Education. *Chinese Journal of Applied Linguistics, 36* (1), 7–28.

Hyland, K., & Wong, L. L. (Eds.). (2013). *Innovation and change in English language education. Routledge.* https://doi.org/10.4324/9780203362716

Jennings, Z. (2001). Teacher education in selected countries in the Commonwealth Caribbean: The ideal of policy versus the reality of practice. *Comparative Education, 37*(1), 107–134.

Kayi-Aydar, H., Gao, X., Miller, E., Varghese, M., Vitanova, G., & (Eds.). (2019). *Theorizing and analyzing language teacher agency.* Multilingual Matters.

Lantolf, J., & Pavlenko, A. (2001). (S)econd (l)anguange (a)ctivity theory: Understanding second language learners as people. In M. Breen (Ed.), *Learner contributions to language learning: New directions in research* (pp. 141–158). Routledge.

Larsen-Freeman, D. (2019). On language learner agency: A complex dynamic systems theory perspective. *The Modern Language Journal, 103,* 61–79. https://doi.org/10.1111/modl.12536

van Lier. (2008). Agency in the classroom. In J. Lantolf & M. Poehner (Eds.), *Sociocultural theory and the teaching of second languages* (pp. 163–186). Equinox.

Index

A

Advanced university students of Spanish, 14
Affordance(s), 12, 97, 113, 152–155, 161, 164, 166, 167, 169, 170, 178, 196, 207
Agency, 5, 11–13, 17, 111, 179, 205, 207, 208
Alliance Française, 107, 108, 140
Anglophone Caribbean, 23–39, 85, 87–89, 94, 107, 123
Applied linguistics, 17, 84, 87
Assessment, 12, 14, 15, 29, 31–32, 38, 47, 51, 54, 57–59, 61–74, 76–78, 126, 133, 158–160, 180, 190, 192, 210, 211, 213
Association of Caribbean States (ACS), 91, 129
Attitudes, 24, 33, 36–37, 114, 179, 188
Autonomy in language learning
learner autonomy, 10, 59, 153, 180
student autonomy, 14
Aviation industry, 16, 152

B

Barbados, 2, 4, 9, 14, 15, 24, 26–28, 33, 36, 37, 83, 86, 88, 101, 107, 123, 130, 205, 209, 215, 219
Beliefs, 12, 33, 37, 60, 88, 154, 165, 209
Bilingualism, 3, 123
Blended learning, 14, 30, 44, 47, 50, 177

C

Caribbean
Anglophone Caribbean, 23–39, 85, 87–89, 94, 107, 123
Southern Caribbean, 1–18, 203–219

© The Author(s), under exclusive license to Springer Nature Switzerland AG 2023
D. Mideros et al. (eds.), *Innovation in Language Learning and Teaching*, New Language Learning and Teaching Environments, https://doi.org/10.1007/978-3-031-34182-3

222   **Index**

Caribbean Community
(CARICOM), 83, 85, 87, 93,
129, 131
Caribbean Examination Council
(CXC), 38
Caribbean Journal of Education, 6, 8
China, 1, 92, 107–114, 117, 118,
120, 124, 180, 209, 218
Chinese, 2, 92, 107–110, 112–126,
194, 204, 209, 211, 215, 218
Classroom
blended environments, 14, 212
classroom practices, 2, 9,
205, 216
learning beyond the classroom,
16, 151–155, 163–167, 169,
170, 207, 212, 217
out-of-class learning, 16, 153,
196, 214, 217
Collaboration, collaborative, 15, 53,
57, 59, 60, 65–66, 77, 79,
100, 109, 117, 122, 125, 140,
192, 204, 210, 211
Collective teacher efficacy, 59–61,
67, 73–74, 77, 78, 206,
208, 210
Colourism, 35
Common European Framework of
Reference for Languages
(CEFR), 27, 99, 130, 131,
133, 138, 155, 176, 205
Commonwealth Caribbean (CC),
8, 9, 17
Communicative competence, 5
intercultural communicative
competence, 14, 23, 24, 26,
28, 29, 31, 32, 37, 38, 205,
209, 216

Competitiveness, competitive
competence, levels of competency,
5, 11, 23–39, 59, 93, 94, 99,
103, 119, 130, 135, 180, 205,
211, 213, 216
phonological competence, 48
Complex dynamic systems theory, 12
Complexity, 47, 92, 161
Computer-assisted language learning
(CALL), 177–178
Computer-mediated communication
(CMC), 177
Confucius Institute (CI), 15,
107–127, 204, 207, 211, 219
Constraint(s), 12, 44, 97, 113, 121,
147, 152, 184, 196, 207,
209, 217
Constructive approach to teaching
and learning, 57
Continuing education, 16, 129–148
Control, 2, 5, 48, 78, 91, 152, 155,
161, 208, 209
Course-based undergraduate research
experience (CURE), 59–61,
68–78, 206
Course materials, 98–100
COVID-19, Covid-19, 10, 16, 88,
148, 176, 178, 179, 206, 219
Creole(s), 3, 6, 7, 129, 132, 133
Critical and decolonial language-
teaching orientations,
87, 94, 102
Critical cultural awareness, 24
Critical pedagogy, 86
Critical thinking, 8, 11, 88, 89
Cultural diplomacy, 110, 111, 113,
124, 125, 209
Cultural stereotypes, 14

Index 223

Culture
  highbrow culture, 25, 27–30
  lowbrow culture, 25, 27,
    28, 30, 31

D

Decision-making, 57, 95, 152
Decolonial, decolonozing, decolonial
  and transformative approaches
  to language learning, 15
Digital tools, 14, 47, 51, 52, 54, 210
Diploma in French language
  (DELF), 130–132, 147

E

Education
  higher education, 11, 57–60, 76,
    78, 90, 108, 109, 131,
    175, 197
  Ministry of Education, 10, 110,
    122, 132, 133, 137
  primary education, 62
  secondary education, 8, 10
  tertiary education, 10
Emergency remote teaching (ERT),
  16, 175–182, 188, 194–196,
  206, 213
Empathy, 24, 29, 36–37
Empowerment, 86
Engagement, 12, 59, 65, 68, 74–75,
  90, 93, 94, 97, 103, 110, 111,
  114, 117, 123, 125, 153,
  167–168, 191, 206
English as a foreign language (EFL),
  2, 45, 179, 180, 215
English-based Creole-speaking, 6

English language teaching, 2
English-speaking countries, non-
  English-speaking countries, 2,
  7, 9, 130
Environment, 4, 12, 14, 16, 31, 44,
  47, 50, 57, 61–63, 98, 129,
  141, 161, 166, 169, 179, 180,
  185, 186, 188, 193, 195, 198,
  212, 216
Experience(s), 2, 3, 7, 13, 16, 23–39,
  60, 73, 74, 77, 84, 88, 90, 95,
  99, 101, 116–118, 126, 130,
  131, 138, 139, 154, 156, 157,
  162, 166, 169, 176–178,
  182–189, 193–195, 198–199,
  205–208, 211, 214
Exploration, 8, 18, 99, 153, 195

F

Face-to-face (F2F) mode, 47,
  167, 176
Facts, folklore, food and festivals, 25
Feedback, 7, 43–54, 60, 74, 76, 93,
  101, 122, 143–144, 146, 147,
  154, 180–184, 188, 195–197
First language (L1), 4, 123
Foreign language education, 1–18,
  85, 108, 111
Foreign language policy, 15, 204
Foreign/second (L2)
  English as a foreign language, 2,
    45, 97, 179, 180, 215
  French as a foreign language,
    129–148, 207
  languages, 2, 3, 11, 13, 203–219
  research, 4, 6–10, 13, 17
  Spanish as a foreign language, 210

224 **Index**

Formality, 152, 154

French

French as language of exchange, 129–132, 134, 135, 143, 144, 147

French-speaking territories, 131

Future, 9, 12, 16, 17, 26, 38, 77, 84, 126, 127, 130, 133, 136, 145, 147–148, 170, 177, 182–185, 194, 196, 199, 203–219

G

Global citizenship, 24, 91, 93, 211

Glocal, 108, 123, 211

Guyana, 2, 4, 5, 9, 61, 130, 206

H

Hanban, 108, 110–113, 115–121, 124, 125, 127, 204

Higher education, 6, 57–60, 73, 76, 78, 90, 96, 108, 109, 131, 175, 197

Hispanic, 34, 36, 39, 205, 216

Human

human capital, 4, 13, 206, 207, 219

human resource, 9, 164, 165

I

Identity, 7, 11, 15, 24, 29, 36, 85, 99, 110, 114, 162, 198, 209, 219

Ideology/ideologies, 85, 86, 90

Innovation/innovative

pedagogical innovation, 14, 59, 147, 192

process of innovation, 15, 16, 86, 154

value-based innovation, 83–103

Institution/institutional, 14, 15, 24, 26, 44, 57, 72, 73, 76, 84–87, 89–92, 94–98, 102, 108–111, 116, 118–120, 125–127, 178, 179, 181, 182, 196, 197, 204, 205, 207–209, 211, 218

Instruction, 57, 63, 65, 72, 84, 112, 133, 140, 145, 152, 154, 156, 177, 178, 184

Integrating French as a language of exchange (IFLE) program, 129–132, 206

Intercultural communicative competence (ICC), 14, 23, 24, 26, 28, 29, 31, 37, 38, 205, 209, 216

J

Job market, 6, 211

L

Language learning and teaching, 1, 11, 16, 203–219

Language(s)

arts, 15, 62–70, 72, 74, 76

East Asian languages, 124

education, 1–18, 57–79, 85, 87, 102, 107–127

policy, 10–11, 15, 38, 44, 90, 91, 94–96, 204, 205

skills, 8, 26, 29, 38, 44, 179, 180, 193

regional languages, 6

South-Asian languages, 6

Index **225**

Language teachers, 2, 12, 13, 25, 117, 121, 211, 218
Latin America, Latin American, 24, 27, 29, 94, 95, 111, 209
Learners
  learner attitudes, 179
  learner autonomy, 10, 59, 153, 180
  learner engagement, 16, 17, 153, 154, 167–168, 191, 206
Learning
  approach, 49
  blended learning, 14, 30, 44, 47, 50, 177
  learning beyond the classroom, 16, 151–155, 163–167, 169, 170, 207, 212, 217
  learning management system, 137, 155, 156, 161, 175, 176, 207, 208
  learning opportunities, 29, 68, 134, 154, 169
  out-of-class learning, 16, 153, 196, 214, 217
  student-centered learning, 86
  styles, 8, 186, 187
Linguistic insecurity, 135, 139
Listening, 7, 29, 30, 32, 35, 36, 38, 131, 152, 156, 158, 162
Location, 4, 70, 71, 90, 108, 121, 152, 154, 160, 213

M

Martinique, 2, 4, 5, 14, 131, 206, 210, 215
Ministry of Education, 10, 110, 122, 132, 133, 137

Mobility, 16, 23, 118, 120, 125, 129, 130, 206, 215
Moodle, 45, 49, 52, 53, 63, 155–157, 162, 166
Multilingualism, 3, 91, 130
Multisensoriality, 44, 210

O

Online, 45–47, 97–99, 122, 130, 136, 138, 140, 142, 153, 156–158, 160–164, 166, 167, 169, 170, 175–194, 196–199, 205, 208, 212, 213, 217, 218
Online curriculum design, 177
Online platform, 157, 159–161, 163, 167–169, 212
Online training, 16, 135, 139, 142
Organization of Eastern Caribbean States (OECS), 129

P

Parents, 9, 123, 133, 215
Partnership(s), 15, 91, 107–127, 207
Pedagogical implementation, 14
Pedagogical innovation, 14, 43–54, 147, 192
Pedagogy, 13, 58, 84, 85, 97, 99, 102, 112, 120, 130, 132, 135, 138, 144, 147, 152, 155, 177, 188, 197
Perceiving, discrimination, appropriation, expression (PDAE), 47, 50, 51, 210
Perceptions, 2, 12, 16, 25, 27, 69, 97, 99, 135, 165–167, 169, 175–197, 206, 215

226   Index

Personalisation, 153
Philosophy of language teaching/
  learning, 84
Phonological competence, 48
Plurilingualism, 130
Policy, language policy, 3, 8–11, 15,
  17, 38, 44, 85, 90, 91, 94–96,
  110, 121, 123, 126, 204,
  205, 218
Postcolonial pedagogy, postcolonial
  language-learning contexts,
  15, 83–102
Prejudice(s), 35
Problem-solving, 57, 61, 67, 73–74,
  77, 88, 210
Proficiency, proficient, 2, 6,
  121–123, 130
Project-based assessment, project-
  based learning, problem-based
  projects, 14, 15, 57–59,
  61–65, 67, 68, 70–74, 76,
  206, 210

R

Racism, 35, 88
Reading for pleasure, 15, 65, 78, 206
Reflection, 11, 28–30, 32, 35, 53,
  61, 67, 93, 103, 109, 154,
  181, 183, 198, 208, 209, 213,
  214, 217
Reflexivity, 44, 210

S

St. Lucia, 2, 4, 16, 130, 132–134,
  138, 146
Self-concept, 24

Self-reflection, introspection,
  14, 15, 28
Service-based learning, 15, 59, 71,
  73, 77, 78, 208, 210
Skills, 5, 11, 16, 24, 27, 34–35, 44,
  48, 57–59, 62, 73–75, 77, 78,
  89, 91, 93, 102, 116, 126,
  131, 162, 176, 179, 180, 192,
  193, 208, 211–213
Small island developing states,
  small-island states, 7, 13, 87,
  100, 203
Sociocultural, 5, 11–13, 17, 26, 38,
  99, 110, 188, 207
South
  Global South, 2, 13, 94, 95, 110,
    111, 196, 218
  South-Asian languages, 6
  Southern Caribbean, 1–18, 203–219
Spain, 27, 29, 33, 35, 36, 99, 111, 209
Spanish
  Spanish-speaking, Spanish-
    speaking country(ies), 14, 26,
    27, 30, 35, 94, 101, 156,
    211, 216
  varieties, 27
Stakeholder(s), 10, 15, 59, 64, 65,
  67, 68, 70, 73, 74, 78, 85, 97,
  111, 113–119, 123, 126
Student-centered learning, 86
Student engagement, 177
Student responses, 16, 213
Study abroad, 7, 10, 86, 117, 153, 154
Study skills, 183
Support, 9, 29, 46–48, 52–54, 59,
  72–74, 99, 109, 116, 137,
  140, 154, 157, 178, 180, 191,
  208, 216

Index 227

T
Target culture, 14, 23, 25, 34
Teacher
  beliefs, 154, 165
  of Chinese, 112, 117, 119, 120,
    125, 211, 218
  collective teacher efficacy, 59–61,
    67, 73–74, 77, 78, 206,
    208, 210
  dominance, 9, 10, 216
  education, 7, 14, 15, 58, 59,
    120, 207
  of English, 8
  of French, 16, 129–148, 206,
    207, 212, 215
  narrative, 155, 158, 166–167
  and practitioners, 2, 10,
    12, 13, 17
  of Spanish, 210, 215
  support, 14
  training, 8, 16, 125, 140,
    191, 213
Teaching
  beyond the classroom,
    14, 57–79
  English as a foreign language, 179
  French as a foreign language,
    2, 133–134
  materials, 8
  methodologies, 8
  pronunciation, 14, 47
  Spanish as a foreign
    language, 2, 17

Technology, 7, 9, 10, 45, 46, 88,
  122, 140, 153, 154, 156, 165,
  181, 182, 190, 193, 196, 197,
  207, 208, 216–218
Transformative pedagogy, 58
Trinidad and Tobago
  Trinidad and Tobago Deaf Sign
    Language, 11
  Trinidad and Tobago Standard
    English, 10
  Trinidadian English lexicon, 10

U
University of Guyana, 15, 61
University of the Antilles
  (Martinique), 14
The University of the West Indies
  (UWI), 4, 15, 16, 24, 26, 30,
  31, 38, 83–102, 107–127,
  155, 175

V
Values
  mission and values, 84, 92–96,
    98, 204, 207, 208, 211, 214
  value-based innovation,
    15, 83–102

W
WhatsApp, 142, 164, 193

Printed in the United States
by Baker & Taylor Publisher Services